Travesty Actors

SRLT NORTHWESTERN UNIVERSITY PRESS
Studies in Russian Literature and Theory

SERIES EDITORS
Caryl Emerson
Gary Saul Morson
William Mills Todd III
Andrew Wachtel
Justin Weir

Travesty Actors

Self and Theater in Stalinist Culture

Boris Wolfson
Edited by Simon Morrison

NORTHWESTERN UNIVERSITY PRESS / EVANSTON, ILLINOIS

Northwestern University Press
www.nupress.northwestern.edu

Copyright © 2026 by Northwestern University Press. Published 2026. All rights reserved.

Printed in the United States of America

10 9 8 7 6 5 4 3 2 1

ISBN 978-0-8101-4925-0 (cloth)
ISBN 978-0-8101-4924-3 (paper)
ISBN 978-0-8101-4926-7 (ebook)

Cataloging-in-Publication Data are available from the Library of Congress.

Contents

Prefatory Note		vii
Introduction		3
Chapter One	Travesties for Stalin's Children	26
Chapter Two	Yuri Olesha's Theatrical Experiment	46
Chapter Three	New Soviet Drama: Performing (for) Stalin	79
Chapter Four	Aleksandr Afinogenov's Acceptable Ambiguities	92
Chapter Five	Remarkable Lives and Soviet Stage Deaths	123
Chapter Six	Mikhail Bulgakov's Theatrical Everyday	137
Conclusion		168
Notes		171
Index		211

Prefatory Note

Boris Wolfson (1975–2024) had been working on this book for twenty years. By 2013, it was essentially complete; research had benefited enormously from the decade and a half of opened archives in Russia after 1994, a thaw that began freezing up after the annexation of Crimea and is now, of course, a distant memory. The thesis of this study—that 1930s Soviet theater was more about the proper, state-sanctioned transformation of the *audience* than about the creativity of the playwright or director—is disturbingly relevant to Russian performing arts today. The three gifted Stalin-era playwrights at its core tried earnestly to fulfill this mandate. The Putin regime, while technologically far more sophisticated in manipulative tools, can only envy their success.

The text has been only minimally edited and updated. Much good work has appeared on Soviet theater over the past decade, and special note should be made of two complementary titles published by or forthcoming from Northwestern University Press: Dassia Posner's *The Actor's Revolution: A History of the Moscow Kamerny Theater*, and Alisa Ballard Lin's *Theatrical Consciousness: The Actor's Mind in Russian Modernism*. I am grateful to Alisa Ballard Lin for her indispensable comments on the final edited Wolfson manuscript, and also to Caryl Emerson, who read through the chapters with a keen eye. My special thanks to Amanda Walling, Boris Wolfson's widow, and to Faith Wilson Stein, Anne Gendler, Madeline Schultz, Neill Bogan, and Michael Kunichika for making the publication of this book possible.

—Simon Morrison

Travesty Actors

Introduction

LIGHTS UP ON AN EMPTY STAGE. A man is waiting in the wings, his words memorized, actions rehearsed. He takes in the silence that has descended on the hall. And steps forward.

> As soon as I entered from the offstage darkness, the full glare of footlights, spotlights, and floodlights stunned and blinded me. The lighting was so bright that a curtain of light formed between me and the auditorium. I felt protected from the crowd and breathed a sigh of relief. But my eyes soon became accustomed to the lights, and then the blackness of the auditorium became even more frightening and the pull of the audience even stronger. It seemed to me that the theater was full of people, and that thousands of eyes and opera glasses were being trained on me alone. It was as if they were piercing their prey all the way through. I felt myself becoming a slave of that thousand-wide crowd—obsequious and unscrupulous, prepared to compromise on every issue. I craved turning myself inside out for them, finding some way to flatter them all, to give them more than I had or could in fact have given. But inside I was emptier than ever before.[1]

This account was published in Moscow in 1938. To interpret the traumatic experience described by the narrator in that time and place is to confront the power of the Stalinist era in our historical imagination. Many details in the text evoke the period's most famous and sinister spectacles: the public interrogations of influential functionaries, scientists, and professionals. These show trials were conducted in the glare of spotlights, with large audiences, in venues normally used for musical and dramatic performances. The year in question, 1938, saw the last of the three "Moscow trials" that received international coverage. The conventions of the show trial as a genre of Soviet public life had been refined over a decade, in a series of carefully staged and documented events beginning with the trial of suspected saboteurs from the industrial town of Shakhty in 1928.[2] And many of these conventions are in evidence here.

Introduction

Consider the threat that emanates from the audience whom the speaker is about to address, his sense that he is the spectators' prey even before he opens his mouth, his eagerness to please at any cost. These could be the sentiments of defendants, a prominent Bolshevik like Aleksei Rykov in 1938 or a respected scholar like Professor Leonid Ramzin in 1930, as they prepare to confess to acts of treason or sabotage they never committed. The anxieties and desires that fuel the intensity of the narrator's onstage crisis recapitulate the dynamic of the Stalinist show trial engulfing both the accused and their accusers. An acute sense of exposure to public judgment, an intense desire to gain the approval of those whose almost unlimited authority derives from that judgment, fantasies of becoming something more than one could ever be in order to satisfy these demands: this combination of sycophancy and anxiety, along with the knowledge that the "curtain of light" offers no protection from the demands of the world beyond the stage, drives the hysterical rhetoric of a state prosecutor such as Andrei Vyshinsky.

So who is speaking in the passage quoted above? And to whom?

This account was not offered by a show-trial participant. It was invented, a fact openly advertised. To understand what it meant for a fictional character to articulate such thoughts, consider other texts from the period that take onstage experience as their theme. For example, Mikhail Bulgakov's unfinished book about the theater, *A Dead Man's Memoir* (*Zapiski pokoinika*, 1937), features a vivid account of a first encounter with the stage. Boris Pasternak's *Doctor Zhivago* does not devote much attention to the theater, but readers will recognize references to the stage. "The hum dies down. I step out on the stage," is the opening of "Hamlet," the poem that prefaces the novel's final section. The lyrical hero of this soliloquy is by turns an actor preparing to perform the title role in *Hamlet*, Hamlet (the character) himself, and the poem's putative author—the protagonist of Pasternak's novel, Yuri Zhivago.[3] A meditation on life as drama, the poem invokes the world-as-a-stage metaphor: "The night's darkness focuses on me / thousands of opera glasses." The ghostly yet inescapable presence of an audience, the condition of being examined through a specifically theatrical lens, is an existential threat for the narrator of the poem. It is also an anxiety that prompts his plea to be spared from taking part in the regularly scheduled performance because "a different drama is going on." Panicked rebellion then famously gives way to a terse acknowledgment that "the order of the [drama's] acts has already been thought out" and cannot now be changed. Zhivago dies in the summer of 1929, on the cusp of the Stalinist era (the first major public sabotage trial had already taken place; the first major celebration of the Stalinist cult of personality followed a few months later). The novel's narrator speculates that Zhivago's "Hamlet" belongs to a cycle of "city poems" written at the end of his life, citing as evidence Zhivago's remark that "the street outside [his wall] is as closely connected with the contemporary soul as the opening overture is with the theater curtain, filled with darkness and mystery, still lowered, but already set aglow by the flames of the footlights."[4] Pasternak names the city street in question: Kamergerskii Lane—just a few houses away from the Moscow Art Theater building. The street that leads to the theater is recast as a portal to the inner world of an entire generation of the novel's contemporaries. And when that curtain rises and the starry multitudes become "thousands of opera glasses," what emerges, in a *mise en abyme* construction, is a fictional character who becomes an author in order to imagine through his poetry what it is like to behave as another fictional character and actually to be that character—that is, to act simultaneously in both principal senses of the word. The city is the overture, not the performance, and the stage is not the world; rather, it is where one comes to terms with one's anxiety about the limits of human beings' autonomy by learning to be seen by the world in a way that makes it possible to perform the will of the director.

If we use Pasternak's metaphors from 1946, when *Hamlet* was written, to make sense of the text with which we began, we glimpse a story about the intervening decade. The world peering at the actor through thousands of opera glasses is still perceived as a threat. But the presence of an omnipotent audience that instills such terror in the heart of the performer in 1936 has been tempered, if not sublimated, into a sense that an actor's onstage powerlessness is not occasioned by scrutiny from beyond the "curtain of light." It stems instead from the very arrangement that allows the actor to be seen by his audience in the first place. The larger-than-life force that shapes the stage is also the source of the actor's power—here presented as the power of an author, twice removed. And that power is what Pasternak's character bequeaths to the generation that, unlike him, is meant to live on, past 1929, into the age of Stalin. And as we now know, into the age of Putin as well. Julie Cassiday followed her pioneering book *The Enemy on Trial* (2000), about Stalinist courts (or show trials) on stage and screen, with a sequel in 2023, *Russian Style,* which analyzes Putinism and performance genres as a twisted descendant of the travesty actor, tied to the current regime's trademark homophobia and sexual hyperbole.[5]

The passage that opens this introductory chapter is not simply a re-enactment of a visceral experience. Consider that the passage in question is excerpted neither from the testimony of a historical actor nor from the pages of a novel. It comes from an acting manual. The narrator in this excerpt, whose last name is Nazvanov, is invented. But there is a key difference between him and a character like Yuri Zhivago. Nazvanov was invented exclusively for the purposes of demonstrating, through a series of lessons in the form of diary entries, the principles of an acting technique developed by the author of the book, Konstantin Stanislavsky (who founded the theater in Kamergerskii Lane, up the street from Zhivago's final apartment). The

Introduction

passage describes Nazvanov's experience at a performance of a scene from Shakespeare's *Othello*. It is a case study of the psychological effect known as "stage fright" and comes from the first chapter of Stanislavsky's 1938 book *An Actor's Work Upon the Self* (*Rabota aktyora nad soboi*).

Suddenly, the account becomes much more literal and yet trickier to read. Both options considered—documentary testimony and work of fiction—presume that the setting (stage, lights, audience) is important and interesting only insofar as it is invested with some kind of symbolic meaning. For a show-trial participant, that meaning lies above all in perceiving the proceedings as a performance—relying on a playscript, responding to the presence of an audience, becoming aware of the setting and the choreography. Judgment, argument, testimony are then reconfigured in terms of the theatrical idiom, and emotions become differently legible as part of a performer's affective state. An understanding of what it might have meant for an actual historical actor to take part in a trial is captured through analogy. For a character in a novel, of course, the set of concerns is different—some meta-literary, others more broadly existential or more narrowly historical. The theatrical setting assumes, however, that meaning emerges only when serving as a pathway to another realm of experience or thought.

And what if, as is the case in this excerpt, the text is (only) about learning how to be a better actor, how to function on a conventional theatrical stage, in a traditional theatrical space with a darkened audience separated by a proscenium from an illuminated performance area? If the aim of describing the onstage experience in this passage is (only) to teach the narrator how to become a better performer, what use is there in trying to understand the time and place when it appeared? A further complication with this passage is that it comes from a manuscript that was years in the making; before it appeared in the 1938 Soviet edition it had been published in an English translation, in the United States, in 1936. The dates for the entries in the fictional protagonist's journal are left blank, so the narrator could be speaking to the book's readers from any time—including, but not exclusively, their own. So how does the preoccupation with a particular performance anxiety on the pages of an acting manual matter in understanding the meanings assigned to their experiences by those who lived when this text was published? What does stage fright have to do with the Great Terror?

THE THEATRICAL ANALOGY AND SOVIET HISTORY

Theater is at the center of writing and thinking about modern Russian culture, especially in the early Soviet period. The Bolsheviks' explicit attempts to theatricalize reality in the immediate aftermath of the 1917 Revolution,

Introduction

complete with extravagant street festivals and restagings of historical events as mass spectacles, have prompted scholars to see the Stalinist era as cultivating its own brand of theatricality.[6] In the 1930s, the ornate rituals of the Stalinist cult of personality and the famous images of militarized, intricately choreographed athletic parades on Red Square suggest that all Soviet citizens participated in some sort of collective performance for the sake of their own comrades and, indeed, the world.[7] The show trials and culture of duplicity cultivated by Stalinist censorship enhanced, or shifted the perception of, the theatricality. Life was a show—a deadly farce with a well-known director and a ludicrous, tasteless playscript performed by large and small groups and sorrowful individuals, all compelled to act out the roles they had been assigned under various degrees of duress.

That the stage was central to understanding the workings of the Soviet cosmos was recognized in the 1930s. In 1934, the British journalist Malcolm Muggeridge published a thinly veiled account of his recent travels in the Soviet Union, *Winter in Moscow*, wherein his semi-fictional alter ego sets out "in quest of the real Russia." Muggeridge explains that "everyone had impressed on him that at all costs he must connect with the real Russia. He began with the theatre."[8] The journalist's irony here is transparent: on the one hand, theater is not the place to connect with anything "real"; on the other, everything "real" about Russia turned out to be a kind of theater. Muggeridge's fictional stand-in is invited by an enthusiastic Soviet bureaucrat to a play that proves mind-numbingly boring: the acting is stilted, the plot contrived, the "message" transparent and predictable. And from that point on, the world he observes through his traveler's lens is just a ludicrous work of stage business mounted by a regime that valued uniformity and simplicity in thought and action but lacked the taste, as well as the basic theatrical know-how, to make the show in any way compelling.

It's a harsh, inaccurate polemic, no less so than the gross misrepresentations of the historical record put out by Soviet officials before and after Stalin's death on March 5, 1953. As we have learned more about the workings of Soviet society under Stalin, scholars of history and culture continue to find that the events of the period resist reductive characterizations on all sides. Over seventy years since Stalin's death, the specific forms of everyday life in the society associated with his reign continue to provoke vigorous scholarly debate. Efforts to reconstruct the meanings of the Soviet world for those living in it have portrayed a culture more brutal and poignant but also more complex and surprising than previously understood. And the more we learn about the mechanisms of that society, the more problematic the terms of Muggeridge's theatrical analogy become.

The political, social, and aesthetic realms were entwined in ways that made some links among these different kinds of performance seem trans-

Introduction

parent. But, as one scholar of Stalinist celebrations puts it, we now know that the organizers of those infamously choreographed Red Square parades "could not always successfully produce a symbolically disciplined citizenry, never mind an actually *self*-disciplined one."[9] The slogans were insufficiently prescriptive and overly aspirational, plus vague enough to alarm both the participants in these staged events, and the observers of them. At the same time, those tasked with promoting Stalinism saw these celebrations as deeply constitutive of their sense of self. Their status as Soviets was intimately linked, in a set of beliefs with inescapably theological overtones, to the revelation of the Great Leader's superhuman persona as the ultimate embodiment of a just common cause, and to the redemption—moral and historical—offered through his genius, in word and deed. The stakes were high on both the stage of the street and the stage inside the theaters, which provoked deeply ambivalent reactions in those who thought about it and appeared on it. The disappointing night at the theater that provoked Muggeridge's scathing review led him to conclude that the "real Russia" can only be found "at the theater" because he cannot imagine the viewer who would be sincerely engaged by the performance he saw. But to understand how the performances of the time were invested with meaning by those who appeared in front of "thousands of opera glasses" and those whose eyes peered at them from the darkness, we need to grasp the very particular ways in which theater itself was conceived and practiced in the Soviet 1930s.[10] The connection between the stage and the world beyond, which Muggeridge takes to be self-evident, is legible only in that historical context. Rather than using the notions of "real Russia" and "the theater" as transparent terms in an axiomatic formula, we need to make sense of Stalinist theater and its context, of the period's surprisingly complex stage spectacles and those who encountered them.

PERFORMANCES AND THEIR REMAINS

That is a tall order.

Any scholar of the theater confronts a fundamental problem: the actual object of study can never be accessed. All historical evidence is fragmentary, and the theatrical event seems especially, almost perversely, elusive. Few performances were documented, and any documentation is partial, including eyewitness recollections, rehearsal transcripts, and episodic images like production stills or brief film strips. Theater historians habitually acknowledge the limitations of their research before bringing that research to light: playscripts, treatises on acting theory, set and costume designs, and such intimate documents as diaries and letters.[11] I too recognize these limitations and

Introduction

work within them while also drawing on microhistories of theater companies and theatrical movements, descriptions of directorial practices, analyses and interpretations.

But the problem is not only that the evidence is incomplete; it is also misleading. Production photos are often staged by a photographer, not the director, and sometimes represent events that no individual performance contained. For productions that survived into the age of film (including a few from the Soviet 1930s), recordings are only marginally more useful. A filmed production is, at best, a skillfully edited compilation of different camera angles, so the viewer of the filmed version sees what no single member of the live audience had observed. And the written sources—promptbooks, rehearsal transcripts, reviews, memoirs (both those recorded immediately after seeing the production and those offered retrospectively)—no matter how thorough, often disagree on crucial points of design and mise en scène as well as the tempo, phrasing, and accentuation of the lines delivered by the actors. Even when the sources concur, they can never be more than textual traces of a physical event that in its totality is unconstrained by a single frame of vision and perception. The evidence represents theater as something that it is not: either a kind of written text or as a kind of image, moving or still. Understanding theater on its own terms means taking stock of a live spectacle during which a performer's behavior, the physical arrangement of the stage, and the makeup of the audience come together to produce a set of meanings and feelings that cannot ultimately be reproduced or archived. Thus, the goal of this book is not to reconstruct the world of Soviet theater in the 1930s (an impossible task), but to consider how the people of that time understood the theatrical experience.

We cannot recapture it, but the available evidence allows for an assessment of the effect of Soviet theater of the 1930s on performers and spectators, so rather than sidestepping the ungraspable qualities of performance to focus on more easily legible (or seemingly "stable") evidence, I keep them at least partly in mind.[12] I also keep in mind the habitual dismissal of all performances in the 1930s as bland, conventional, and staid—the perspective Muggeridge crudely captures. Stalinist productions are a source of embarrassment for those drawn to the experiments of the early 1920s, which challenged the limitations of the stage. For students of performance as an irreproducible art, dramatic theater continues to function as a site of frustration or apathy: a lost cause.

Built into the terms of this antagonism, however, is the possibility of a dramatic reversal.

Theater has, in the past, served as an object of denigration or condescension by those outside the community of performers. But some of the most direct attacks on the mimetic confines of the stage originated with

Introduction

artists and thinkers whose militant anti-theatricality made possible groundbreaking developments in drama. Modernism could not have reinvented the theater, as it did, were it not for the anti-theatrical prejudices of key modernist figures, the focus of Martin Puchner's 2002 book *Stage Fright: Modernism, Anti-Theatricality, and Drama*. Or, as Nicholas Ridout puts it in the similarly titled *Stage Fright, Animals, and Other Theatrical Problems*, his 2006 account of the conflict between "theater" and "performance," the famously anti-theatrical playwriting practices of Samuel Beckett or Peter Handke prove "unavoidably theatrical in their engagement with the question of theater."[13] Even as their plays undermine what they considered to be the staidness of the theater of their time, they bring to the attention of the audiences the elements of the broader theatrical experience that scholars of performance most privilege: its instability, elusiveness, irreproducibility. Their critique, in the end, sidesteps the opposition they are trying to uphold. Comparing the arguments against theater reveals a common concern with the insufficiently ordinary and uninterestingly excessive. Ostensibly mundane or uninspired kinds of dramatic action (seen earlier as antithetical to "genuine" performance) emerge as fruitful areas of study.

Ridout thinks about theater from the perspective of someone seeking to move beyond theater. His first case study includes the passage with which we began: Stanislavsky's fictionalized account of an actor experiencing stage fright. Immobilized, speechless, facing the darkness of the auditorium, an actor who finds himself unable to perform crosses all sorts of experiential divides. Ridout identifies other seemingly mundane elements of the theatrical experience that cause discomfort on both sides of the proscenium: real animals on stage, the embarrassment of the spectator who meets the gaze of an actor, the predicament of actors "breaking character," the complex performative give-and-take of actors and spectators during the curtain call; this list can be extended. His attention to theater's imperfections allows us to see "how theater discloses the weaknesses and blind spots in its own structures."[14] The performance becomes self-conscious. Ridout takes one of his cues from Heinrich von Kleist's influential 1810 discussion of puppet theater, which summarizes several puzzling instances of flawed performances. Kleist proposes that the power in the experiences lies in their failure to accomplish what they meant to do flawlessly, and in turning the tables on the spectator by forcing him to consider the role that he is supposed to be performing.[15]

"Performance"—taken as an abstract category, in both the academic and aesthetic senses of the term—claims a kind of innocence by seeking an arrangement where nothing distracts the spectator and performer. There is no room for embarrassing side effects. "Theater," in contrast, cannot hide its secrets—those awkward moments when the entire theatrical enterprise is laid bare, the artifice exposed. Beyond compelling storytelling and convinc-

Introduction

ing representation, "theater" privileges side effects—or, rather, side *a*ffects, which are the truest, most real part of the theatrical experience.

THEATERS AND SELVES

Words spoken from the stage, décor, lighting, the many signs that are produced and decoded over the course of a theatrical performance—all these details and factors, to the extent we can reconstruct them, matter. There are, however, additional sources of meaning and insight: the misfires—things that make it all (in some important way) "right" by going wrong (for those self-consciously attuned to the mundane qualities of theatrical happenings). Still, focusing on theater's side *a*ffects does not in itself offer a framework for capturing the connection between stage action and historical circumstances—between stage fright and the Great Terror, to return to the matter with which we began.

Although Ridout's interpretation of stage fright as experienced by Stanislavsky's semi-fictional protagonist is historically contextualized, it is only vaguely so, and excludes the fraught context of Moscow in 1938. In Ridout's interpretation, the paralysis induced by stage fright is emblematic of the condition of an actor shaped, as a human being and as a performer, by the conventions of nineteenth-century bourgeois culture.[16] We learn much from Ridout's account about European cultural and intellectual history, from the Industrial Revolution to the birth of psychoanalysis, and what prompted this actor to (fail to) act the way he does. But these are not the circumstances prompting our interest in the stage fright scene. Katerina Clark takes a different tack in her reading of it. Unlike Ridout, she is not interested in diagnosing the actor's psychological condition, but rather in thinking through the cure prescribed for it, which involves accessing a kind of primal state, becoming "a pure, quivering self."[17] The self-affirmation envisioned by Stanislavsky as the actor's transcendent achievement, Clark explains, requires stepping out from the moment, setting aside the given circumstances, becoming "ahistorical."[18] Clark here recalls the title of Stanislavsky's book: the work that an actor is expected to undertake "upon the self." But the "self" involved in the "performance" still exists in a particular time and space. Becoming ahistorical is in and of itself a response to historical circumstances.

In Russian, the word "performance" can be rendered as *ispolnenie* (execution, enactment), *predstavlenie* (representation, spectacle), *igra* (play, game), or *vystuplenie* (participation, contribution)—and in a few other ways (including, recently, the loanword *performans*, used primarily to refer to performance art, which boomed in Russia beginning in the early 2010s). The Russian word for "self" in Stanislavsky's title—*soboi*—is an inflection of a

Introduction

reflexive pronoun, *sebia* (oneself), that does not exist in the nominative case. For this reason, the first English translation of Stanislavsky's book appeared under a different title: the actor doesn't work upon the self but simply "prepares."[19] Translation challenges like this inform Russian selfhood studies,[20] and so too studies of Russian performance practice.[21] In this book I swap out the terms when needed, replacing them with language more in keeping with the context of the 1930s and the self-understanding of playwrights, actors, and directors. The overarching question: How did the actions performed on the stage in the 1930s influence events beyond the stage? What were their side *a*ffects in the lives of *historical* actors?

In one of his famous lectures on "how to do things with words," J. L. Austin dismissed theatrical speech as "non-serious," "infelicitous," and "etiolated."[22] *Theatrical* utterances *cannot*, he suggests, make things happen—they are unable to perform a wedding, for example. Words spoken on stage are always in this sense inactive. Austin's extreme stance has been challenged in several ways, perhaps most famously by Andrew Parker and Eve Kosofsky Sedgwick. Words that "do things," they argued,

> cannot be distinguished from the hollow utterances of the stage on the basis of originality, as though nontheatrical speaking were more authentic, less repetitive, than stage speech. Performatives [in everyday experience] can work "felicitously" only to the extent that they, like theatrical performance, are reiterable, signifying through a process of citation; utterances perform actions only when they iterate familiar verbal behavioral regimes.[23]

The problem with Parker and Sedgwick's argument, according to W. B. Worthen, is that they treat all forms of performance as "conventional theater," with "a darkened auditorium, a bourgeois drama, [and] performance conventions that confine the play behind the fourth wall of a box set onstage." The concept Worthen offers to avoid the pitfalls of "anti-theatrical performativity" is "dramatic performativity": "the relationship between the verbal text and the conventions, or 'regimes,' of behavior that give it meaningful force as performed action."[24] In his view, one *can* in fact "do things with words" on stage. The words spoken by an actor during a theatrical event transform the text into something else—into stage behavior that possesses special significance, "force," in theatrical performance. This pattern, this mechanism of turning words into actions that matter to those who perform and witness them, can be sustained when we consider fully the implications of treating what happens on the theatrical stage as an *event*.

Besides expanding our definition of the theatrical experience, Worthen considers how the repetitions of certain actions, on stage and off, contribute to self-understanding. I enlist his notion of "dramatic performativity," along with his earlier work on the "force" of performance, to highlight different ways of performing—different modes of behavior that give specific, palpable *force* to performance on and off stage. The performance Muggeridge witnessed had no such force for him; but the performances that took place on Soviet stages in the 1930s left deep marks on the lives examined in this book. The passage from Stanislavsky's acting manual allows us to see that the stakes of existing on either side of the "curtain of light" separating the Soviet stage from its audience are indeed high and complex. Dramatic performance allows historical actors to "do things"—real things—with their bodies and their words.

NEW SOVIET PEOPLE AT THE THEATER

My sense is that theater's place in the culture of the 1930s can be best understood when considered from the perspective of its unmasked, obvious "secrets"—the conditions, to return to Ridout, that make us appear as we truly are—as opposed to its representational possibilities, limitations, and accomplishments. In this way the study of theater and history can benefit from the study of performance, elusive as it might be. Exploring these secrets—moments of strangeness or discomfort (for audiences, actors, producers, playwrights)—allows us to have a better sense of the stakes of performing theater in fraught conditions. The exploration involves thinking through what it meant to take part in the production of these plays and what it meant to experience them from beyond the stage. Each experience, of giving and receiving, is paradoxically unique each time it is repeated.

In the Soviet 1930s theatrical performance was an engine of discomfort, not because it was aesthetically or ideologically subversive, but because its strangeness made its affect, in a sense, real—that is, it made fear and loathing, but also belief and commitment, *work*. Seeing our "quivering" selves on the stage, there is always a risk that feelings and meanings will not match up—a disturbing possibility in a political system that sought from its subjects a firm allegiance to a coherent (if sometimes vaguely expressed) set of ideas. But without allowing for the risk, theater could not "do things with words"—it had no performative force, could not shape feelings, thoughts, and events.

The Soviet 1930s sought the creation of a New Person through art. For the cultural elite of the first half of that decade—for writers, scholars, artists, and performers, many of whom were soon to form the core of the so-called new Soviet intelligentsia—the task of becoming a model Soviet citizen was inseparable from the creation of an aesthetic.[25] Theater lay at a crucial intersection of these concerns. Its purpose in the 1930s was to represent

Introduction

Power, both figuratively and literally. Stalin and his aides regularly attended plays. Encounters with the authorities, simultaneously public and intimate, could take place at any moment. Meantime, theaters struggled to define true, proper Soviet behavior for their audiences. The repertoire represented the ideological and artistic anxieties of its many authors—playwrights, directors, designers, and actors. To understand the "theatricality" of the historical events in which they all took part, we must consider how theater gave force to Soviet conceptions of art, authority, and self-understanding.

The later 1920s and early 1930s witnessed cataclysmic transformations in Soviet life. Free experimentation was over. The utopian project of fashioning a new Soviet (and by extension global) citizen came to the fore. It entailed a radical transformation of all aspects of human existence, from child-rearing and communal living to physiology and ethics. The changes were interrelated and art was at the heart of them. Few passages capture the zeal of this vision better than the conclusion of Leon Trotsky's *Literature and Revolution* (*Literatura i revoliutsiia*, 1924):

> The human being will make it his purpose to master his own feelings, to raise his instincts to the heights of consciousness, to make them transparent, to extend the wires of his will into hidden recesses, and thereby to raise himself to a new plane, to create a higher social biologic type, or, if you please, a superman . . . Social construction and psycho-physical self-education will become two aspects of one and the same process. All the arts—literature, drama, painting, music and architecture will lend this process beautiful form . . . Humans will become immeasurably stronger, wiser and subtler; their bodies will become more harmonized, movements more rhythmic, voices more musical. The forms of life will become dynamically dramatic. The average human type will rise to the heights of an Aristotle, a Goethe, or a Marx. And above this ridge new peaks will rise.[26]

In the later 1930s the fashioning of a new Soviet man dominated debates about the future of Soviet theater, with the rhetoric undergoing an important change. The cultural imperative was the creation of a "genuine Soviet person" (*nastoiashchii sovetskii chelovek*), and the focus shifted from shaping a new-and-better future for all of humanity to designing paradigms for Stalinist society. What this meant in practice, however, remained unclear. Adding "genuine" to "Soviet" increased the danger of being branded "disingenuous" and "anti-Soviet," terms associated with the obsessive pursuit of double-dealing enemies in the run-up to the public trials of 1936–38. But what were the limits of being "genuine" and "Soviet"? The arts played a crucial role in providing the answers, literature first and foremost. Developing a new aesthetic—Socialist Realism—aligned with the construction of Soviet

Introduction

Andrei Zhdanov and Maxim Gorky at the First Congress of Soviet Writers in August 1934. Russian State Film and Photo Archive, Krasnogorsk. Credit: Album / Alamy Stock Photo.

literature and, more specifically, the Soviet writer as a cultural institution. The famous definition of Soviet writers as "engineers of human souls," attributed to Stalin in Andrei Zhdanov's speech at the First Congress of Soviet Writers in 1934, formally and firmly linked aesthetics and authorship to the mechanisms of true, proper Soviet selfhood. But the exact meaning of that slogan, like that of Socialist Realism, remained to be worked out by the artists themselves, at least until they were criminalized for doing so.[27]

To be an artist of any kind under Stalin was a high-stakes profession. Literature was the first field of creative endeavor to be explicitly annexed by the Party-state and anointed as the central ideological institution of cultural and social life. Nowhere—not even in film—was the promise of cultural stardom so great; and almost nowhere (perhaps only in high politics) were the repercussions of failure as dire. Engineering human souls was a profession that offered housing and vacation perks and a potential presence in the pantheon of Soviet heroes—though making a wrong move in pursuit of literary fame could, and frequently did, have fatal consequences. Writers were tasked with coming up with true, proper Soviet protagonists. But the protagonists given the most attention were not fictional characters but the writers themselves. In contrast to literature, which was restricted to author, reader, and a line of print, Soviet theater provided a constant, visceral reminder of the complex and precarious negotiations between writers, actors, roles, and their ideological overseers, who were often in attendance at the performances.

Introduction

Soviet theater had its rituals, but these were not the rituals of athletic demonstrations or May Day parades. Red Square celebrations offered participants a chance to affirm their connection to the larger whole, representing a common cause, general beliefs, and the truth. Soviet theater ritualistically worked through these beliefs. Its power resided in its small but crucial degree of unpredictability; every new performance was a product of a unique combination of text, interpretation, and countless invisible backstage maneuvers. The performance was heuristic, guiding audience members toward the truth, in whole or in part, and encouraging them to absorb it into their daily lives.

Side *a*ffects mattered more in the theater than elsewhere. Aesthetics, the careers of the production's creators and participants, and strategies of behavior for the genuine Soviet person were at stake in every performance and for every new audience.

What kind of self was being shaped in the Stalinist era, how, and by whom? For the answers, historians have turned to intimate diaries, public confessions, literary theory, fiction, and visual artifacts.[28] This study contributes to the conversation by focusing on the stage and its tensions: how actors both shaped the Stalinist worldview and at the same time were shaped by it. Theater could make the submission of the self to a powerful cultural institution attractive, desirable, or inevitable, while demonstrating with every performance that meaning did not reside in words or images alone—and could be genuine in different ways across the length of a play's run. Active theater thrived on ambiguities that could allow an existentially potent self-conception to acquire agency in the very performance that appeared to cede it.

TRAVESTY ACTORS

This book centers on Soviet writers who both wrote for the theater and reflected on their experiences writing for the theater. I consider their efforts to harness the force of the performances in their own lives—their attempts to survive the Terror by learning from their own experience with stage fright. My title for this book refers to a self-conscious acting practice that remained popular throughout the 1930s. A "travesty actress" (*"aktrisa-travesti"*) is a cross-dresser, skilled at performing roles for boys. This type of performer is more generically known in English as a "breeches" actress. To refer to the figures discussed in this book as "travesty *actors*" is to highlight the displacement, or disjunction between person, character, and role, on stage and off, in the Stalinist context.

The identity of the travesty actress (and actor) is advertised, not concealed; her skill at realizing her stock type, or *emploi*, is scrutinized. And her stock type is a character she is patently not: a young pioneer from a children's story, for example. Theatrical realism assumes authenticity in the performances, which means a transparent appeal to convention. But there are side *a*ffects. One gazes at the performer, and at the role the performer is performing, and one cannot help but consider the person behind the makeup, inside the costume. There is signification, and there is being. The travesty actress is not who she appears to be, not because the appearance is fake—that is a given—but because she invites the audience to experience the disjunction between what she is and what she claims to be, to experience the displacement.[29]

Theater is a rhetorical art. It addresses itself to a viewer and seeks to conquer and manipulate the attention, thoughts, and feelings of those in attendance. But theatrical practices differ when it comes to acknowledging their rhetorical drive, their coveting of the audience's engagement.[30] Theatrical realism as theorized by Stanislavsky (considered in detail in chapter 4) privileges emotional authenticity and poetic realism. Within that paradigm, an actor who fails to connect is the actor who exposes what should have been hidden. In the 1920s in contrast, in the work of Vsevolod Meyerhold (featured in chapter 2) and Aleksandr Tairov, fantasy and illusion were privileged.[31] The travesty actress occupied the middle ground, neither authentic nor artificial, existing in the interspace between realism and caricature, type and person, normal and abnormal.

The travesty actress is not a product of the Stalinist stage alone; she first appeared on the stages of Russian theaters before the Russian Revolution and had become a fixture of Soviet theater by the mid-1920s. But it is in the 1930s, when the question of becoming a genuine Soviet person, a true, proper Soviet writer, a fully Soviet artist becomes imperative, that the effect of the travesty actress's presence on the stage acquires full cultural significance. It serves to alert the audience to other stranger disruptions, unconventional moments on the conventional stage that can change perceptions, alter lives. Such, in the Stalinist theatrical context, was what one could do with words.

ACTORS AND AUTHORS

To be sure, making words matter onstage is not in the actor's power alone. But an actor's life on stage is the engine of the theatrical event—and never more so than in the Soviet 1930s. So the question of how performers act—what (or who) compels them, what they experience, how they engage their audiences—fascinates, to a point of obsession, all of the Soviet writers whose theatrical careers feature prominently in this book. The words they write and publish are not necessarily the words that are spoken during any given performance—directors change the playscript, actors forget and/or improvise, the censors weigh in.[32] Yet writers still hoped their words would survive. They were credited as the production's author. Their texts are essential to what takes place on stage, but how exactly do they matter from the perspective of a theatrical event? The words are, as playwrights quickly realize, neither the governing playscripts for what happens (because they do not prescribe most of the specific actions) nor its "score" (to be interpreted, say, as a musical work). If we see performance as an event (act) taking place within a specific setting (scene)—a particular theater on a particular day—then we can apply to it Kenneth Burke's model for analyzing the structure of actions. In his framework, the play can be understood as the *agency* of what takes place—"an instrument for organizing, prioritizing, and implementing a set of values in action."[33]

As the text is spoken by an actor, it is transformed into stage behavior that possesses special significance, or force. The actor lives *in* and *through* their lines. The Russian modernist writer and theater theorist Sigizmund Krzhizhanovskii draws a distinction between a *poetics* (which is directed at the speaking person) and an *ethics* (directed at the acting person). In his view, actors are a privileged breed of people who turn *words* into *acts*: "On the stage not only deeds act but also words, which, thanks to stage technique, are transformed into deeds. The stage does not speak words but acts through them, strikes up a beat."[34] Reimagining the relationship between the text and the active (powerful, striking, performing) word leads to a different understanding of the literary and cultural authority of texts and their creators. To see the play as the *agency* of the performance that can succeed or fail at becoming an event is to address the question of embodiment not only to the actors (whose technique has been the primary focus of earlier studies), but to the texts as well, especially because these texts take upon themselves the arduous task of making fictional lives acquire force on stage.

The playwrights featured in this book tried to keep *their* words from getting churned up in the theatrical machine. Soviet writers learned to become both authors and performers, not by reluctantly submitting to convention but by embracing the opportunity to do so, for it allowed them to become shapers of cultural policy. The assumption is that a particular theatrical event would generate a particular effect. But as the experience of the playwrights grew, they sought to loosen the one-to-one relationship, to make their texts porous, hollow enough for the knowing creation of side *a*ffects.

The kind of cultural authority Soviet theater offered to its would-be authors was quite specific and circumscribed, but no less coveted for that. Theater was not an art for the masses. For a brief time after the Russian

Revolution, theater was considered a potential replacement for religion.[35] In the end, however, Vladimir Lenin assigned that role to cinema, which became the most powerful instrument for mobilizing and educating the populace. Theatrical productions, even at the country's leading theaters, could hardly compete with motion pictures in terms of viewership. Manufactured to appeal to a remarkably broad range of spectators, Stalinist films are justifiably seen as the culture's central, most openly declarative channels for ideology. Chapter 3 discusses the fascinating, albeit brief, moment in Soviet culture when writing plays received the endorsement of the most important theatergoer in the land—Stalin himself. Even at that time, however, the power of Soviet theater did not lie in conquering the hearts and imaginations of millions. It had a different function and, in a trend that became more and more prominent as the 1930s wore on, addressed itself to a specific subset of the citizenry. Interpreting a work of literature *by* an institution of the elite (a title theater claimed over cinema) and *for* that elite was just one aspect of the Stalinist theatrical experience. Other pieces of the puzzle included the personality of the director (as in the case of Yuri Olesha and Vsevolod Meyerhold's *A List of Good Deeds* [*Spisok blagodeianii*]); the composition of the audience, especially the presence of the powers that be; the spectators' reactions to the onstage spectacle, and their interactions with each other (as in the case of Aleksandr Afinogenov's *Fear*, examined in chapter 4); and even the audience's awareness of the backstage gossip surrounding the production's producers or performers (as in the case of Mikhail Bulgakov's *Molière*, discussed in chapters 5 and 6). Theater was a shifting, changing complex of attitudes and strategies for those either seeking to preserve their position as the intellectual and social elite, or to become part of it.

Writers *for* the theater had different careers than other writers. The challenges, too, were different, theater being less subject to policy decisions than literature (cases in point: the spring 1932 Central Committee resolution disbanding the proletarian writers' associations in favor of the Union of Soviet Writers, and the First Congress of Soviet Writers in the summer of 1934). When the highest authorities spoke to writers about the theater, they did so (as we see in chapters 3 and 4) in private.

Still, since most playwrights joined the Writers' Union, developments on the literary front affected them and exacerbated the tensions between the word as written (and venerated) and as performed. In search of a new aesthetic, playwrights found themselves at odds as to what should and could be done and what was out of bounds. There was a positive and a negative canon. Theater proved the most difficult of the narrative arts to regulate. It was elusive, ineffable, and no two performances were alike.[36]

At the start of the 1930s, influential Bolshevik playwrights engaged in a protracted polemical confrontation about the style and form of a truly

Soviet, ideologically sound theatrical production. The camp headed by Vsevolod Vishnevskii and Nikolai Pogodin argued for a grand epic style and representations of the power of the collective—as illustrated by Vishnevskii's *An Optimistic Tragedy* (*Optimisticheskaia tragediia*, 1933) and Pogodin's *A Poem About an Axe* (*Poema o topore*, 1930). The competing group, represented by Aleksandr Afinogenov and Vladimir Kirshon, sought to focus on the individual and the moral decisions that a person must make in a rapidly changing world. Examples of this trend included Afinogenov's *The Eccentric* (*Chudak*, 1929) and Kirshon's *Bread* (*Khleb*, 1931). Historians of Soviet theater considered Afinogenov and Kirshon the victors in this "debate."[37] Ironically, perhaps, Vishnevskii and Pogodin had the more lasting influence on the repertoire. They adopted from others what suited their needs, and they were savvier operators than their opponents.

The disparities between the two camps' aesthetics were not as significant as the playwrights advertised: both specialized in melodrama (though not the kind of melodrama that Anatoly Lunacharsky and Maxim Gorky had in mind in the late 1920s).[38] As leaders of the Russian Association of Proletarian Writers (RAPP), Afinogenov and Kirshon attacked the Moscow Art Theater (MAT) in the late 1920s for its conservatism and apparent inability to generate ideologically suitable content. The theater's most important new production was Mikhail Bulgakov's *The Days of the Turbins* (*Dni Turbinykh*, 1926), which RAPP subjected to withering critique.[39] The unlikely alliance of proletarian playwrights and the theater (MAT) most associated with the pre-1917 cultural elite forced a rewrite of the playscript in rehearsal. The premiere was a success with the public, but the Soviet press panned it, and in 1929, the production was canceled. Bulgakov repeatedly petitioned Stalin for a revival. His appeals were ignored until 1932, when suddenly, unexpectedly, performances resumed.

Such was the life of the playwright in an era of ideological arbitrariness. Performances were approved before being canceled and canceled before being approved. Moscow's Second Art Theater was closed in 1936 and the State Meyerhold Theater shut down in 1938 for political misdeeds. Meantime, MAT's 1937 production of Nikolai Volkov's adaptation of a classic novel, *Anna Karenina*, was lavishly praised.[40] The narrative content of the production was hardly Soviet, but the realist treatment was considered exemplary. MAT, a storied theater, became the premier company of the new era. The decision to endorse the staging of a novel by Leo Tolstoy flew in the face of the efforts to establish Maxim Gorky, the no. 1 Soviet novelist, as the no. 1 Soviet playwright. The plays he wrote both before and after the Russian Revolution were performed in several theaters, including MAT, and the theater was renamed after him in 1932.[41] But the productions were underwhelming and some of them even failed. Irrespective of Gorky's fame, his career in the theater was subpar. The page didn't always translate to the stage.

For Soviet cultural luminaries, then, cultivating a new theatrical idiom meant developing a new repertoire. In February 1932, Gorky wrote to the Art Theater's literary manager, Pavel Markov, from Italy to express his dissatisfaction with the plans for the large-scale production in commemoration of the fifteenth anniversary of the Bolshevik revolution. "I have," he wrote, "all sorts of ideas and topics that I would like to bring to the attention and for the judgment of our most talented playwrights: Bulgakov, Afinogenov, Olesha, and also Vsev[olod] Ivanov, Leonov, and others . . . I'll tell you about them in Moscow."[42] Gorky had come up with the list of top playwrights in consultation with MAT. In September 1931, Markov had informed the Art Theater's cofounder Vladimir Nemirovich-Danchenko that during his meeting with Gorky at the House of Writers, Gorky told him that the theater should be "relying on the principal group of our writers, by which he means Leonov, Vs. Ivanov, Olesha, Afinogenov, Erdman, and Bulgakov." Four months later, Nemirovich-Danchenko informed Stanislavsky and Markov of his interest in commissioning a "simply excellent" play (or two) that would be suitable for the celebration of the October revolution. (Nemirovich-Danchenko's exact expression is *"stoprotsentno-oktiabr'skaia"*—an imprecise and suggestive formulation that might be aptly rendered as "one-hundred-percent October-fit.") He imagined them asking "from whom?" He answered that

> of all those writing for the stage I perceive a true playwright only in three people: Bulgakov, Afinogenov, and Olesha. In view of the "one-hundred-percent factor" I would put Afinogenov first. I would commission one from Afinogenov and one from Olesha. Which one happens to be more appropriate for the anniversary—that we'll see later. But we can perform both of them.[43]

Olesha (1899–1960), Afinogenov (1904–1941), and Bulgakov (1891–1940): writers with little in common save for their prominence, in the early 1930s, in the Soviet theater world. They had had dozens of articles and several book chapters written about their accomplishments by respected Soviet critics. In Nemirovich-Danchenko's ranking, Afinogenov was the closest to the ideal (closest to being one-hundred-percent October-fit), even though he had decadent, expensive tastes in clothes and cars and longed to live in Paris. Olesha, who came from a family of ruined Belarusian nobles, occupied second place in the ranking, and Bulgakov, the son of a prominent religious writer, was a distant third. Most post-Stalinist histories emphasize Bulgakov's resistance to Bolshevism and see him as a victim of the world he rebelled against. Olesha's posthumous reputation among the liberal post-Stalin elite, strongly influenced by Arkady Belinkov's research, is that of an apolitical artist who ultimately succumbed to official ideology. He kept silent during the darkest years of Stalinism and so emerged relatively unscathed.[44] Colleagues remembered him as "a kind of bohemian alcoholic joke-teller."[45] As for Afinogenov, who died from a bomb blast at age thirty-seven, he is best known for a trifling comedy called *Mashen'ka* (1941), but it's hardly representative of his output. His published and (especially) unpublished diaries fill in the details of a career defined by the Stalinist repressions.[46]

These three writers had obvious creative differences, mooted, one presumes, at conferences and other official events. Bulgakov and Olesha worked together in the early 1920s, writing feuilletons for *Gudok* (*The Whistle*, which began as a newspaper for railway employees before expanding, prominently, into culture and politics). In the mid-1930s Olesha still felt comfortable calling Bulgakov to discuss his anxieties, neuroses, and bouts of depression.[47] Afinogenov and Bulgakov met at events organized by the Art Theater, the Playwrights' Section of the Writers' Union, and the U.S. embassy in Moscow; both benefited from Gorky's patronage. Olesha wrote an influential review of Afinogenov's play *Fear* (*Strakh*) and discussed Afinogenov's work in occasional articles on playwriting. These interactions, of course, did not prevent Afinogenov from attacking Bulgakov and "Bulgakovism"—something he began to do in the late 1920s as an officer for RAPP. In 1936 Afinogenov and Olesha were among the first of Bulgakov's colleagues to criticize the MAT production of *Molière*, and they did so in the same issue of the theater's in-house newsletter (which also bore Gorky's name). Olesha denounced Afinogenov's work in private, and the diary of Bulgakov's wife Elena suggests that Bulgakov resented both Afinogenov's efforts to ingratiate himself and Olesha's opportunism.[48]

What, then, accounts for Gorky's and Nemirovich-Danchenko's belief in a bright future for these three playwrights? In the chapters that follow I assess both the ups and downs of their careers and the complexities and ambiguities of producing one-hundred-percent October-fit plays. Through these case studies, I describe the coming-into-being of the new Soviet theater,[49] the new Soviet writer, and the new Soviet self. Approaching the material from writers' perspectives, rather than those of performers or producers, allows me to construct an argument along two axes, considering both the power of the stage and the power of the state. I bring together personal accounts (diaries and memoirs) with summaries of playscripts and critical analyses of specific productions.

Though we may now remember them for other accomplishments—Olesha for his short prose works of the 1920s, Afinogenov for his intimate writings and tragic end, and Bulgakov for *The Master and Margarita*—in the 1930s the three of them were best known, and most often identified themselves, as playwrights. The 1931–32 Gorky-Markov-Nemirovich-Danchenko exchange confirms their elite status in the MAT sphere, despite, or because of, the differences in their aesthetics.

THEATERS, WRITERS, SELVES

Focusing on the word as written and then as performed, on the careers of those seeking to harness the power of the stage, and on the politics governing that effort, I have organized the book in pairs of chapters that move between the particular and the general. The careers of the three writers are explored, along with their special theater-specific concerns: the stage in Olesha's case, the audience in Afinogenov's, and the backstage in Bulgakov's.

Chapter 1 considers Olesha's earliest dramatic experiments, which included educational plays, within the framework of a unique cultural institution—a state-sponsored children's theater seeking to shape the next generation of Soviet citizens. Travesty, side *a*ffects, and the representation of genuineness informed Olesha's 1931 collaboration with Meyerhold on the production of *A List of Good Deeds*, discussed throughout chapter 2. The collaboration helped Olesha to achieve what had eluded him in his earlier fiction writing. Olesha sought to cleanse himself of those aspects of his identity that conflicted with his "mission" as a Soviet author.

Chapter 3 turns to Afinogenov's similar attempts to define himself as a genuine Soviet playwright by examining the debates about the future of theater at the start of the 1930s and the concurrent search for an "official" no. 1 playwright. Both activities came to a head at the First Congress of Soviet Writers, which Afinogenov played a leading role in organizing. The chapter focuses on the search for an ideal Soviet playscript—a play that would receive the biggest stamp of official approval—and the effects it could exercise on the audience. Stalin's conversation with writers at Gorky's apartment (with Afinogenov in attendance) is central to the discussion of the future of theater.

Just a few months after that conversation, Afinogenov, whose theatrical career is the focus of chapter 4, sent Stalin a draft of his new play, *The Lie* (*Lozh'*). Stalin responded with detailed comments, and Afinogenov produced another draft, but did not heed the Leader's instruction to eliminate an ideologically problematic scene. Instead, Afinogenov changed the scene's context and drafted a set of instructions to the play's directors to accommodate it. Neither the revisions nor the instructions saved *The Lie*—but the efforts to do so prove a point: what was considered politically inadequate on the page might come across altogether differently onstage, and could, in fact, change the political calculus. Afinogenov was basking in the spectacular success, just a few months earlier, of his previous play *Fear*. Banned shortly after it premiered, it was resurrected in 1931 after Afinogenov appealed the decision, and it became more than a hit. According to the theater historian Il'ia Veniavkin, it was a total sensation. "The curtain was raised 19 times, the author, director, and troupe were called to the stage. Then Afinogenov was invited to the Party leaders' box, where they shook his hand and shared their impressions of the play."[50] *Fear* went into production in hundreds of theaters across the Soviet Union, and an emboldened Afinogenov approached composer Sergei Prokofiev, then living in Paris, about supplying incidental music for it (Prokofiev declined). At that time, the fall of 1931, "playwrights were paid royalties for each act—and Afinogenov earned 171 thousand rubles the following year."[51]

The Moscow Art Theater production of *Fear* was supervised by the theater's founder Konstantin Stanislavsky, and it brought one of Stanislavsky's techniques—playing the subtext—to the forefront. Although Stalinism privileged firm statements and clearly spoken words, the power of theatrical performance in the 1930s resided in discovering and disclosing that which the word did not express, what language cloaked. In 1937, at the height of the Stalinist purges, Afinogenov was expelled from the Communist Party and the Writers' Union. In his journal, he steels himself for arrest and imprisonment. Interspersed among his talk of survival and his readiness to bare the innermost recesses of his soul to the authorities are his ruminations on what the classics of Western theater might teach audiences about living under terror.

Theater allowed Olesha and Afinogenov to fashion genuine selves, to become that which other forms of writing denied them. Mikhail Bulgakov is a contrasting figure insofar as he belonged to the theatrical elite from the start. He was the most prominent Soviet playwright of the 1920s but faced, in the 1930s, the end of his career—no more publications or performances. Chapter 5 anticipates his exile to the margins of the Stalinist cultural establishment by examining his biographical plays, those that stage both life and death (the latter in full view of the audience). Chapter 6 shifts to Bulgakov's backstage activities, how he worked his connections at MAT and the Bolshoi Theater in hopes of burnishing his credentials and reestablishing himself as a cultural leader. I consider Bulgakov's *A Dead Man's Memoir* and the MAT production of *Molière* (1936).

Together, the six chapters present a broad range of writings and discussions, public and private, about the purpose and function of theater and literature in Stalinist society. I present Olesha, Afinogenov, and Bulgakov on their own terms, and complement their accounts of their experiences as playwrights with those of others. The chronological limits of my study are determined both by the turning points in Soviet social and cultural history and the biographical milestones of my three protagonists. The year 1929 marked

Introduction

the "Great Break," the beginning of the "cultural revolution," the First Five-Year Plan, and the first major commemoration of Stalin's rule. Afinogenov and Olesha scored their first major theatrical successes in that year—the former with *The Eccentric* at the Second Moscow Art Theater, the latter with *A Conspiracy of Feelings* (*Zagovor chuvstv*) at the Vakhtangov Theater—just as productions of Bulgakov's plays (three already running and the fourth one in rehearsal) were canceled. Meyerhold and Tairov were the leading Soviet stage directors, while the Moscow Art Theater struggled to reassert itself as a major theatrical company. By the fall of 1939, at the outbreak of the Second World War, MAT was firmly established as the country's preeminent theater. Stanislavsky had died, Meyerhold's theater had been closed and the director himself arrested. That year Afinogenov was once again a member of the Communist Party and the Writers' Union, working away on a new play; Olesha abandoned all attempts to write a new play for MAT; Bulgakov saw the premature demise of *Batum*, his biographical play about Stalin's youth, and was diagnosed with a deadly hereditary disease from which he would die a few months later.

The story that emerges within, and despite, these many constricting boundaries is the story of an ambiguous, nervous, and surprising world. It is a story of Russia under Stalin, and a story of the theater and its travesty actors—writers, performers, directors, and designers attuned to the destabilizing effects of their actions both on and off the stage.

Chapter One

Travesties for Stalin's Children

LATE IN THE EVENING of May 2, 1936, Galina Shtange, a fifty-year-old Moscow homemaker, wrote in her diary about a stroll with her husband:

> After a full day's work, Mitya and I decided to take a walk and enjoy the sights of Moscow celebrating the holiday [Day of Labor]. It's not that simple these days just to go out for an evening stroll! All Moscow has turned out to celebrate, and the streets and squares are clogged with cheerful people in their holiday best. Decorative lights illuminate the streets and there's music everywhere. All the streets have been decorated, some more than others, but the center of the city is simply indescribable. In the central squares the artists tapped deep into their imagination to illustrate the theme of this year's celebration: "A Happy Childhood." Stalin loves children dearly and does absolutely everything he can to make their lives happy. By the way, they've recently opened a children's theater in the building of the former Second Moscow Art Theater. The company of this theater was sent out into the provinces, since it was of inferior quality, and the facility was promptly made over to accommodate the children's theater. The organizer of the theater is Nataliia Sats. Our young artists Irina [Shtange's daughter] and her husband helped paint the murals.[1]

Shtange's passing mention of Stalin's love for children seems out of place in a passage otherwise devoted to chit-chat and personal matters. Her daughter and son-in-law, struggling professionally and financially and long reliant on her, are finally going to get paid for their work at Nataliia Sats's children's theater. The opening of that theater, symbolizing Stalin's boundless affection for his country's frontier generation, is a big moment for Shtange. No longer needing to support her children, she can devote herself, full-time, to her true passion: "community work." And indeed, Shtange soon assumes a community leadership position, becoming the head of a women's group affiliated with the People's Commissariat of Communication and Transportation. Most of the members are wives of transportation workers, and their work consists, in the main, of agitprop. Shtange sees this work as her most important and personal undertaking and thinks of her commitments to her family as overwhelming, stifling, and even alienating.[2] She becomes part of the Stalinist establishment and the greater family of the Communist Party.

The opening of Sats's theater (officially known as the Central Children's Theater (*Tsentral'nyi detskii teatr*, or TsDT) was a major event in Soviet cultural life. Back-page articles in the Communist Party newspaper *Pravda* and the official newspaper of the Soviet government, *Izvestiia*, praised Sats's creative gifts and ideological foresight amid announcements of the opening of the TsDT. Nataliia Sats herself wrote for *Pravda*,[3] and her creative activities received extensive coverage in *Soviet Art* (*Sovetskoe iskusstvo*). She was deeply embedded in cultural life as an actress, director, playwright, the wife of the People's Commissar for Internal Trade, Izrail Veitser, and the longtime head of another, smaller children's theater that operated out of a movie house on Gorky Street (the Moscow Theater for Children, or *Moskovskii teatr dlia detei* [MTD]). Her company moved into spacious and opulent quarters right across the square from the Soviet Union's most prestigious theater: the Bolshoi. Children were the sole privileged class in the USSR, Stalin made clear, and Sats was put in charge of their cultural edification.

Her perch, however, was precarious. Nothing culturally or institutionally was safe in the 1930s, and indeed the space that TsDT moved into had recently belonged to the Second Moscow Art Theater. The latter was denounced in the press and ordered closed, and Sats, a canny political operator in the early 1930s, took over the premises.[4] Sats also indirectly benefited from the war that the newly formed Committee on Arts Affairs, the bureaucracy overseeing the creative unions, had begun waging against formalism in creative activity. On January 28 and February 6, 1936, for example, the composer Dmitri Shostakovich was scorned in a pair of unsigned reviews—not editorials, as is often claimed—which were first published in *Pravda* before being republished in music periodicals. The first of them concerned his opera *Lady Macbeth of the Mtsensk District* (*Ledi Makbet Mtsenskogo uezda*, 1934), and the second his ballet *The Bright Stream* (*Svetlyi ruchei*, 1935). Vicious attacks were also mounted against filmmakers and visual artists.[5] Thus, the TsDT opened only steps away from the Kremlin in an atmosphere of uncertainty, which raised the stakes of everything that Sats commissioned, created herself, or produced. (The best known of her productions is Sergei Prokofiev's symphonic fairy tale for children *Peter and the Wolf*, first performed on May 2, 1936, with the composer's older son Sviatoslav, age eleven, in attendance.) Sats unexpectedly lost her directorship in the fall of 1937 just after the arrest of her husband. He would be executed for counterrevolutionary activities. Sats was herself arrested and sent to Moscow's Butyrka prison, the backstage holding center for prisoners in the show trials, and then to a labor camp in Siberia for five years. She didn't make it back to Moscow until after Stalin's death in 1953. "It was her strong will, courage and innate feeling of dignity that helped her to survive through all the hardships," Itar-Tass drily reported of her ordeal.[6]

CHILDREN'S THEATERS AND THEIR AUDIENCES

Children's theaters were the most blatantly ideological institutions for children, outside of the school system itself. They were central to the correct ideological upbringing of Soviet youth and had greater heuristic influence than books and films. Going to a play was a special treat, but a nutritious one. Technically, the children's theaters were educational institutions, and each one had a school outreach program or pedagogical department (*pedagogicheskaia sektsiia*) staffed by professional educators involved in repertoire and casting decisions. Artistic councils passed judgment on performances and advised creative collectives on the most effective ways of manipulating ideological content.[7] Taking regular field trips to the theater with one's classmates and teachers, participating in post-show discussions, filling out surveys, and sending letters to the actors and directors of one's favorite plays—such were the features of a golden Stalinist childhood. At the end of the 1930s, some seventy-one professional children's theaters were operating in the Soviet Union. Most of the companies toured, spreading the fun across the mountains and through the steppe, beyond the wheat fields, gold mines, and timber operations into the farthest reaches of the Soviet Union, where the ideological power of the regime was weakest.[8]

To be successful, a production needed to be interpreted correctly. The children in the seats needed to draw the correct lesson from the plot, recognize the positive versus the negative characters, and understand the allegories and symbolism. If they did not do so, the play had failed. Still, some of the shows, holdovers from either the imperial era or the first years of Soviet power, went against the grain: their messages weren't clear; they trafficked in ambivalences. The theaters performed genuine Soviet dramas—plays written by Soviet authors specifically for Soviet children—but also experimental (ultra-revolutionary) works, and, to fill out the season, Russian and Western classics. The latter included plays by Ostrovskii, Gogol, Griboyedov, Shakespeare, Molière, Schiller, and Calderón, as well as stage adaptations of non-Russian works of fiction: *Don Quixote, Tom Sawyer, Uncle Tom's Cabin, Oliver Twist, Les Misérables*, the fairy tales of Hans Christian Andersen, and *Arabian Nights*. The repertoire was diverse, and exposed children to alternate realities: ancient kingdoms, the exotic near or far East, hallucinatory dreamscapes. But the more diverse and cosmopolitan the source, the greater the risk. Each performance held the potential for undermining the didactic message its creators (playwrights, directors, performers, designers, musicians) were supposed to be fashioning. Then, like now, the theatrical experience was elastic: the signs produced on stage were counterweighed, and often subverted, by how a particular action was experienced in the hall. Unpredictable behaviors meant alternative readings. Even as they participated in the ideological conditioning of the well-behaved Soviet child, then, theaters like the two (MTD and TsDT) indefatigably directed by Nataliia Sats undermined that conditioning, representing experiences and attitudes at odds with the regime's agenda.[9]

There were fault lines, then, in Soviet children's culture of the 1920s and 1930s. Focusing on these, however, distracts from the broader aesthetic and political goals of this time and place, as well as the sustained efforts to embody, as perfectly as possible, the playwright's intentions.[10] But a couple of questions arise: What could children's theater accomplish above and apart from children's literature, film, and music? How did Sats's performers represent Galina Shtange's shift from a focus on her own family to broader social concerns—her community work?

These issues preoccupied Sats herself, as they did her colleagues across the Soviet Union. Conferences, festivals, polemical articles, and quasi-academic studies returned over and over to the twin problems of distinguishing theater for children from theater about children and keeping children's theater relevant as film became more sophisticated, easier to distribute, and better suited to the upbringing of socially and politically conscious youngsters. And the theater did remain relevant. The first years of Soviet power witnessed the emergence of a coherent and subtle idiom of child-centered theatricality.

EARLY SOVIET CHILDREN'S THEATER AND THE PROBLEM OF *THE BLUE BIRD*

In May 1934, the Cooperative Publishing Society of Foreign Workers of the USSR put out a handsome hardcover album containing hundreds of glossy black-and-white photographs and a dozen hand-drawn sketches. The album appeared simultaneously in three separate foreign-language editions—English, French, and German—to be distributed in New York, London, Paris, and Zurich; the print run of the 1934 English-language edition was 54,000 copies. The title of the album was *The Moscow Theater for Children / Das Moskauer Theater für Kinder / Le Théâtre pour les enfants à Moscou*, and

Chapter One

it chronicled the productions and outreach activities of what was described in the foreword as "the oldest permanent professional theater for children."[11] Moscow in the early 1930s had four well-appointed children's theaters, and there were nationally prominent companies in Leningrad and Kharkiv, each over-subscribed and with a record of long-running, well-received original productions, many of which had influenced the work of other children's theaters across the Soviet Union. Most of these regional theaters were older than the Moscow Theater for Children (MTD). The album served as the strongest official endorsement of the MTD and Sats and marked the triumph of the "synthetic" approach she championed in debates with other directors, pedagogues, critics, and Communist Party officials over a dozen years.

The album featured production stills from more than a dozen MTD successes, but one production received particular attention as emblematic of Sats's vision, even as its racism was overlooked.

> Children must not be generalized. That is, the six-year-old must be distinguished from the fourteen-year-old. Every play of the Moscow Theatre for Children is written with a certain age in view. A play for six to-eight-year-olds is "The Little African Boy and the Monkey." The youngsters greatly enjoy the story of Nagua, the boy, whose life was saved by the monkey, Yirka, and the story of their friendship. They eagerly follow the kidnapping of the monkey by a circus owner, Nagua's adventures in search of his simian friend and the boy's arrival in Moscow; and they are glad to find out that the working-class little African is a friend of Soviet children. Nataliia Sats wrote the text in collaboration with [the Russian and Soviet children's writer Sergei] Rozanov.
>
> "In this play there will be no talking. Why should there be? You couldn't understand African language anyway. But the Nice African Girl will explain everything to you. She speaks Russian, and can read Russian, too. So after the show you should write a letter to the Nice African Girl and tell her how you liked 'The Little African Boy and the Monkey.'" This speech the Nice African Girl—N. V. Ostapova—makes from the proscenium before the rise of the curtain.
>
> "The Little African Boy and the Monkey," a play with dance and song, circus interludes, animated cartoons, and running comment by the Nice African Girl, has had a run of over three hundred performances—and is still going strong. It always draws a full house. And long after they have gone home the kids remember "Auntie Natasha" (Nataliia Sats) and the Nice African Girl and send them letters and drawings and stories of how they play at "Little African Boy and the Monkey."[12]

This account reveals as much about Sats's aesthetics as it does about theater's role in the socialization of children. Music, movement, animated sequences,

Nataliia Sats (1903–1993). Private collection. Credit: Album / Alamy Stock Photo.

and "circus interludes" are intended to transmit similar messages and to stimulate role-playing games in imitation of the production (the album contains a photograph of two children engaged in one of these games). Variations on the idea of children's theater as ideological *Gesamtkunstwerk* (total work of art) appear in the descriptions of other productions in the album. But in *The Little African Boy and the Monkey* (*Negritenok i obez'iana*), theatrical convention is heightened by the authors' decision to eliminate dialogue: the spoken text belongs to the narrator, the Nice Girl, and the bulk of the action is pantomimed.[13] This arrangement assigns a substantial interpretive burden to the six- to eight-year-old spectators: the narrator and then "auntie Natasha" comment, explain, and direct, but the narrative they construct competes with the actions of the two- and three-dimensional characters on stage.

The anointing of *The Little African Boy* as the most important production at Moscow's finest children's theater (and thus a model for other children's companies) was reinforced soon after the appearance of the album by a series of high-level governmental endorsements.[14] When the People's Commissariat for Internal Trade (headed by Sats's husband) sanctioned the production of a series of themed gift sets of assorted chocolates and commissioned prominent Soviet artists to design boxes and wrappers for them, the gift set called "The Theater" featured characters and scenes exclusively from *The Little African Boy*.[15] The decision to turn the MTD into the Central Children's Theater in a prestigious new space was preceded by a surprise

Chapter One

Cover of the 1930 edition of S. Rozanov and N. Sats's *The Little African Boy and the Monkey* (Moscow: Gosizdat). Photograph by the author.

visit to the MTD, in December 1935, by high-ranking Party officials who took in a matinee performance of *The Little African Boy*.[16] The support was unusual given the show's "exotic" subject matter, the privileging of theatrical action over dialogue, and the fairy tale–like structure of the narrative.

These matters were at the center of debates about the direction of Soviet children's theater after the Russian Revolution. What kinds of performances should children experience? How were ideological education and entertainment to be blended? The 1920s witnessed a movement against the publication of fairy tales, and the MTD could be said to have resisted this development. Sats needed to both diversify her offerings and come up with a politically correct alternative to the most popular children's play of the years before the Revolution: Maurice Maeterlinck's mystical fantasy *The Blue Bird* (*L'Oiseau bleu*), which the Moscow Art Theater had started performing in 1908. Under Stanislavsky's direction, it became a big hit, lasting three decades in the repertoire.

The Moscow premiere of that play was, unusually for a foreign (Belgian) writer of Maeterlinck's stature, the world premiere. Maeterlinck tells the story of poor siblings, the boy Tyltyl and the girl Mytyl, who are visited by a fairy on Christmas Eve and sent on a search for the magical blue bird that will cure the fairy's ailing daughter. Aided by the materialized souls of domestic animals and household goods (bread, milk, sugar), the children set out on a journey that takes them to, among other places, the land of the dead and the land of the unborn. They look in vain for the bird that will bring health to the fairy's little girl, and in the process engage in lengthy conversations with those they meet about the meaning of death, human beings' fundamental loneliness, and the profound social inequalities in the world. If anything made the play suitable for the New Soviet Child it was its didactic structure: at every point in this quest-cum-picaresque, Tyltyl and Mytyl receive advice from others or find themselves teaching others a lesson. The play builds to a final revelation about the elusive nature of happiness. The mystical search for answers to the most fundamental philosophical questions about happiness, reality, appearance and essence, and the life of the spirit— all of them key Symbolist concerns that preoccupied MAT during the Silver Age—turns out to have been a kind of *Bildungsspiel*. The tensions in the play's genre (fairy tale, philosophical parable, picaresque) were exploited by Stanislavsky and his co-director Leopold Sulerzhitskii (a disciple of Leo Tolstoy) to great effect: *The Blue Bird* became a must-see play for children that adults also admired.[17] In addition to regular and frequent performances in Moscow before 1917, MAT took *The Blue Bird* on tour, and provincial companies picked up the production. For Sats, *The Blue Bird* had an important personal connection: her father Ilya had written the incidental music for the MAT production, which itself became well known and associated with thousands of Russians' first visit to the theater. Besides the music, the production benefited from dazzling costumes and spectacular special effects (including a magical transformation of the set right before the spectators' eyes). This was how Sats herself described her trip to see *The Blue Bird* with her father.[18]

The didacticism of *The Blue Bird* generally suited the post-1917 context, but its mysticism was problematic, no less problematic than the religious-folkloric elements of stagings of the Russian classics that were attacked by leftist critics in the 1920s. For several years *The Blue Bird* was the only title in the MAT repertoire that remained from the theater's Symbolist period, but the anxiety over its suitability for Soviet children increased.

At first, *The Blue Bird* was emulated and became a source of inspiration for post-1917 productions. The First State Theater for Children of the People's Commissariat for Enlightenment Moscow, the MTD, and the Petrograd Theater for Young Spectators opened with successful stage adaptations of fairy tales between 1919 and 1922.[19] Critical responses to all these productions, and to others that sought to recover a theatrical idiom that predated *The Blue Bird*, consistently contrasted them with MAT's production of the play. Aleksandr Briantsev's stage adaptation of *The Little Humpbacked Horse or The Tsar Maiden* (*Konet-gorbunok ili Tsar-Devitsa*) in Petrograd tried to circumvent MAT by going back to a time long before the premiere of *The Blue Bird*, namely 1864, when Arthur Saint-Léon's ballet version of *The Little Humpbacked Horse* was first performed. Briantsev's adaptation was praised for avoiding the mystical excesses of *The Blue Bird* without sacrificing special effects. Adaptations of fairy tales and other well-known works of children's literature formed a significant share of the theaters' repertoire for several years, and *The Blue Bird* continued to serve as a point of reference for judging these productions.

Sats's production of *The Little African Boy* opened in 1927, when fairy tale spectacles were under attack for their sui generis anarchic caprice, and Sats framed her production as a deconstruction of the genre. It paid homage to *The Blue Bird* by stressing pantomime over dialogue and borrowed aspects of its plot: there's a rescue mission, and there's a transformative realization. At the same time, central elements of Soviet ideology—solidarity with oppressed foreign workers, for example—replaced Maeterlinck's reflections on the nature of happiness, reality, and the afterlife twenty years earlier.

Creating a show on a par with *The Blue Bird* became something of an obsession for directors. Writers needed to assist with this task, given the obvious parallels between children's theater and children's literature.[20] Efforts were made during the New Economic Policy (NEP) era to revitalize the fairy tale genre, but these failed and the genre was condemned anew for its unruliness (and its association, in the Soviet press, with writers of suspect politics). There followed the emergence of pedagogical plays about actual events, albeit adhering to the fantastical template of Socialist Realism. I have in mind Leonid Makar'ev's Civil War drama *Timoshka's Mine* (*Timoshkin rudnik*, 1925, premiered in Leningrad); Aleksandr Afinogenov's adaptation of Lev Gumilevskii's novel about class struggle in the village, *The Black Ravine* (*Chyornyi iar*, 1928, premiered in Moscow), and Aleksandr Kron's drama about the militaristic reeducation of homeless people, *Rifle 492116* (*Vintovka 492116*, 1929, also premiered in Moscow). After a transitional period of experimentation, certain theatrical methods were deemed ideologically flawed or pedagogically inappropriate despite their occasional success with audiences; among these were the attempts to develop a "theater of games" ("*igrospektakl'*"); the use of film sequences, masks, montage; and Constructivist designs.[21] Then, with the dissolution of the Russian Association of Proletarian Writers, order was imposed, and stable genres emerged. Plays about school and home life (Valentina Liubimova's *Seryozha Strel'tsov* [1936] and Isidor Shtok's *Building Number Five* [*Dom nomer piat'*, 1939]) took their place alongside dramas about workers, the poor, and ethnic minorities (Aleksandra Brushtein and Boris Zon's *This Is the Way It Was* [*Tak bylo*, 1929] and Sats's *Fritz Bauer* [1928]). Then, unexpectedly, the fairy tale reemerged, infused with references to the concerns of the day: Evgenii Shvarts's *Little Red Riding Hood* (*Krasnaia shapochka*, 1937), and Mikhail Svetlov's meta-theatrical *Fairy Tale* (*Skazka*, 1939).

Such seems to be the chronology, but it unravels quickly. The history of Soviet children's theater is largely coherent, driven by administrative intrigues within the theatrical establishment and the agencies in charge of the arts, power struggles between the main theaters, and personal rivalries. There is also the puzzle of the fairy tale, which hangs on in the repertoire despite being proscribed, and then comes roaring back. Plays "ripped from the headlines"—*Seryozha Strel'tsov* and *Building Number Five*—ran into serious trouble in the late 1930s, while *Little Red Riding Hood* and another Shvarts fairy tale, *The Snow Queen* (*Snezhnaia koroleva*, 1938, based on Hans Christian Andersen), not only emerged unscathed but went on to become the most popular children's productions in the Soviet Union. This resurrection contradicts the official narrative of chaotic experimentation moving to orderliness and coherent ideological messaging, or spontaneity moving to consciousness, vacillation to certitude. Some fairy tales were safer than others, and Shvarts, the leading writer in this arena, had several plays rejected or banned outright, including the first version of *The Naked King*, or *The Emperor's New Clothes* (*Golyi korol'*, 1934), a comedy of manners conceived as an anti-fascist, anti-Hitler commentary, but also and inevitably sensed as potentially anti-totalitarian, that is, anti-Stalinist.[22] The model that emerges by the later 1930s takes its cue from *The Blue Bird*, that of a dazzling but sufficiently flexible production to accommodate different didactic constructs. The fairy tale became an ideological genre, a fairy tale in name only.

COERCION IN *THREE FAT MEN*

I turn here to the tale of a production relegated to the margins of Soviet children's theater. Though well reviewed, it did not have a long run and was not

Chapter One

in fact produced by a children's theater. And yet this elaborate production, Yuri Olesha's adaptation of his novella *Three Fat Men* (*Tri tolstiaka*, 1928) for the Moscow Art Theater, represented the most direct attempt to surpass *The Blue Bird* as the best play for children to date.

MAT approached Olesha about adapting *Three Fat Men* to the stage in 1928, just after the novella was published (a long process; the final draft dates from 1924). Pavel Markov and Nikolai Gorchakov, representing MAT's up-and-coming dramatists, offered him the commission.[23] Olesha was himself a gifted writer, the author of the provocative novel *Envy*, whose stage adaptation was in rehearsal at another major Moscow theater.[24] Adapting *Three Fat Men* seemed obvious given Olesha's talent and ideological sure-footedness, and MAT was under attack at the time for not staging enough agitprop. The plot of *Three Fat Men*, structured around the struggle to liberate the *narod* from the obese, super-tyrannical rulers of an exotic elsewhere, was clearly more topical than that of Maeterlinck/Stanislavsky's *Blue Bird*. At the same time, the didactic content of Olesha's novella was complex and serious enough for it to be favorably likened to children's theater hits of the

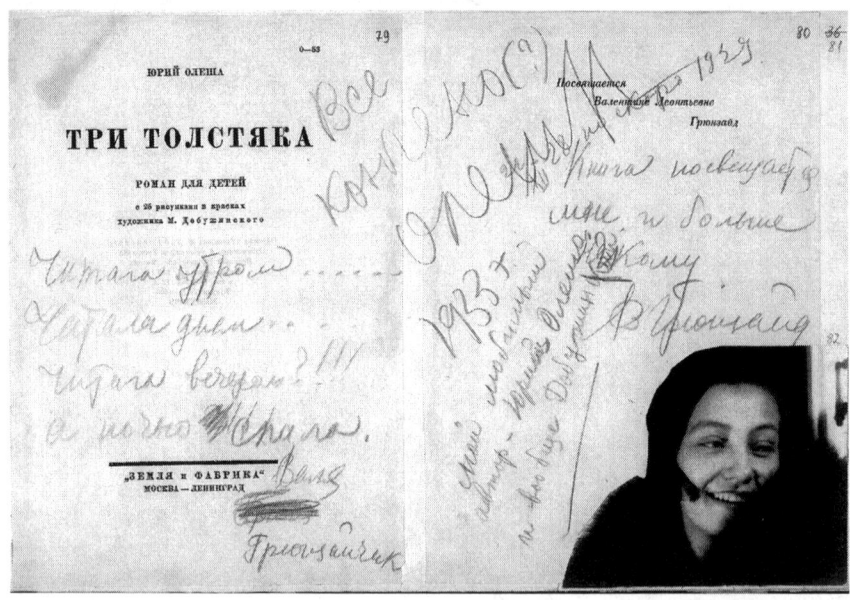

Title page of the first edition of *Three Fat Men* with a photograph and inscription of the dedicatee, Valentina Griunzaid. The author, Yuri Olesha, was smitten with Griunzaid and promised to write a fairy tale for her. Russian State Archive of Literature and Art, Moscow. Credit: Album / Alamy Stock Photo.

1920s (like *Timoshka's Mine* and *Fritz Bauer*). Olesha's language and characters allowed the theater to promote *Three Fat Men* as both aesthetically dazzling and socially progressive.

Writing a playscript for a children's matinee might seem a trifling enterprise, especially for a scandalously fashionable author. Yet for Olesha the production was in some ways the most ambitious project of his career up to that point. He wanted to create something genuinely meaningful, a play that would become a permanent fixture in the Soviet repertoire, used to educate generations of future audiences, just like *The Blue Bird* had in the past.[25] He invested his adaptation of *Three Fat Men* with meta-theatrical and meta-literary references from start to finish, earning praise from arguably the most important theatrical critic in the land—Anatoly Lunacharsky, in a June 30, 1930, *Literaturnaia gazeta* review titled "'Fat Men' and 'Eccentrics'" ("'Tolstiaki' i 'chudaki'").[26] Though recently dismissed from his position as People's Commissar of Enlightenment, Lunacharsky remained an authoritative and ideologically astute writer. He lauded Olesha for having achieved a perfect balance between "reason" and "true class consciousness" on the one hand, and "unmistakable elegance of inspiration and effortlessness" on the other. This was a formidable achievement, and Lunacharsky went out of his way to explain the nimbleness with which Olesha navigated politically fraught terrain, traversing the vigorous Marxism of the RAPP era and Socialist Realism:

> So what—does this mean that the author of the play Olesha is already a New Person, whose class consciousness and his individual "depths" have been brought to complete unity? Or does it mean that he expressed the mood of the bourgeoisie? Neither one nor the other. The gracefulness of Olesha's work is explained by the fact that he speaks on behalf of the "eccentrics," on behalf of the best part of the scientific and artistic intelligentsia.[27]

Lunacharsky posits a kind of ideological purgatory for Olesha and his putative constituency—the camp of the "eccentrics" of the past.[28] But his review avoids the criticism typically leveled at ideological "fellow travelers" to focus on Olesha's remarkable theatrical achievement: he had created a drama that wore its ideological garments lightly; it seemed "free of coercion."[29] (Lunacharsky focuses on the allegories of class struggle in the playscript and brings up the issue of coercion—or its absence—almost as an afterthought.) In the review, the benchmark desideratum of naturalistic theater—authenticity—becomes an ideological tool. *Three Fat Men*, Lunacharsky insists, is "peculiar" in its coerciveness, "since it gives the impression of a lack of violence against itself. It flows like some kind of cheerful joke, carefreely developing its bizarre and motley pattern." But it is also liberating, placing the eccentrics in completely new conditions. They feel the powerful, victorious movement of the working class around them. Of course, there are those among them who are not at all carried away by the firm tread of the workers' battalions, who paint a different picture of the future for themselves and do not sympathize with socialism. But there is a very large layer of artists, people of science, intellectuals in the deepest sense of the word, who, like Dr. Gaspar [the character symbolizing intellectual thought and inventiveness in Olesha's play], will say with conviction: "I'm a learned man, and I can't help but sympathize with the working class." . . . Being people who revolve in the sphere of artistic fiction, scientific theory, they are poorly connected to the earth. Their volatility is beautifully expressed by [Olesha's] character of the balloon seller. They barely touch the earth, and the fantastic nature of their existence, which carries them upward, sometimes prepares the most unexpected surprises for them. Gaspar, losing his glasses, no longer sees anything at all, although he considers himself the main witness of historical events.

All these are very nice and apt touches. Olesha keeps saying: "Don't take us seriously. We are not the same people as gunsmiths." But he adds: "However, we love you, we are with you, we can be extremely useful to you." . . . The meaning of the performance lies in the artistic intelligentsia wholeheartedly accepting the revolution.[30]

Such is the lesson, according to Lunacharsky, that Olesha's Fat Men can teach the eccentrics, members of the intelligentsia, and fellow travelers in the Moscow Art Theater audience. The play's extremely light ideological touch, its freshness and spiritedness and natural (non-coercive) guiding of the audience to the right conclusion, lent it lasting significance.

What, then, is the play about? *Three Fat Men* involves a group of working-class revolutionaries in a fictional, exotic country. They're busy trying to overthrow a tyrannical regime controlled by corpulent despots. The play's protagonist, a young girl named Suok, is a friend of the revolutionaries. She's arrested by the Fat Men when she tries sneaking into their palace in the guise of a magic doll that belongs to the Fat Men's heir apparent. (As it turns out later, the doll looks exactly like Suok because it had in fact been modeled on her.) Suok, a circus performer, does a superb job imitating the doll, but she's unmasked by one of the play's numerous villains and sentenced to a hideous death: drawing and quartering. Act 4 begins with a graphic execution scene: Suok's body is methodically ripped apart in plain view of the audience, and her limbs are thrown into a pool, which is said to be full of sharks (this part is left to the audience's imagination). Only at the very end of the play, when the revolutionary forces storm the Fat Men's palace and arrest the tyrants, does it become clear that Suok has not in fact been murdered. Her execution was faked by one of her friends from the circus, who cleverly disguised himself as the executioner and "killed" the lookalike doll. The dismemberment scene was conceived specifically for the stage adaptation; the graphic details are absent from the novel.[31]

The spectacle of execution followed by a miraculous resurrection of the girl who was never actually harmed aligns with the play's meta-theatrical conceits. The first is bodily. The Fat Men constantly discuss each other's absurdly large physical dimensions, chomp on each other's ears and fingers, and try to consume one of the characters alive when he accidentally ends up in the middle of a cake.[32] Corpulence is suspect, and bodies are constantly put in danger. Yet no damage is ultimately done: the Fat Men munch on each other without any loss of flesh, and the hapless character who is served to them for dessert manages to escape unscathed. This pattern overlaps with the other major conceit. Each of the play's acts, and nearly every scene, begins and ends with the actors referencing some aspect of stagecraft. "We need more light!" exclaims a character—and the house lights turn on; "Pull the curtain, I need to change my clothes!" exclaims another—and the stage curtain falls.[33] The repeated consumption/mutilation of vulnerable yet invincible bodies in a fictional world where any action could breach the proscenium prepares and justifies Suok's resurrection in the play's finale.

In 1920 Olesha had written a play in verse titled *Playing Execution* (*Igra v plakhu*).[34] In an imaginary country whose features prefigure the fairy-tale land of the Fat Men, a troupe of famous actors arrives at the palace of a tyrannical king who fancies himself a great connoisseur of theater. The actors suggest that the king showcase his skills as a tragic actor by performing with them. Since their specialty is improvisation, they invite the king to play himself, and then, under the pretext of devising a plot that befits a great tragedian, they dupe the king into staging his own hypothetical execution by a rebel general (a "friend of the people" whose troops are storming the capital). The king realizes that this is no mere play, but the executioner's axe, held by one of the actors, is already coming down on his neck.

The final scene of *Three Fat Men* extends and complicates Olesha's parable about performed versus experienced reality. In *Playing Execution* the division between representation and enactment is dissolved, restored, and dissolved anew. *Three Fat Men* inflicts violence upon the positive characters and suggests that the physical transformation they experience is itself only temporary. In both plays, protagonists manipulate the belief of their spectators within the world of the play—and, in the case of *Three Fat Men*, the belief of the MAT audiences observing the performance—to negate the physical consequences of symbolic violence. This, I argue, is the crucial meta-theatrical effect, and one that connects to the broader political context of the MAT production. In Olesha's theatrical fantasies, coercion is hidden in plain sight.

Chapter One

Playing Execution was not produced in Olesha's lifetime; its theatricalized violence wasn't shown in an actual theater. *Three Fat Men*, in contrast, was commissioned by a theater, written with that theater's concerns in mind, and adjusted in rehearsal. The illusion of a lack of violence/coercion, which Lunacharsky noticed and praised in his review as the source of the production's "effortless grace," was created by the actors and the décor. The illusory violence in Olesha's playscript was echoed and amplified in rehearsals and design meetings by the production's other authors.

The production Lunacharsky lauded was Constructivist in aesthetic, with dazzling visuals of the kind MAT's founders had once ridiculed.[35] The "magical," grotesque elements of Olesha's playscript were emphasized by designer Boris Erdman's amalgam of geometric shapes that abstracted buildings, rooms, and pieces of furniture. The exaggerated angular costumes, the grotesque makeup, and the sharply syncopated musical accompaniment reflected director Nikolai Gorchakov's eschewal of the "excessive psychologizing" of previous MAT productions. The violence—the coercive element—in the play is absurd, impossible to believe, which is exactly the point, since violence and coercion are the absolute worst means of bringing one's opponents around. In this instance, Stanislavsky's conservatism got the better of him. He didn't understand the point of the play and pulled *Three Fat Men* from the stage because he considered the designs too radical. (He was just told this about the production; he himself didn't see it.)[36] It soon returned to the stage, however, and became a successful ballet, then a musical, and then an animated film.

That *Three Fat Men* was devised to replace *The Blue Bird* was, in some respect, secondary. Its high-minded absurdism was what mattered, as did this quality in other children's plays of the 1930s. Violence was omnipresent in theater, and it wasn't limited to the destruction of enemies (kulaks, Whites, saboteurs, and assorted counterrevolutionaries). One of the MTD's most popular productions at the end of the 1920s, Liudmila Vepritskaia's *The Snitch* (*Liagavyi*, 1929), concerns a group of homeless boys learning the benefits of snitching on each other to the police. As the review in *Izvestiia* explained, the play set up a simple opposition between the law of the streets and the law of the new Soviet order. To snitch on one's brothers-in-crime is to serve the "new morality" and "healthy society."[37] Vepritskaia filled her play with fight scenes, but the protagonist emerges unscathed, having shed his past and detoxed his mind to become a model citizen.[38] Liubimova's play *Seryozha Strel'tsov* gives a related subject intensely melodramatic treatment and received a positive review in *Pravda*. The review was written by the secretary of the Central Committee of the All-Union Leninist Young Communist League:

Travesties for Stalin's Children

There's great pleasure to be had from the new play of the Moscow Children's Theater, "Seryozha Strel'tsov," staged under the direction of Honored Artist N. I. Sats and V. D. Korolev and based on V. A. Lyubimova's play.

This is the first serious production on the subject of Soviet school life, about the leaders and teachers who devote their strength, knowledge, and love to the communist education of the new generation. The performance represents certain negative aspects of our schools (weak discipline, incorrect attitude toward the teacher), but this does not detract from its merits. To the contrary, the play calls for further strengthening of conscious labor and discipline in our schools.

The roles of Seryozha Strel'tsov and Lova Safronov speak to the role of family and one's neighborhood in a child's upbringing. The performance confirms that without consideration of family and the world at large, finding the correct approach is unthinkable. It's precisely in those schools where these influences are not taken into account in the educational program that we sometimes experience ideological dislocations.

The performance certainly engages the consciousness. It is sufficient here to note the numerous discussions among schoolchildren about the characters of the play. A thirteen-year-old schoolboy sitting next to me openly stated that he sees himself in some of the characters.

Does the play reach adults? Certainly. Let's just say that the play is of value to young and old alike. This is its great merit.

The directors and the entire team did a masterful job, worthy of the Moscow Children's Theater 15th anniversary, which is being celebrated this year.

I would like to express my wishes for a few improvements in the play. There needs to be more explanation of Seryozha Strel'tsov's mother's departure to Alma-Ata, which, in fact, causes him to lose his moral balance. In the form in which it is given, the explanation sounds unconvincing. It's also necessary to emphasize the role of the pioneer organization in the school, showing examples of conscious discipline in the effort to learn. It's rather primitive that almost the entire class wears pioneer ties and speaks in the language of the "honest pioneer."

In general, the play teaches the correct approach to the education of children and their organization. Seeing this play is a must not only for students, but also for directors, teachers, Komsomol organizers of the Central Committee, Komsomol and pioneer workers.[39]

Missing, here, is the plot: about a boy who is saved from illness and suicide by a caring teacher and realizes that he too is of value to society.[40]

Each variation on the reeducation story used force not to coerce but to demonstrate the opposite: force is unable to coerce. Violence, to put it simply, solves nothing. The protagonist of Afinogenov's *Black Ravine*, Egorka, is murdered by a kulak in plain view of the audience, only to be resurrected in the finale.[41] Effortless coercion became the central concept of children's theater. In 1933 the State Central Theater for Young Spectators in Moscow premiered a new play by Dmitri Shcheglov called *Juggernaut's Chariot* (*Kolesnitsa Dzhaggernauta*). It told the story of an actual historical personage—James Hargreaves, an English weaver who invented the "spinning jenny," a weaving machine that brought the Industrial Revolution to the textile industry—and his calamitous upbringing (including forceful eviction from his home and regular beatings in a workers' barracks). It was a period drama for teens about the life of oppressed workers.[42] But the production had a much broader ambition: it tried to make Karl Marx's *Das Kapital* meaningful for children. Hargreaves's experiences are emblematic of the advance of capitalism, which Marx (following Hegel)[43] famously likened to the unstoppable chariot of a Hindu god, Juggernaut.[44] The chariot moves from temple to temple, crushing worshippers who have thrown themselves, or been thrown, under its wheels.

SATS, THE CHILD, AND TRAVESTY

Nataliia Sats spent the summer of 1937 at an exclusive sanatorium for the political and cultural elite in Barvikha, outside Moscow, but in August her vacation was cut short. She was ordered back to the capital and arrested for her inconvenient political connections.[45] One of her regular interlocutors at Barvikha was Stanislavsky: aged, battling a myriad of ailments, and aloof. As the daughter of MAT's first in-house composer, Ilya Sats (1875–1912), Nataliia had known Stanislavsky since childhood, but she had had little contact with him after the Revolution. He was working at the sanatorium on his treatise, *An Actor's Work Upon the Self*, and held daily public readings from his drafts with Sats in attendance. According to her memoirs—an idiosyncratic and patently selective account—Stanislavsky offered her his thoughts on the future of her craft.[46] He was in favor of a new kind of children's theater—a theater whose actors would be trained, and would begin performing, while they were themselves children. It was a utopian vision, intended to ensure freshness and boldness in representing a child's surreal perspective on the world.[47]

For Sats this was an awkward moment. She respected Stanislavsky's authority in all matters theatrical and felt obliged to endorse the old man's vision. She confirmed doing so in her memoirs. Elsewhere, however, in books, articles, and lectures, she ruled out having children on the stage. Hers was a polished operation, no rough edges, no unintentional caprice, with adults performing all the parts for their youthful audiences.[48]

There was an additional ideological factor, however. Sats and most of her colleagues in the Soviet Union considered children's plays performed by children a form of child labor. The shows were exploitative and amateurish.[49] Over and over, Sats in Moscow, Briantsev in Leningrad, and the chroniclers of Soviet children's theater elsewhere insisted that the only kind of spectacle for children worth cultivating was one where everyone involved—directors, designers, and above all, actors—came from professional training programs. This insistence carried over to the names of the theaters: the older ones were called "children's" (*detskie*) companies, but Sats preferred "theater for children" (*teatr dlia detei*), because the modifier *detskii* (which can mean "child-like," "immature") belittled the whole endeavor, tainting it as unserious, childish in the worse sense. The name that seemed most appropriate was Briantsev's "theater for young spectators" (*teatr iunykh zritelei*), which, in a slightly modified form ("theater for the young spectator"—*teatr iunogo zritelia*) became the standard term for a children's theater. (The creation of the Central Children's Theater in 1936 was one of the few exceptions to the rule.)

The model for Sats's operation was the troupe of adult actors trained by Stanislavsky for *The Blue Bird*. The acting technique was, for the time, experimental and fantastical, as befitted the dramatis personae, which included the Souls (or Spirits) of Water, Bread, Dogs, and Cats. A young woman took, *en travesti*, the part of an adolescent boy. The vocal music, moreover, was set in a soprano and alto range for female singers dressed in male costumes.

As children's theaters flourished, the problem of performing the roles of young and teenage boys had to be solved institutionally. And, in the 1930s, it was: theaters across the Soviet Union trained travesty actresses.[50] The demand for these actresses increased as the repertoire expanded. Makar'ev's *Timoshka's Mine*, Sats's *Little African Boy*, and a later work, Aleksei Tolstoy's *The Golden Key* (*Zolotoi kliuchik*, 1936, TsDT's inaugural production), all involved women dressed as prepubescent or adolescent boys. These actresses were valuable members of the theatrical troupes and were better known to their audiences than the playwrights themselves. Since their *emploi* was so specific, these actresses got caught in a double bind: once they'd reached a certain age, they could no longer convincingly play the parts of children; but because they had spent so much time doing just that, they couldn't easily make the transition to "adult" roles. A typical trajectory for a travesty actress was to shift, almost overnight, from playing ten-year-old street urchins to lumpy, grumpy grandmothers.[51]

The prominence of travesty actresses in Soviet children's theater is acknowledged in the sources. A 1972 anthology of writings about the genre includes memoirs of prominent directors and playwrights and the reminiscences of the famous travesty actresses Klavdia Koreneva (1902–1972) and

Chapter One

Valentina Sperantova (1904–1978). And yet, tellingly, neither the contributions of the actresses themselves nor the writings about them consider the reliance, in Soviet children's theater, on cross-dressing and the sublimation of fantasy into reality. Sperantova came closest in her conclusion: "It was bitter, painfully bitter to part with my boys. Later I understood that it was not really a separation; I reunited with them only in a different way. I also understood that the calling of the travesty actress is lifelong [*I eshcho ia poniala: ampula 'travesti'—eto na vsiu zhizn'*]."[52]

Koreneva began her career at the MTD, and Sats devoted a separate chapter in her memoirs to admiring descriptions of Koreneva's major roles: the Monkey in *African Boy*, Fritz Bauer, and, most importantly, Buratino in the 1936 production of *The Golden Key* at the TsDT.[53] Sperantova, who joined the TsDT after World War II, was the original lead in Afinogenov's *Black Ravine*, Kron's *Rifle 492116*, Shvarts's *The Treasure* (*Klad*; the lead was a female role), and Shtok's *Building Number Five*. In the late 1940s and 1950s she went on to play both Kai and Gerda in Shvarts's *Snow Queen* at the TsDT, and recorded radio play versions of the most popular productions; these versions, distributed on LPs for decades (and now available in digital remastering), ensured that several generations of Soviet children identified Sperantova's voice, as it sounded back in the day, with the most famous characters of children's fiction.[54] Just between these two women, then, we have a catalog of Soviet children's theater's most important, ideologically challenging, and problematic roles. Sperantova was also famous for prevailing upon playwrights to rewrite the dialogue of her characters to match the lines she improvised in rehearsal.[55]

For Koreneva and Sperantova, and for those who wrote about them, the measure of their success was their ease on stage with their boyishness. Soviet children were told, repeatedly, that the characters created by travesty actresses were ideal people, more real than reality, but should also be thought of as role models. In this kind of ideological operation, the more the entity likened to the spectator is unlike that spectator, the stronger the effect. Identification is an exercise in fantastical self-coercion. To recognize a thirty-five-year-old mother of two as an eleven-year-old boy just like yourself means, above all, acknowledging that the most fundamental categories of life, including gender, are subject to manipulation by forces unseen.

The swapping of gender, then, is a metaphor for a process of ideological conditioning. One of the passages Sats liked to cite in the various editions of her memoirs was an excerpt from an article reporting a conversation between a young spectator and her mother, overheard in line for tickets to *The Little African Boy and the Monkey*. The mother tries to convince her daughter that since she has already seen the production once, and since the next show was sold out, they should just go to the zoo and look at a real monkey. The girl replies in indignation: "That's not the real one. The real one's right here! [*Zdes' nastoiashchaia!*]"[56] The "real" monkey in question was played by Koreneva, and the child's insistence upon identifying the actress so completely with the animal suggests that the real and the represented had swapped places. In a provocative study of Aleksei Tolstoy's *The Golden Key*, a true relic of Soviet children's theater, Mark Lipovetsky suggests that Tolstoy's Buratino, an archetypal trickster, is markedly different from the other characters of the mid-1930s because in Tolstoy's narrative there is no privileging of the "real" human over the "fake" marionette. The counterexample, for Lipovetsky, is Olesha's *Three Fat Men*, with its clear ideological distinction between the oft-malfunctioning mechanical doll and the healthy flesh-and-blood Suok.[57] But he's talking about the novella, not the playscript. On stage, in the proper realm of Soviet children's theater, the distinction between the real and the fake dissolves. In MAT's production of *Three Fat Men*, the girl Suok was played by the same actress who played the doppelganger doll. Tolstoy's marionette Buratino was performed by a travesty actress, and so too was the "real boy" at the heart of Olesha's play (the Fat Men's heir apparent).

This fundamental malleability, this counterintuitive and absolute identification with the other as the self, is what ultimately brought together fairy tales and school tales, melodramas and period dramas. Soviet children's theater did not merely teach, convince, or agitate. Drag and its correlative (breeches) naturalize and sublimate the violence done upon the self in the process of identification and transformation. Experiencing Soviet children's theater meant identifying travesty as a source of authenticity. For children and for the adults in the audience, it also meant treating every story as a potential chariot driven by a Juggernaut.

Chapter Two

Yuri Olesha's Theatrical Experiment

A PHOTOGRAPH preserved in Yuri Olesha's archive shows an attractive short-haired woman in her mid-thirties. Her outfit is stylized, old-fashioned. The elaborate velvet jacket over a loose white blouse with a pointed collar and wide cuffs, the cloak draped over her left shoulder, and a beret in her hands immediately tell us that she's in a costume, that of Hamlet. The handwritten inscription reads: "Iurochka, it was you I played. Radek said I played myself. Not true. I'd like to play myself [*Khochu sebia*]. I'd like to bond with you, one more time, through your art. Zinaida."[1]

The woman in the photo is a famous theatrical talent, Zinaida Raikh. In 1932, the year she made the inscription, Raikh was the leading actress of the Meyerhold Theater, the wife of Vsevolod Meyerhold himself, and the star of *A List of Good Deeds*, a play written by Olesha and directed by Meyerhold. The photograph Raikh autographed for Olesha belonged to the promotional materials for *A List of Good Deeds*, in which she played the part of a fictional Soviet actress/director who takes on the title role of her own stage version of *Hamlet*. Raikh's inscription is both provocative and ambivalent. To observe that an actress is playing herself is, in effect, to accuse her of lacking in skill, of failing to turn into her fictional character, dissolving into the role. Raikh refers in this context to a scathing review of *A List of Good Deeds* by Karl Radek, a high-ranking government official who fancied himself a theater critic. The review was published in *Izvestiia*, the official daily newspaper of the government, and it accused Raikh of lack of preparedness: she had "played" not her character but "herself." But then Raikh invokes a different, more openly metaphorical and far-reaching meaning of this criticism. Her future collaboration with Olesha is about finding an onstage simulacrum, a character just like her. Raikh's ambiguous formulation *"Khochu sebia"* suggests that she needs Olesha to develop this simulacrum, to invent the self that she has not yet become, the self in waiting. She had played the part of "Iurochka" on stage, and now she wanted "Iurochka" to create the ideal role for her, a better version of Zinaida Raikh.

But what does it mean for an actress to claim that, instead of playing

Yuri Olesha's Theatrical Experiment

Vsevolod Meyerhold and Yuri Olesha. Credit: Magite Historic / Alamy Stock Photo.

Olesha's character (also an actress) playing Shakespeare's character (the single most iconic and coveted role in Western theater), she is in fact playing a character she essentially created herself and called "Yuri Olesha"? What happened to Olesha's and Shakespeare's characters in the process? And what does it mean for Raikh to suggest that "playing oneself" is not just an inadvertent side effect of inferior acting technique, but instead a desirable mode of relating to the stage and comprehending one's personal experience? Her reference to Radek shows an awareness of how her work (and by extension Olesha's and Meyerhold's work) is informed by the historical setting in which

Chapter Two

it was performed—the Soviet 1930s. *A List of Good Deeds* was conceived, written, and staged during the time when a distinctly Stalinist society was taking shape—in the years of the First Five-Year Plan for accelerated economic development, the early show trials of so-called bourgeois specialists accused of sabotaging that development, and the ascendancy of RAPP and other militant "proletarian" artists' organizations that would serve as prototypes of the "creative unions" established later in the decade. The omnipresent rhetoric of reconstruction, renewal, and cleansing of ideological allegiances rendered the innocent theatrical metaphor of playing (impersonating) someone inherently problematic,[2] and the notion of playing oneself especially precarious. How, then, can we understand an attempt to enact, and stage, the self within the context of the Soviet culture and society of the early 1930s?

In this chapter, I approach these questions through the story of the writer whom Raikh claimed to have embodied on stage, Olesha, and what he referred to as his theatrical "experiment." In 1932 Yuri Olesha (1899–1960) was the well-known author of three plays, two novels, a dozen short stories, and several hundred poems (these of very uneven quality), with another play commissioned and another novel in the works. As it turned out, *A List of Good Deeds* (1931) would be the last of his plays produced in his lifetime.

Meyerhold's production of *A List of Good Deeds*. Private collection. Credit: Album / Alamy Stock Photo.

Olesha's star turn in the theater was brief—five years—but intense: his plays were shown in major Soviet theaters. His theatrical pursuits were deeply personal; he was seeking to transform himself into a "true" Soviet artist, a model for his generation. The stage would help him do that.

I will first consider Olesha's abandonment of highbrow, "belles lettres" writing. His diaries of the 1930s witness, in tortured guise, his efforts to re-create himself, and he describes his plays as the therapeutic tools for surviving his personal crisis. I then consider Olesha's thoughts in general about the theater as a cultural and political institution, and then focus on his difficult experiences at the Moscow Art Theater, which forced him to reconsider his place in the Soviet cultural sphere. Finally, I take up Olesha's most ambitious theatrical project—his collaboration with Meyerhold on *A List of Good Deeds*. The collaboration took on enormous personal importance for him; what he failed to achieve in his personal writings became Meyerhold's task to realize in public, on the stage. At its core, the production represented a member of the intelligentsia—Olesha himself—cleansing himself of aesthetic, ideological, and personal weakness to become an ideal Soviet citizen. At issue in Olesha's theatrical experiments was not only his success as a playwright but fundamental suppositions about the relationship between literature, dramatic theater, and the self-perception, the self-conception, of the artistic elite.

SEEKING ANOTHER SELF

Olesha began keeping a diary on May 5, 1930. He did so, he says in the first entry, as an antidote to "belles lettres." He's not referring to writing of the past, the Silver Age or the decades before, but to recent Soviet novels, which have become vile to him, forcing him to rethink the entire genre. "I despise belles lettres . . . they rot away [in the hands]! Their pages give me boils! Reading them has become disgusting!"[3]

At this point in his career, his reputation rested on the success of his short novel *Envy*, which had provoked animated discussion in the press because of its ambivalent representation of the conflict between the old Russian and the new Soviet world. That wasn't the success he needed, he decided. He needed to overcome its form, style, and subject matter to become a "new Soviet man."

How to do so was a problem he solved by abandoning novel-writing altogether. His diaries were the substitute. This impulse was hardly new in Russian literature; it began with the eighteenth-century Sentimentalists. And like the faux confidential "friends' letters" (*"druzheskie pis'ma"*) of Pushkin's time, Olesha intended his diaries as public not private documents, showing his colleagues that he was still an active member of the profession but going through a process of Stalinist redefinition. From the start, his diaries served as records of excruciating conversations with himself. The process of self-education had him frequently abandoning his diaries only to resume them again, leaving them fragmentary, unpolished, pitted out. The diary entries vary greatly in length, form, and style, and many are undated. Still, he intended his diaries to be read by his contemporaries, both his supporters and foes, as well as by future generations of Soviet readers. They give new meaning to the personal in a time and place that had resolved to re-motivate previous conceptions of the private and the intimate.

The diaries weren't published in his lifetime. Five years after the writer's death, in 1965, a novel-memoir-treatise appeared under the title *No Day without a Line: From Notebooks* (*Ni dnia bez strochki. Iz zapisnykh knizhek*).[4] The mysterious coda to his career, *No Day* tends to be published alongside his masterpiece *Envy*. In 1999, the Russian theater historian Violetta Gudkova published a revised edition of Olesha's diaries under the title *A Book of Farewell* (*Kniga proshchaniia*). This complicated publication history underscores the diaries' experimental nature.[5]

Olesha carefully addresses the delicate matter of the relationship between literature and the ideology of the new state. Even as he questions the value of fiction that seeks to "reflect" reality, Olesha frames his understanding of the alternative in the quasi-scientific terms of Marxist dialectics, which had become prominent in the public language of literary and cultural politics of the post-NEP years.

> Hardly a week passes before yet another campaign is announced, and here we go—a new crop of short stories appears, complete with plots, characters, human types—whatever your heart desires: collectivization, purges, constructing new cities. It's crucial, you see, that literature reflect modern-day concerns. But how timely is this form of "reflection"? A short story? A narrative poem? A novel? I think something else is more useful and valuable: nothing can be *synthesized* in one week, that's just *antiscientific*; and the meaning of art lies in *synthesizing* . . . So wouldn't it be better (and more interesting)—instead of writing about how an imaginary character was purged [*chistilsia*; literally, "purged himself"], to preserve the writings of any one of those who have been subjected to a cleansing [*kto podvergalsia chistke*] . . . Three cheers for diaries! (Writing fiction is getting to be too easy). (*KP* 36/20; emphasis added)

Olesha seeks to reconcile the impossible, skirting the fundamental tension between the imperatives of capturing "objective reality" (in Marxist terminology), on the one hand, and privileging the highly subjective medium of diary-writing (and self-changing) on the other. In Olesha's improvised dialectic utopia, synthesis is reserved for a new literature. As he relates his conception of non-"belletristic" literature, Olesha refers repeatedly to purging, which is of course a term associated with the NKVD (the People's Commissariat for Internal Affairs, the secret police) and the Stalinist repressions. Olesha broadens the definition of purging to include the systematic weeding-out of undesirable members of the Party, collectivization, and industrialization ("the Great Construction").[6] Purging, then, is a "modern-day concern," and serves a rhetorical purpose for Olesha as he talks about "belles lettres." But for Olesha purging is also—and above all—an operation he is carrying out in his diaries.

The diaries move backwards and forwards in time, embed narratives within narratives, and include fictional characters writing about other fictional characters. Like a hangman attending the hanging of another hangman, Olesha purges—cleanses—an author just like himself. The starkly impersonal constructions (passive voice, infinitive-imperatives, reflexive verbs)[7] in "his" narrative of self-cleansing are a riposte to the assumption that diaries are hopelessly subjective, unable to reflect reality with anything approaching objective accuracy. Olesha wants to believe that literature can reflect reality through the individual experience without falling prey to the vicissitudes of the writer's personality. To accomplish this in a journal, the writer must aim not merely at producing an account of how things really were or what really happened. He must also attempt, in Olesha's words, to expunge the fictional from the self (*vytravit' iz sebia belletristicheskoe* [*KP* 36/21]). The diary's specific charge is to develop a paradigm for writing that transgresses the conventional understanding of literature, turning it into a synthetic act where fiction and reality intersect on a higher plane. Hence Olesha's interest in scrubbing his craft of anything suggesting "belletrism": "It would be great to write a diary as a work of literature. That is, not a fictional diary, but a genuine, bona fide diary [*samyi nastoiashchii dnevnik*], and, after having kept it, say, a few years, then publish it as your new work."[8]

According to this vision, the diaries *become* "literature" by avoiding, and in effect rejecting, typical plot-units. The endeavor relies on metaphors borrowed from Soviet ideology, endowing the diaries with crucial new meanings. Olesha's experiment involves exploring and conceptualizing his self-understanding, his vocation as a writer, and his historical circumstances—that is, his existence as a member of the intelligentsia (an *intelligent*) in the new Soviet world.

The metaphors of bodily decay ("rotting," "burning") that launch his rhetorical assault on "belletrism" indicate the depth of his investment in fashioning a new "literature." He links his creative capacity to physiology,[9] and admits that his turn to diary-writing is rooted in anxiety:

I'm trying, intentionally, to be as lapidary as possible when I write—trying to expunge the fictional out of myself . . . Or maybe I no longer know how to write. "The glue of the epic does not flow freely from my quill." I tried to write a novel, describing the rain in the opening, and realized I was just *repeating myself* [*eto povtorenie samogo sebia*]. So I gave up, depressed and afraid. What if *Envy, Three Fat Men, A Conspiracy of Feelings*, a few short stories—what if that's all I was ever meant to have written? (*KP* 36/21; emphasis added)

Olesha is stuck trying to figure out (1) how to adapt to a new reality; (2) how to create a new literature for this new reality; and (3) how to create a new primary self that follows the truths unearthed by this new literature. His diaries describe his predicament, and that act of confessing becomes the synthesizing vision. In theory, Olesha can't repeat himself in a diary entry: the writer's self is inextricably linked to time, and time keeps moving, and time structures the reality he's recording. His diaries move deliberately and inexorably toward an unknown future. Every sentence is original insofar as it gives shape and meaning to something that did not, indeed *could* not, exist before.[10] The attempt to escape "bad" literature, then, parallels the project of articulating a new self and discarding an old one.[11] To write is to live, to be a writer is to be.

As Olesha's vision of professional, personal, and ideological rehabilitation through diary-writing takes shape, he also dissolves it. At one point he interrupts his musings on the virtues of diary-writing to acknowledge that the opening May 5, 1930, entry represents his second attempt to begin a diary in as many months. At several crucial points throughout the 1930s, Olesha claimed that he was "beginning anew," "starting over" with the entire project. He wrote on loose sheets of paper rather than in a notebook, ignoring evidence of previous work but also recycling and reshaping discarded material. This method allowed him to manufacture an appearance of immediacy and authenticity.[12] Olesha says that he began his first diary on the evening of April 13, not May 5, but the news of Vladimir Mayakovsky's suicide the following morning stopped his project in its tracks (*KP* 36/20–21). That his writing faltered in the face of an event of such "profound historical importance" (36/21) seems to contradict Olesha's promise to use his diaries to chronicle the events of his epoch.[13] He had provided a description of Mayakovsky's funeral in a letter to Meyerhold and Raikh but decided that it didn't belong in his journal.[14] The reason: lack of spontaneity. He composed three different versions of the letter before mailing it to Meyerhold and Raikh in Berlin.[15]

Besides lack of spontaneity, Olesha worried about his diary degenerating into fiction. "Sometimes I think that writing the diary is just a trick out of desire to use unusual material of some kind as a steppingstone for rediscovering novelistic form, i.e., going back to belles lettres" (*KP* 36/21).[16] This self-awareness was a crucial distinguishing mark of the new literary form he was creating. His silent editing of the "unusual material" in the first few paragraphs is counterweighed by the detailed, persistent critical ruminations on the form and the content of the work-in-progress. The passage where he accuses himself of trying to "cheat" his way back to fiction is one of the less forceful instances of self-awareness, self-criticism. Others are highly dramatic, with a generous use of parentheses and dashes. "Drumroll, please! Creativity is a profoundly physiological activity! (Of course that's well known, and has been for a while, it's been discussed for a while, it's been formulated before—there must be books written about it—so why am I repeating this?!)" (36–37/21; note Olesha's interest in purging repetitions). The parenthetical comments focus on the weaknesses Olesha perceives in his style,[17] and yet he allows these weaknesses to coexist with passages of stronger thoughts. His diaries include "wooden" language, "trite" thoughts, and repetitions that should have been excised. The presence of the imperfections makes the diaries seem authentic. There would be "no striking out, no crossing out, under any circumstances—[he would just be] writing down everything that comes to mind—no refining, straightforwardly [*lapidarno*]" (33/17).[18] His self-conscious fault-finding extends from the parentheses to invade the general texture of the narrative, as this passage about dying illustrates:

> I've had to interrupt writing—went to take a bath. It's hard to avoid Rozanovism in a diary. In the tub. Hot—fear of death—have to listen closer: is it the heart? is there something happening to my brain? or isn't there? *I think about death* a lot. Some old man determined, by looking at my handwriting, that *I think about death* a lot. Morbidly, *I think about death*—too often (almost constantly). It's disgusting, I want to get rid of it. (*KP* 37/21; emphasis added)

The remark about needing to avoid the aphoristic style of Vasilii Rozanov (1856–1919), a controversial conservative essayist and journalist, is linked, banally, to taking a bath which is in turn linked, even more banally, to death. To write about death in a diary is to confirm the self's inability to transcend the limitations of one's former self in the context of the "new," Soviet world. Instead of helping the writer appease the fear of death—one of the main motivations of diary-writing in general[19]—the May 5 entry seems to present death as the only definite source of the self: "I've thought this through and come up with the following conclusion: the only real thing in this world is my death. The rest is accidental, maybe it's there, and maybe it isn't—a specter; whereas my death will happen come what may" (*KP* 37/22).

Chapter Two

Olesha is alternately self-critical and reflective in his diaries, and aspects of the character he constructs can be likened to Dostoevsky's Underground Man and that famous antihero's "self-surveillance."[20]

The design of his diary also allows Olesha to reframe two fundamental categories of autobiographical writing: sincere expression and catering to an audience. Because the writer holds the authority to construct the narrative but is censured by that narrative, the notions of "lying" and "inventing" in their conventional sense cannot be directly applied to Olesha's diaries. As he implies, if he engages in either, he does so only to the extent that these devices help him create a more revealing account, establish a more powerful and far-reaching control over his putative weaknesses as a human being and man of letters. Is this dynamic catering to his old self, or helping him to forge a new one? It is telling that Olesha's analysis of the way (other) diaries are made relies heavily on third-person verbal forms, implicitly contrasting Olesha with the generalized other authors whose predicament he discusses:

> No diary is absolutely honest. People want to spare their friends' feelings. They are embarrassed. There's always the chance of the diary being read by someone else. People come up with tricks. Secret codes. Who knows, what if there's a police search. You can have secrets from the wife, too. What if the wife finds it accidentally—and is going to spend the whole evening, red and out of breath, swallowing page after page . . . So people lie straight out, invent things. (And you do want to look intelligent in front of your offspring.) (*KP* 47/32)

Olesha doesn't experience the common anxieties of diary-keepers. His journal is meant to be "read by someone," and the process of being read while one is writing is part of his account. Olesha oscillates between public confession and private assessment: he is writing for publication; he is writing for himself.[21]

> The idea that the self can be understood and captured in writing—
> So who am I? Who? This question must be resolved, must be answered—
> (*KP* 71/57)

The question coexists with a perception of the self as radically mutable. "I'm sick of being myself [*Nadoelo byt' samim soboi*]," Olesha confesses. "I want to be someone else. I *could even* change physically" (*KP* 59/44; emphasis added). Physical transformation is neither necessary nor sufficient; it is secondary to another, as yet unspecified, means of altering identity. Finding a surrogate, becoming the Other, defines Olesha's journal. In one entry, he adopts the persona of a bland *chinovnik*: "I am a Soviet civil servant. Today

I resolved to begin writing a diary. My name is Stepanov. Grigorii Ivanovich Stepanov. 1934. April 16" (116/104). Elsewhere, he represents himself as a peasant-worker hero:

> Saw a man at the barber's—the kind I would like to have been myself [*kakim khotelos' by samomu byt'*]. He was getting a shave. A peasant, probably. The face of a soldier, maybe forty years old, healthy, lips like Mayakovsky's, blond. It's the kind of face you want to call modern, internationally masculine: the face of a pilot—the modern type of manliness.[22] A man like that stands somewhere between courage, magnanimity, and technology. He flies across the ocean, he loves his mother, he stops a car sliding into the river by grabbing on to one of the wheels, he turns up when an electric cable falls on the street, and he materializes atop the fire ladder that has arrived on the scene of the accident, wearing his rubber gloves. (*KP* 37–38/22)

Olesha's 1927 novel *Envy* engages, satirically, with the utopianism of the first decade of Soviet power. In his diaristic vision of a near-mythical, elusive New Person (*KP* 39/23), physicality and ideology come together: admirable (even enviable) masculinity is inseparable from a thoroughly Soviet identity.[23] Yet, just as "Grigorii Stepanov," certainly a figment of Olesha's imagination, is identified above all as a "Soviet public servant," the barbershop client Olesha wants to become is first described, and defined, as a peasant. His "would-be-selves" exist at opposite sides of the sociopolitical spectrum.

The April 13, 1930, entry moves from a brief discussion of Olesha's creative hopes to an acidic passage about getting older and physically declining—he was just thirty-one—and then moves into a critique of his peers: "Our generation, the generation of thirty-year-old *intelligenty*, is an uneducated generation" (*KP* 33/18). Then, on May 5, 1930: "Difficult is the life of a thirty-year-old *intelligent* in the era of the Great Construction" (37/22). Each time he uses the word *intelligent* he is expressing disappointment and frustration.[24] The reference to the "Great Construction" ("*Velikaia Stroika*") of the First Five-Year Plan underscores his failure to adapt. "I am a Russian *intelligent*," he continues, and this "moniker"

> is a product of Russia and Russia alone. There are engineers, writers, politicians in the world. We have a profession of the *intelligent*. He's the one who doubts, suffers, finds himself split in two [*razdvaivaetsia*], takes the fault, repents and knows the precise meaning of "heroic deed," "conscience," etc. My dream is to stop being an *intelligent*. (*KP* 55/41)

That being an *intelligent* is a matter of professional affiliation and occupation for Olesha becomes clear when he describes self-criticism—blaming oneself, self-reflexivity (his term is *razdvoenie*: duality, literally "being split-in-two"), confessing—as a preoccupation of the intelligentsia. The desire to remold himself paradoxically makes him consider abandoning his diaries, which were supposed to help with this process: "I'm sick of being an *intelligent*, sick of this Hamletism. It's an occupational hazard of being a writer. The subjectivistic essence of the writerly profession: digging within oneself" (*KP* 37/22); "Boring diary, self-digging, Hamletism—I don't want to be an *intelligent*" (39/24).

Whether Olesha begins with a discussion of his craft, of the events of the day, of his decaying physical condition, or of his future, he is unable to sustain the narrative because it ultimately doubles up on itself. Olesha abandons his journal, and then, after a pause, returns to it, hoping to avoid the same dead end. In a telling passage of self-surveillance, he writes the same phrase twice: "*Chut' podlinnee. Chut' podlinnee*" (*KP* 77/63). The first phrase, "*chut' podlinnée*," means "just a little longer," while the second, "*chut' pódlinnee*," comes out as "just a little more authentic." Can he find a new format for his diary, a format that would allow him to expand the scope of his inquiry without undermining his goals?

On January 20, 1931, Olesha began his diary anew, this time explicitly referencing the theater:

> Let me inform the future aficionados of memoir literature that the most remarkable man I have ever known in my life was Vsevolod Meyerhold. In 1929 he commissioned a play from me. I wrote that play in February–March of 1930. In the winter of 1931, he began working on it. I want to write a book about Meyerhold directing my play. (*KP* 25/9)[25]

Questions arise: how much room can there be for the story of the self in another man's undertaking? What relevance did studying a theatrical production have for Olesha's project of "writing more *authentically*"? The answers reside in his diaristic account of the Meyerhold production and the Meyerhold–Olesha relationship.

AT THE MOSCOW ART THEATER: THE STAGE AS PROMISE AND CHALLENGE

What an era! A play of mine is being done by the Art Theater. Me—an author of the Art Theater. Maeterlinck, Chekhov, Andreev and me. Imagine that. Even Andreev thought it an achievement: to have a play open at the Art Theater. And here's me, a tiny schoolboy, a denizen of Odessa, Daddy's and Mommy's little son—I, too, have become an author of a famous theater. (*KP* 42/27)

Gingerly, Olesha tries the new identity on for size. The ambiguous genitive construction *"avtor Khudozhestvennogo teatra"* holds the promise of something more than mere institutional affiliation. Like other modernist authors involved with MAT, Olesha wanted to be a co-creator of the institution. As discussed in the first chapter of this book, he conceived *Three Fat Men* as a replacement for Stanislavsky's production of Maeterlinck's *Blue Bird*, which had been popular with children since 1908.[26]

The author of a play manipulates the theater staging the play, and the theater staging the play manipulates the author of the play. Just as Olesha expected to transform a crucial institution of Russian cultural and intellectual life—MAT—so he looked forward to being transformed by it. To be (quite literally) stage-managed: this experience is available to the playwright but not to the prose writer, poet, or diarist. In a sense, then, Olesha sought an escape from the anonymous creativity of literature even though his playscript belonged to literature. Reconciling the writing of the self with the staging of the self are part of a bigger project: becoming a New Person. At the same time that he was asking himself questions about the meaning of his diarist writings, searching for a new sense of self, the same process was unfolding at MAT. "A feeling of boundless, tender gratitude takes hold of me," he wrote,

> when I listen to, and watch, the actors perform the roles I invented. *This, then, is what I came into this world for: to compose roles*, to create that very strange entity called art whose origins and aims are ultimately inscrutable. My dear, darling actors, we have all been fused together—me with my ability to articulate thoughts by putting them into words, you with your capacity for giving shape to what I have thought up, that is, to *my very own life* as it has been transformed on the page. (*KP* 101/89; emphasis added)[27]

In his formulation, "writing parts" (or "composing roles") serves as both a metaphor and a potential justification for his craft. Olesha's identity as an author, then, is defined in terms of his experience of being embodied and even resurrected onstage, as an experiment in staging his self.

The passage referencing the fame of Chekhov and Maeterlinck is dated May 7, 1930, two days after Olesha resumes his diary, and only a few days before *Three Fat Men* goes into dress rehearsals. Olesha attempts to describe a *Fat Men* rehearsal, but it becomes a discussion of MAT as a cultural institution and what it was like to be a playwright for MAT before the Revolution. In Olesha's telling, getting a play accepted at MAT before 1917 allowed the aspiring young writer to "solidify his situation" (improve his finances) and increase his "personal dignity" (*KP* 43/28). Dignity is the true measure of fame and the attribute of an author of authority (the wordplay is distinctly Olesha's: "*avtoritetnyi avtor*"). The intelligentsia gave the author this influence through "a special kind of attention—sympathetic, thoughtful, compassionate—in other words, *the attention of someone very much like yourself*" which was fixed by default on every new MAT production (43/28, emphasis added).[28] The prominent, progressive writer, by contrast, did not have to compromise his "personal dignity."[29] In Olesha's diaristic fantasy about the life of a MAT playwright, access to material privileges (wearing tails at a fancy reception) comes with a license to challenge the institution that had provided the privileges:

> At a soirée in the capital, among the pillars of society—in a tuxedo, stylish—I could have uttered words that would spread like flames on a safety fuse, leading to an explosion. *I could have uttered words directed against the very people who had created me, against my own kind.* I could have said: "I detest people." And the people whom I detested would have forgiven me and even called me a philosopher. That's the thing of it. (*KP* 44/29; emphasis added)

The thoroughly theatrical configuration of this fantasy world—a good costume, a pithy line of dialogue, an attentive audience—reflects Olesha's vision of the intelligentsia as the culture of its own kind (*svoi*). It is a close-knit circle of pretentious elites subjecting each other to verbal abuse. As noted in the previous chapter, MAT's production of *Three Fat Men* portrayed just such an abusive community. The characters lauded by Lunacharsky in his review as representing the finest attributes of the intelligentsia are impervious to the abuse they've received (and meted out).[30]

Olesha is just one of the authors of the production of *Three Fat Men*. His playscript accrues different meanings, and so in a sense does he, because the playscript is an expression of the self and now the playscript has changed. Olesha relished the chance to shape the future of the theater just as the theater shaped him. He was also interested in changing the theatrical experience for the audience, especially the intellectuals writing the reviewing and paying the closest attention to the play. He worked at a theater, and the theater worked at him.

Still, even as Olesha enumerates the privileges of involvement with MAT, he senses a divide between what that institution promised and what sociopolitical circumstances demanded. He alludes to this division in different passages in his diaries. Before 1917, MAT existed, as it were, outside of time, offering its authors not relevance or immediacy or even authenticity but a place in the canon, the status of a Classic:

You were invited to join an exceptionally select set, haughty and arrogant by definition—the nation's [cultural] vanguard, the "cream of the crop." All of Russia was provincial, small-town. And then—somewhere up there, beyond it all—there was *stolichnost'*: big-city lifestyle, the way they live in the capital. *Stolichnost'* was the pinnacle of all your aspirations. Becoming an Art Theater author meant turning into one of the luminaries of *stolichnost'*. (*KP* 43/28)

"*Stolichnost'*" is Olesha's shorthand for a hierarchical cosmopolitan culture that fosters dissent even as it dictates the latest fashions. The concept helps him imagine the collapse, in the Soviet context, of the cultural metaphors upon which the theater's authority had been premised. With Moscow's political and economic dominance challenged by the rise of the new industrial cities (like, for example, the muscular iron-smelting town of Magnitogorsk in the Ural Mountains), the opposition between center and periphery dissolves. Every place, every theater, serves the same truth—the only truth, as it is revealed to them in an overarching plan.[31] According to Olesha, the body politic does not yet have enough "fat and flesh," but even in the new society's nascent state the Moscow Art Theater, like Moscow, was losing the dominance it had in the first years of the Revolution:

The idea takes shape, becomes flesh, and—what do you know!—does not incorporate the Moscow Art Theater. And so I, having only now become one of the Theater's authors, feel truncated, two-dimensional. MAT has been deprived of one of its dimensions. That is why I feel neither joyous nor triumphant as my play opens at the very theater where Chekhov's plays ran, at the theater whose troupe includes—do you hear?—Kachalov himself! (*KP* 44–45/30)

As this passage shows, Olesha's self-understanding is bound up with his role as an "author of [and for] the theater." But MAT's loss of status in Soviet culture has deprived Olesha of an entire side of himself. His hopes have been dashed; he realizes that his expectations have been misplaced. The themes Olesha built into *Three Fat Men* are transformed in his diaries into metaphors of discontent. The power of embodiment, theater's ability to manufacture layers of meaning unavailable to language, are aligned in Olesha's thinking with the realization of the Soviet Idea. His attempts to become a genuine Soviet citizen through his work in the theater are thwarted by the theater's diminished relationship with Soviet reality. If MAT forfeits its privileged position in the construction of the new world, Olesha's work loses relevance. It becomes suspect, and he becomes disenchanted.

Olesha translates his observations into the Marxist language of class struggle and recoils in disgust. The yearning for the attention of a like-minded *intelligent* camouflages a deeper craving for the return of a world in which cultural institutions served the interests of Olesha's own class, the bourgeoisie: "I am a petty bourgeois . . . in my blood, in my braincells" (*KP* 45/30).[32] Olesha's somber assessment of MAT's prospects for being successfully absorbed into the new body politic and maintaining its cultural relevance points to lingering doubts about the theater's possibilities as a ground for articulating an adequate self-conception. Contrary to Lunacharsky's claim, in the review of *Three Fat Men*, that Olesha had transcended polarizing ideological categories through theatrical means,[33] Olesha claims that he had failed at the effort, and had come to a dead end: "Having become an author of a theater built by a bourgeois, I am in a state of total bewilderment: I am neither a bourgeois nor a New Person—so who am I? Nobody. A function in time. I am my own thought hatched in childhood" (46/31).

Olesha arrives at this cul-de-sac through his scathingly self-critical unraveling of his affiliation with MAT. He writes in a confessional mode with no shortage of self-accusation and self-surveillance, even though nothing has yet gone wrong in his career.[34] Every time Olesha begins to articulate his understanding of the theater's function and possibilities, the rhetoric of the diary takes over. Olesha's experiment in writing the self, as it were, undercuts his staging of the self.

Olesha's disenchantment with MAT increased when the production of *Three Fat Men* was canceled in the 1931–32 season. The end of its run validated the acerbic observations about MAT he expressed in his diary. But while being an "Art Theater author" no longer seemed viable, Olesha didn't abandon his interest in performance as a mode of self-reflexivity. His exploration of transformative violence, both on stage and in the diaries, led Olesha out of his limbo (the condition of being "neither a bourgeois nor a New Person"). If he was to succeed, however, Olesha needed to find the right language for self-reflection and self-observation. He began to use his diaries in the service of theatrical experiment, not as a corrective to it.

While Olesha was attempting to synthesize the contradictory ideological and aesthetic imperatives of literary self-inquiry—and attending rehearsals at MAT—he was drafting a new, as yet untitled dramatic work, the future *A List of Good Deeds*.[35] Olesha's various preoccupations—stimulating artistic production, articulating a self-conception, taking stock of being staged by MAT, and writing for the stage—all came together in his journal.

In his review of *Three Fat Men* Lunacharsky called Olesha the self-appointed spokesman for the "eccentrics," describing them as "the best representatives of the intelligentsia." But as noted, Olesha's relationship with the intelligentsia was far more complicated and uneasy than Lunacharsky signals. Recall Olesha's earlier definition of writing and self-reflexivity as the occupational hazards of being an *intelligent*. In his play, Olesha altogether avoids the word "intelligentsia." Circumlocution is more than a narrative device: it is an important aspect of Olesha's attempt to purge the person of the *intelligent* from reflections about his own present and future. This move works well in the theatrical context, where action, rather than narrative, defines the character's relationships, and mentions of rank or title or status can be omitted without hindering dialogue. How a character behaves can matter far more on stage than the badge he wears.

Olesha makes a distinction between proletarian *"obshchestvennost'*,*"* the community of proletarian organizations, labor unions, and the press—and another, parallel *"obshchestvennost'.*"[36] This second category is characterized by the absence of characteristics:

> This community [*obshchestvennost'*] is regulated by no one; it functions according to intrinsic laws legislated with no regard for labor unions, newspapers, etc.; its constant transformations are as unpredictable and its heartbeat as irregular as the fluctuations of free-market prices. A product of nobody's deliberate design, it is supported by a powerful mechanism which everyone knows about—a mechanism whose gears shift on their own, even though no one is standing by the lever waiting to push it; in fact, it's not even clear where that lever is or what it looks like. (*KP* 40/25)

Here, then, is what Lunacharsky called the "appearance of lack of coercion." Alternative but not necessarily adversarial (because it, too, works for the benefit of the new state), Olesha's unnamed second *"obshchestvennost'"* is able to wield authority *and* perpetuate itself without being led or governed by anyone. This "nameless" (unnamable?) community is Olesha's "new intelligentsia," though, to be sure, it has been represented before in his work, in *Three Fat Men*, and, to a lesser extent, in *A Conspiracy of Feelings*.[37]

Still, Olesha recognizes the need to distinguish his new theatrical project from those that came before. He defines *A List of Good Deeds* as a "Soviet-(hu)man comedy" (*KP* 41/26).[38] The outline for the play lists five character "types," who represent different factions of the community he is putting on stage.[39] Each of them comes with a slogan, a catchphrase explaining their relationship to the state.[40] The play's intrigue centers on finding the lever that controls these representatives of the parallel *"obshchestvennost'"*:

> Construction of socialism in a single country serves as the background. The conflict revolves around the problem of dual existence, the life of the self [*sobstvennoe ia*, literally "one's own 'I'"], the profoundly *kulak*[41] nature [*kulacheskaia sushchnost'*] of that life, and the need to construct socialism, under which any and all varieties of the will to property [*sobstvennicheskaia sushchnost'*] will be de-kulakized. (*KP* 41/26)[42]

Chapter Two

This passage demonstrates the shifting function of the diaries. Much as he did in earlier entries, Olesha grafts terms for self-exploration ("dual existence," "the life of the self") onto the discourse of class warfare ("de-kulakization"). The formulation is also a product of Olesha's reflections on theatrical embodiment in *Three Fat Men*. In the MAT production of that play, absurdist violence is transformative, even liberating. In the plans for the new play, "de-kulakization" allows for the constitution of the parallel "*obshchestvennost'*"—the new world Olesha identifies with. The question arises: Having distanced himself from the traditional intelligentsia, could he in fact replace it with a genuine Soviet intelligentsia? One in which the "I" was one's own (*sobstvennoe*), but somehow not one's personal property (*sobstvennost'*), as was the case earlier?

The effort leads him to the eminent director Vsevolod Meyerhold.

OLESHA AND MEYERHOLD AND THE CONTRADICTIONS OF PERFORMANCE

Meyerhold is sitting behind Olesha. They are both at the Moscow Art Theater, taking in a performance of *Three Fat Men*. On stage, the absent-minded professor, Doctor Gaspar Arneri, asks the fat men to commute the death sentence of the rebel leader Prospero. When the Fat Men refuse, Arneri enlists the circus performer Suok to impersonate the magical doll. She goes limp and collapses: the doll that had just been magically resurrected in front of the Fat Men is broken once more. In the audience Meyerhold taps Olesha on the shoulder and whispers something to him.

That this incident should become, in Olesha's diaries, a paradigmatic revelatory moment is telling: his collaboration with Meyerhold on *A List of Good Deeds* was transformative. In the incident, Meyerhold apparently whispered: "The heart is kind" ("*Serdtse dobroe*"). The power of the human heart is a point of focus in *Three Fat Men*,[43] and Meyerhold could be merely acknowledging a striking metaphor.[44] But Olesha interprets the remark not as a comment on his play but as an appraisal of his character; he is convinced that in the play's action Meyerhold has "discerned the kindness of [Olesha's] own heart" (*KP* 104/92). To Olesha this experience suggests that his self can, in effect, be made legible to others on stage—and that the man in the next row who convinced him of that possibility is "Meyerhold the omniscient, the genius, the child, and *my own self*" (104/92; emphasis added).[45]

If Meyerhold *is* Olesha, one might ask, does Olesha see himself, in turn, as an omniscient and/or childish genius? As Olesha announces his radical identification with Meyerhold, he consistently avoids addressing this question. The focus is instead on Olesha's willingness, even eagerness, to surrender his aesthetic and ethical authority to the great director. Olesha's descriptions of his encounters with Meyerhold range from admiring to obsessive. He pleads for reciprocity of feeling: "[Meyerhold] is a strange, wonderful human being, a man of the stage whom I love terribly. And I terribly want him to love me as well" (*KP* 104/92). He defends what he believes to be Meyerhold's vision of the future of theater—even if that means scolding Meyerhold's wife (Zinaida Raikh) for doubting her husband.⁴⁶ Olesha's attempts to rhetorically possess Meyerhold inevitably involve upholding "the Master" (the form of address Meyerhold cultivated, and one Olesha gladly appropriates) as the most important standard for his own understanding of art and life: "Meyerhold is my yardstick for judging character. You scoff at him—you're an idiot. You have to worship geniuses unconditionally, worship those who invent things, the visionaries—worship their subtlety, their surprising insights" (104/91). By conflating originality of creative vision with strength of character, this ranking system implies, in turn, that Olesha's achievement can be measured in degrees of his acquiescence to Meyerhold: "He will direct my play, *A List of Good Deeds*. That's how far I've come!" (104/92).⁴⁷

Here is the culmination of Olesha's self-staging and self-writing projects. He recognizes Meyerhold's power and wants to join his Russian-Soviet theater.⁴⁸ He knows that it will be a different experience than joining MAT. In 1930 Meyerhold is a recognized, if controversial, leader of avant-garde theater, a bold experimenter who has redefined "doing theater." Just as important for Olesha, Meyerhold has embraced the Soviet world and has contributed to the building of Soviet culture. Even when Meyerhold clashes with critics and government officials, even when his productions receive bad press or are not allowed to open (which happened several times in the late 1920s and early 1930s), Meyerhold's authority isn't contested.⁴⁹ What's not accurate is the representation of him as *the* most authoritative director. Aleksandr Tairov earns that title.⁵⁰

There is another important difference. Olesha is now working for a single creator, "the Master," rather than a troupe. He is not being initiated into an organization where everyone has a role in shaping the repertoire. Rather, he is humbly submitting to Meyerhold, who is known for radical productions of the Russian classics, with each part subordinated to the director's obsessions. Meyerhold made the plays of Gogol, Ostrovskii, and Griboedov almost unrecognizable; he also, against the odds, turned the Futurist poet Mayakovsky into a successful playwright. The program for the opening night of *A List of Good Deeds* declared Meyerhold, not Olesha, the "author of the production" ("*avtor postanovki*") and calls it *his* "OPUS 1931" (*OM* 507). Olesha's staging of the self became Meyerhold's staging.⁵¹

The plot of *A List of Good Deeds* concerns a fictional Soviet actress and director, Elena Nikolaevna (or Lelia) Goncharova. The Soviet government sends Lelia to Paris on a kind of research trip: to study Western theater and meet with her foreign colleagues. Lelia's frustration with her life in the Soviet Union leads her to consider defecting. Before she leaves Moscow, Lelia tells a friend that she's been keeping a special sort of diary, a political journal, a chronicle of everything that has happened in Russia since 1917. It includes two lists: a list of the Soviet regime's crimes and a list of its good deeds.[52] Knowing the journal will place her in great danger if found in her Moscow apartment, Lelia takes it with her to Paris. There Lelia is invited to an "international actors' ball" hosted by a millionaire sympathetic to the Soviet cause. She doesn't have a proper gown; an émigré Russian journalist—the play's villain—offers her the services of his dressmaker mistress. She's broke, so the journalist allows her to pay for the dress on credit. He steals Lelia's journal as she's writing the promissory note.

Short on funds, Lelia pays a visit to Margerette, the manager of the Globe Music Hall, to see if he might be interested in her services as an actress. In the Soviet Union, Goncharova had become famous for her performance, *en travesti*, of the title role in *Hamlet*. In the prologue to *A List of Good Deeds*, which takes place during a post-show discussion at Lelia's theater in Moscow, she performs act 3, scene 2, of Shakespeare's tragedy at the request of a proletarian spectator. She performs this same scene for Margerette, taking on the parts of both Hamlet and Guildenstern. Margerette is so perplexed by the performance that he withdraws his offer of employment. Shocked and upset, Lelia storms out, but not before an unpleasant encounter with the star of the Globe, an androgynous cabaret singer named Ulalume.

The Russian reporter who has stolen her journal publishes excerpts of it in his newspaper, which makes Lelia persona non grata back home. Lelia has long since realized that the capitalist world is crueler than the Soviet world, and that "freedom" in the capitalist context is just another form of bondage. But all the same, she's trapped in Paris. ("Olesha's essence is homelessness and a longing for a home," Slavist Helen Muchnic observed in an overview of his work, and that longing made him a "craftsman of unrest.")[53] The French police enlist Lelia to help arrest a French communist leader, but she defends the man instead, taking a bullet for him—that is to say, a bullet for her Soviet homeland's "deeds"—and then she dies on the streets of Paris just as a workers' march is getting under way. The play, then, is "an optimistic tragedy" (to borrow Vishnevskii's title) about the search for an authentic and meaningful Soviet identity. Lelia speaks on behalf of a larger artistic and intellectual community that remains nameless, much like the parallel "*obshchestvennost'*" described in Olesha's outline.

By the time *A List of Good Deeds* opened in June 1931, the playscript had gone through at least three major revisions, and it would be further edited for publication.⁵⁴ In the process, the playscript evolved significantly from the outline in Olesha's journal. One of the most noticeable changes, introduced by Olesha himself in the early stages, involved reducing the five character "types" to a single personage, Lelia. Olesha made this decision long before Meyerhold or anyone else saw the full version of the playscript. The play underwent many other changes in the two years of rehearsals. Some were Olesha's improvements, others were recommended by Meyerhold, and still others were mandated by the censorship board Glavrepertkom.⁵⁵ Many of these changes involved revising or excising images of Soviet society as uncultured, intolerant, or arbitrarily repressive.⁵⁶ What do these changes, especially those introduced by the government censors, mean for any attempts to connect the Meyerhold production to Olesha's earlier theatrical experiences and his larger self-staging project?

Previous studies of *A List of Good Deeds* have sought to divine Olesha's intentions, specifically his inclination toward justifying and/or condemning the play's characters in the different versions of the playscript. This line of inquiry relies upon categories borrowed from the language of the play and follows the characters' own definitions of these terms. My reading sees the different versions of the playscript as illuminating Olesha's original diaristic project. Throughout the writing and staging process, as certain lines of dialogue were replaced with somewhat less polemical but often equally ambivalent substitutions,⁵⁷ the project of articulating the self, as it had been conceived and transformed in Olesha's diaries, remained at the playscript's core.⁵⁸ Olesha submitted the playscript to Meyerhold knowing that it would be remade to suit the director's aims. The latter's production foregrounded ideas that could not easily be censored; removing or rephrasing passages that struck Glavrepertkom as too negative or severe did nothing to change these ideas, which remained intact through the various drafts of the playscript.

The premiere of *A List of Good Deeds* was a major event in the cultural and intellectual life of the Soviet capital. At a series of "open" and "restricted" (by invitation only) public discussions and in several high-profile newspaper articles published in June 1931, reviewers of the production offered competing opinions about two things. The first issue was the play's contemporaneousness: What did Olesha have to say about "the fate of the old intelligentsia," and was the play obliged to take up this subject? The second issue was Meyerhold's success or failure in "staging a play the proletariat could understand."⁵⁹ The lack of consensus among the reviewers contrasted with their agreement about Meyerhold's uncharacteristic loyalty to the playwright's text. Those familiar with Meyerhold's previous work were amazed that his production neither resisted nor undermined the playscript. That left Olesha, as much as Meyerhold, on the hook for the production's weaknesses.⁶⁰ For Olesha, the criticism of *A List of Good Deeds* recalled that of *Three Fat Men* at MAT, which was seen as a departure from Stanislavsky's typical approach. His new play was considered untypical of Meyerhold. Of course, how or if Meyerhold transformed the play wasn't clear. The text hadn't been published in advance and so did not exist as an independent work of literature (unlike, say, the case with Gogol's *Inspector General*). *A List of Good Deeds* suggested a different type of relationship between text and performance, text and act.

Transcripts of rehearsals at the Meyerhold Theater and Olesha's drafts find Meyerhold shaping the staging around a single scene. The scene in question was Lelia's visit to the Globe, the vaudeville theater where she hoped to find a job. In the final version of the playscript, Olesha separated out seven episodes of similar length. Meyerhold grouped these into four acts. The scene at the theater, the placement of which he changed during the rehearsal process, now took up most of the third act. This emphasis was noted by the critics and discussion participants: those who approved of the production and those who disparaged it agreed that the scene was the highlight of the evening, showcasing Meyerhold and Olesha at their best. And yet most of them were at a loss to explain what made the scene work. Reviewers instead concentrated on the ideological implications of Lelia's actions at the beginning of the play and in the final scene. The scene at the Globe defied easy interpretation. A closer look at this scene, then, is warranted.

The scene is obviously concerned with styles and techniques of performance—those of Lelia, the theater manager, and the cabaret singer. To see how this meta-theatrical theme, in Meyerhold's staging, relates to Olesha's interest in the theater as a venue of self-understanding, we need to consider the references to the Hamlet character and to *Hamlet* the tragedy, an obsession shared by Olesha, Meyerhold, and the actors in the main roles of *A List of Good Deeds*.[61]

We last encountered Hamlet in Olesha's diaries. There, the name of Shakespeare's self-obsessed, self-narrating, and self-analyzing character is a kind of shorthand for the compulsive introspection characteristic of the Russian/Soviet *intelligent*. Introspection, Olesha makes plain, is the professional hazard of the elite: "I'm tired of being an *intelligent*," he vents, "sick of Hamletism" (*KP* 37/22); "We were once all Hamlets, and we lived entirely inside ourselves" (38/23); "Boring diary, digging into the self [*samokopanie*], Hamletism—I don't want to be an *intelligent*" (39/24). This view of Hamlet echoes a particular tradition of reading the play in Russian culture, codified by Ivan Turgenev in an 1860 lecture called "Hamlet and Don Quixote."[62] For Turgenev, the two characters reflected different types of forces. Hamlet placed himself at the center of the cosmos, with everything relating to him, while Don Quixote existed in relation to other things, seeking to benefit others. Hamlet, Turgenev added, was too skeptical to believe in good and too moral to commit to evil. His inwardness, the "centripetal" orientation of his thoughts, ultimately paralyzed him.[63]

Turgenev's additional claim—that "Hamlet must have kept a diary"[64]—is referenced in Olesha's diaries and literalized in his play. Lelia's crisis of faith, which embraces both resentment of Soviet reality and disillusionment with the myth of Europe, is structured according to Turgenev's model of Hamlet as an intellectual in limbo. However, her strategy for dealing with that crisis involves keeping a journal, and the chain of events that leads to her ruin originates with that journal.[65] There's another connection to Turgenev that would be clear to everyone in the audience. Lelia's death on the streets of Paris evokes the final scene of Turgenev's novel *Rudin* (1855), whose protagonist, a wavering Russian intellectual, dies on Parisian barricades in the waning days of the 1848 Revolution.[66]

The dramatic conflict that Olesha assigns to Lelia closely resembles Hamlet's predicament: the perception of something rupturing in historical time; anxiety over the loss of reason in everyday experience; and sensitivity to language's role in defining the self. For Lelia, all these concerns are interrelated, as she makes clear during her conversation with a Soviet trade representative whom she has met at her hotel in Paris:

> I remember what my personal life was like in the world that you call "new." It was all in my thoughts. The Revolution has taken my past away from me but it has failed to show the future to me. And so *thought became my present*. To think . . . I thought, only thought—by means of thought I wanted to attain what I couldn't attain by feeling. A human being's life is natural when *reason and feelings* are in harmony. I was deprived of that harmony (and so my life in the new world was unnatural. My reason fully comprehended the concept of Communism; my brain believed that the final triumph of the proletariat is in the natural pattern of things to come. But my emotions were against it), I was torn in half. So I ran away here from that divided life, and if I hadn't run away then I *would have gone mad*. In the new world I lay about like a fragment of broken glass. Now I have returned, and the two halves have united. I live a natural life. I have recovered *present-tense verbs*. I *eat, touch, look, walk*. (*OM* 318–19; emphasis added)[67]

Olesha's Lelia is like Turgenev's Hamlet: a skeptic. Thinking and reason are a trap—not because they undermine her abilities to act, but because thought and reason have become instruments of faith rather than critical inquiry. Lelia's vision of personal harmony circumscribes the "centripetal" worldview excoriated by Turgenev, which is also the "Hamletism" referenced by Olesha in his diaries. Lelia transcends the fundamental contradictions of her Soviet "double life" with the help of a syllogism. In the monologue quoted above, thought gives meaning to time, and time gives meaning to language: in the Soviet Union, thought "becomes her present," in the West she "recovers present-tense verbs." If, as the monologue suggests, language can invest the experience of touching, looking, walking, and so on, with profound new meanings, then thought and feeling can be reconciled by recovering the language lost in the temporal cataclysm of the Revolution.

The yearning for a "harmonious" future, epitomized by Lelia's character, becomes a search for lost time. At several points in the play she suggests that verbs conjugated in the present tense are meaningless if one has not been able to recover the language of the past, the "nouns" that the Revolution and the Soviet experiment had rendered obsolete: "bride, groom, guest, friendship, reward, virginity, fame."[68] Each noun related to an aspect of Soviet public or private life that had disappeared, or was in the process of disappearing. When she uses these nouns in a sentence with present-tense verbs—the way she speaks in capitalist Paris, not communist Moscow—Olesha's heroine reconstitutes the cultural mechanisms that disappeared together with those concepts. Recall that in Olesha's diaries a single word can symbolize an entire worldview, linking metaphors of past times and places. (One such word, singled out in the previous section, is *stolichnost'*: "the quality of life in a capital city.") In *A List of Good Deeds*, the word "Europe" has this function. In a tiny room of a Moscow communal apartment and in the foyer of a Paris hotel, Lelia envisions her search for the right sort of language as a quest for "European culture." Europe is emblematized by two names: Charlie Chaplin and William Shakespeare. Lelia idolizes Chaplin, and one of her primary motivations for going abroad is to be able to watch his films.[69] Chaplin represents the Europe that can only be experienced by going to Paris. Shakespeare, in contrast, transcends all borders. Lelia's biggest achievement, Olesha tells us, involved "bringing *Hamlet* to the New Person."[70] Performing *Hamlet* allowed her to recover a certain type of language, language that reconciled thought and feeling.

For the practitioners of Soviet theater in the 1930s and for Meyerhold specifically, *Hamlet* was rich with cultural and ideological connotations. In the first scene of *A List of Good Deeds*, Lelia responds to notes from her audience demanding that she justify her choice to stage a work as archaic and impenetrable as *Hamlet* "in this day and age." She says that her production might be the last time Shakespeare's play is ever seen in the Soviet Union.[71] For the audiences of *A List of Good Deeds*, the most recent Moscow production of *Hamlet* was the Second Moscow Art Theater's 1924 version, directed by, and starring, Mikhail Chekhov, nephew of the writer and an artistic rival as well as close friend of Meyerhold's.[72] In 1928 Chekhov, at the time the artistic director of the Second Moscow Art Theater and an internationally famous Soviet theater personality, went to Germany with his wife on an official leave of absence and did not return. After it became known that Chekhov had defected, *Hamlet* was barred from performance in Moscow. (Meyerhold would be involved in a defection—or possible defection—scandal of his own in 1930. His theater was late returning from a trip to Germany and France in the spring of that year and wasn't allowed to travel abroad again.)[73] The status of Shakespeare's tragedy was an uneasy one, then: though never banned, it had been in a way exiled together with the man who produced the most memorable interpretation of that text in the Soviet 1920s. By structuring the plot of *A List of Good Deeds* around the attempted defection of a famous actress/director who stages *Hamlet*, Olesha and Meyerhold invoked the well-known incident with Mikhail Chekhov and alluded to the fate of his theatrical legacy. They posed a larger question about the cultural and ideological significance of producing *Hamlet* on the Soviet stage.

The fate of *Hamlet* in Soviet theaters preoccupied Meyerhold. After Chekhov's defection, it seemed that it could only be performed in a play-within-a-play context. The Hamlet in *A List of Good Deeds* was the last of the Hamlets seen on a Moscow stage for a long time, and reviewers had a lot to say about the insertion, finding within it a kind of confession on Olesha's part. His career was an extended working out of the "to be or not to be" question—that is to say, should the intelligentsia be with the Bolsheviks or not be with them? The problem was complicated by the nature of the people championed by the government. Having rebelled against the forces of tsarist autocracy and an official church that oppressed "freedom" and "reason" before the Revolution, the intelligentsia now feared the proletariat.[74]

Though one production of *Hamlet* was undertaken shortly after the premiere of *A List of Good Deeds*, Shakespeare's tragedy disappeared from Moscow's theaters for twenty years.[75] Though he never managed to produce a full stage version of the play, Meyerhold discussed his vision for a production with colleagues and students.[76] At the same time, approaching *Hamlet* from the meta-theatrical perspective of *A List of Good Deeds* allowed Meyerhold to revisit his radical interpretations of the classics in the 1920s rather than tackle Shakespeare directly under the new Stalinist conditions.[77] If, as I argue below, Olesha relied on *Hamlet* to take stock of his relationship with Meyerhold, then Meyerhold used the problem of staging *Hamlet* to explore his own past as a theatrical innovator and his future as a "Master" of Soviet theater.

Recall that in *A List of Good Deeds* Lelia performs an actual scene from *Hamlet* at two different points: first in the Soviet Union, as an encore for the proletarian audience of her Moscow theater, and then in Paris, during the crucial scene at the Globe Music Hall. Both times, the central line of her monologue—"Call me what instrument you will, though you can fret me, you cannot play upon me" (act 3, scene 2, ll. 340–41)—has a strong metaphorical charge. In the scene in Moscow, the performance is preceded by Lelia's claim that she "finds it difficult to be a citizen of the new world."[78] At the Paris vaudeville house, Lelia's performance ends with a grotesque proposal made by Margerette:[79]

> Right, you see I'm busy, I don't even have time to drink a glass of milk, and here you are taking up my time. Let's wrap this up. (*Grabs the flute*.) What I'm saying is that an interesting act with a flute could go like this: First you play the flute—a minuet or something—get the audience all sad—right? Then you swallow the flute (*mimes swallowing the flute*). The crowd gasps. Just gasps. Everybody's jaws drop. Then the mood immediately shifts: surprise, alarm. And then you turn your back to the audience and they can see that the flute is sticking out of a part of your anatomy from which flutes usually don't stick out. Listen, this is great! It would be especially kinky considering you're a lady. And then you start blowing the flute with what you'd call your other end—and this time not a minuet but something more upbeat, like "Daisy, Daisy, give me your answer, do . . ." Now that would be a scene! And you show up here with your *Hamlet*! (*OM* 337)[80]

Meyerhold exaggerated the coarseness of the act envisioned by Margerette. Maksim Shtraukh, who performed Margerette, wielded a whip on stage like a lion-tamer. Meyerhold wanted to "saturate" the scene with "blood," as though it were happening in a torture chamber.[81]

Margerette is supposed to produce the effect of torture by redefining the meaning of embodiment offered elsewhere in the play. In the prologue, embodying Hamlet the character meant representing those who embraced the ideal of a more perfect social arrangement but find themselves at odds with the realities of Soviet life. At the same time, Lelia's monologues identify the experience of performing *Hamlet* as the character's principal symbolic means of relating to the present while attempting to recover and hold on to the most valuable elements of the past—and yet not falling prey to paralyzing self-doubt (not becoming a Hamlet) in the process. At the Globe Music Hall, whose very name mockingly evokes Shakespeare, performance refers not to the process of creating a physical representation of a dramatic character, but to the act of contorting one's body in ways that a body ought not to be contorted. From Lelia's perspective, Margerette's proposal is a form of torture because it divests the act of performance of the symbolic function assigned to it earlier in the play. The whip wielded by Margerette amplifies the stage metaphor: Margerette's theater is, above all else, a circus.

The contrast between serious dramatic enactment and grotesque circus performance had a particular resonance in Soviet theater. Physical contortion for expressive/Expressionist effect; the development of actor training methods based on disciplining the performers' bodies; the unexpected, imaginative use of physical objects, including stage props, in building the mise en scène—all these developments were spearheaded in the 1920s by Meyerhold and Tairov. By turning Margerette into a kind of perverse mini-Meyerhold, Meyerhold raises the meta-theatrical stakes of the scene. The spectators of *A List of Good Deeds* are offered an implicit parallel between the effect of Margerette's proposed novelty act upon Lelia (a parody of Meyerhold's own avant-garde practice) and the effect of the scene they are watching upon themselves. In what sense, then, is Meyerhold staging a "torture scene" for his audience? What is he inflicting upon them and to what end?[82]

The Lelia-Margerette exchange has an obvious ideological aspect. As far as we know, Lelia has had no experience with coercion in Moscow; she refuses to be "played upon." Margerette's indecent proposal humiliates Lelia and forces her to rethink her attitude about the Soviet Union's treatment of artists. As staged by Meyerhold, however, Lelia's conversation with Margerette no longer yields such a clear-cut reading. Margerette's lesson on the dos and don'ts of performance is interrupted by a phone call announcing the imminent arrival of the famous cabaret singer, Ulalume.[83] Meyerhold has prepared the audience for Ulalume's arrival: he opened the third act with a brief inserted scene of a telephone conversation between Margerette (onstage) and Ulalume (offstage), in which Margerette urged the performer to hurry to the theater. In the dramatic structure of the act, then, Lelia's audition for Margerette was essentially a buildup to Ulalume's anticipated entrance. But for Lelia, who enters after Margerette's original phone call, the singer's appearance is unexpected, even shocking.[84] To impress upon Lelia the enormity of what is about to transpire, Margerette offers his own assessment of the singer's uncanny talent:

> People have turned him into a god. The world has gone crazy over sexuality. And he's a champion of sexuality, no doubt about that. To men he is a man; to women he's a woman. Maybe he is a god after all? When I hear him sing, I feel as if a woman intended for me were slowly undressing before my eyes. Then I watch the faces of women in the audience. It's phenomenal! He sings, and their eyelids droop like hen's lids, they turn to glass, they are dead . . . they are in ecstasy. And what does he sing? Stupid ditties! But he's got some sort of secret hidden in his erogenous zone.[85]

Following on the heels of Margerette's lecture about performance, this description makes explicit the opposition between the two characters, Lelia and Ulalume. Before Lelia encounters Margerette and Ulalume, her theatrical craft is her defense: she cannot be played upon, exploited, humiliated. Ulalume's claim to greatness, in contrast, resides in his transcending the physical limitations of his body performance and his manipulation—his playing upon—the bodies of his audiences.[86]

In Meyerhold's staging, however, Lelia's encounter with Ulalume emphasized the subtle, crucial parallels between the two characters—an identification which served to complicate Lelia's subsequent discovery of a genuinely Soviet self. The androgynous Ulalume of Olesha's playscript drives members of both sexes into frenzy by embodying for them a peculiar kind of fantasy.[87] At first he makes his audience identify with him: in Margerette's description, he appears to men as a man, to women as a woman. And yet when he seduces them, he heteronormatively provokes their desire by appealing to them as a member of the opposite sex: Margerette imagines a woman undressing before his eyes. This combination of sameness and otherness, of exoticism and vulgarity, brought together by the performer's unique manipulative skill, is enacted in Ulalume's encounter with Lelia.[88]

As she stands before Ulalume, Lelia is still wearing her Hamlet costume. At first, Ulalume takes her to be a man. Elsewhere in *A List of Good Deeds*, Lelia has to account for her decision to play a male role, and she denies the claim that her interpretation of the role is informed by her own femininity; when she plays a man, she implies, she *is* a man.[89] It is only at the moment when she faces the androgynous singer, then, that she is shown to be a kind of androgyne, attractive because she is both male and female. Ulalume is drawn to Lelia for this reason. He sings to her—and then, having mesmerized Lelia with his performance, kisses her. Meyerhold turned Lelia's seduction into the act's, and perhaps the production's, most vividly ambiguous moment. The two actors' gestures, during the song, the kiss, and the wordless exchange of intimate gestures that followed the kiss, were stylized and meticulously choreographed: part dance, part mating ritual, watched by the rest of those present on stage (the audience within the play) in "rapturous silence" (*OM* 339). Reviews and discussions reflected the audience's surprised, puzzled reactions to the portrayal of Ulalume in general and to the seriousness with which this moment was performed.[90] Typical of Meyerhold, there followed a scene of grotesquerie: a rapid-fire exchange of obscene jokes, at Lelia's expense, between Margerette and Ulalume. Yet the contrast intensified, rather than undermined, the effect of Ulalume's kiss: even as she recoiled from the insults, Lelia was shown to be under the spell of the singer's powers. In Meyerhold's staging, Ulalume's kiss formed a bridge to the culmination of the act—Lelia's soliloquy in which she finally reasserted her Soviet self: "I want to go home. Homeland, I want to hear the roar of your public discussions. Worker, only now do I understand your wisdom and magnanimity . . . Forgive me, Land of Soviets, I am coming to you. I don't want to go to the ball. I want to go home. I want to stand in a [bread] line and weep" (339–40).

During rehearsals, Meyerhold described this moment as "the ecstasy [*ekstaz*] of Soviet Power" (*OM* 438). This kind of ecstasy is, in Margerette's description, precisely what Ulalume—and Ulalume alone—provides to his audiences. In *A List of Good Deeds*, the longed-for, mythologized, painful assertion of Soviet identity came from Ulalume's seduction of Lelia, which was an extension of Margerette's "torture" of Lelia.[91] The entire scene at the vaudeville theater, then, was built on a series of provocations. Humiliation and obscenities intertwined with moments of powerful tension leading to emotional transcendence. Sexual manipulation became ideological revelation. I noted that Margerette represented a perverse version of Meyerhold, and the attempt to manipulate Lelia acquired a meta-theatrical dimension: it signaled to the audiences of *A List of Good Deeds* that they, too, were about to be assaulted with an indecent proposal. The substance of that proposal was only made palpable in the performance's side *a*ffects. Olesha and Meyerhold defined the successful embodiment of the Soviet self through its opposite: the anti-Soviet, decadent, histrionic world's acts of seduction. Lelia, it seemed, was not actually rejecting, overcoming, purging the Hamlet—that is to say, the *intelligent*—within her.

Instead, through the kiss and the epiphany that followed, she was revealed to be like Ulalume: a consummate performer who learns to manipulate opposing categories of being—similarities and differences—and manages to circumvent them through her craft.[92] In Meyerhold's clever realization of Olesha's playscript, the results of this transformation were affirmed even though how it happened was not enunciated.

To embody the Soviet self does not mean living happily ever after. At rehearsals, and later during public discussions of *A List of Good Deeds*, Meyerhold emphasized his efforts to add a tragic sensibility to the staging, especially in the run-up to Lelia's death.[93] The crucial scene at the Globe Music Hall motivated the tragic finale. The heroine dies not because she fails to embody a Soviet self or because she does so too late, but because becoming Soviet has the same relationship to violence and humiliation that acting has to inspiration and insight. Lelia hangs on to her identity as an actress and a representative of an intellectual elite, and doing so makes her execution—which some viewers interpreted as suicide—inevitable. Violence catalyzes an epiphany in the scene with Margerette and Ulalume; but its intimate link to performance makes violence, coercion, and constraint in the play omnipresent and literally inescapable.

These disorienting, disquieting effects were emphasized in Meyerhold's production through transformations of the performance space. One of Meyerhold's justifications for calling himself the production's "author" was his scenic design work.[94] His vision for the play, outlined at a cast meeting in late March 1931, involved redefining the relationship between the stage and the audience:

> I noticed that whenever our actors move to center stage, they always try to find the exact geometrical center for their position . . . If an actor tries to find this precise central point, an audience member perceives equilibrium. That kind of equilibrium is unnecessary for this piece. For this piece, maybe, what we need is that there be no equilibrium . . . One wants to take the road of constant deformation, something our eyes are not used to. (*OM* 259)

By creating, with the tall rectangular columns, a line stretching diagonally from the upstage area (the back of the stage) to the audience, Meyerhold shifted the geometric center of the performance area. The audience watched the play from a sharp angle.

Meyerhold experimented with staging and seating arrangements in most of his productions. Compared to his Constructivist stagings of the 1920s, *A List of Good Deeds* is a tame affair, though it represented the first time that Meyerhold had decided to limit the audience's ability to see the show. Earlier, he had been interested in opening up the stage space. Quite the opposite happened in *A List of Good Deeds*: the sides of the stage were pushed in, and the ceiling was pulled down (a large overhang extended over the stage and the front rows of the audience). Tension increased; it was as though the director had located an invisible lever and was pushing on it, changing the contours of the performance, inhibiting the characters.[95]

Everything in the production was out of balance, just as the director wanted it to be. Meyerhold's production recalled the governing metaphor of Olesha's earliest draft of *A List of Good Deeds*. In his outline of the project Olesha fantasized about staging a "hidden mechanism," a metaphor for his reconstruction of the power of the elite.[96]

The intelligentsia tried to hang on to their authority in the new Soviet world while also recognizing the need to transform themselves, to be remade. How to do so eluded them. Lelia emerges from her ordeal at the Globe as a genuine Soviet Person. And yet she retains her Hamletian, *intelligent* self-understanding, which no longer stands in direct opposition to the project of becoming a "citizen of the new world." After her climactic monologue, Meyerhold has her exit the stage using the same spiral staircase that Ulalume had used for his entrance. Especially as performed by Zinaida Raikh, Lelia's slow, silent exit in Hamlet's costume, tracked by the spotlight, was an exquisite counterpoint to her monologue. The past and the present were intertwined in Lelia's transformation.

Lelia is, of course, a "breeches" actress, an heir to a distinguished tradition of women performing Hamlet.⁹⁷ The biggest insult in Margerette's monologue is the implication that Lelia's behavior is somehow unprofessional, that she is not good at what she is supposed to be doing. Ulalume, by contrast, is represented as the ultimate professional—except, unlike Lelia, he does not *enact*, does not seek to inhabit another; he performs a *kind* of "authenticity"—he acts by being, in some complicated sense, "himself." Lelia's encounter with Ulalume is an encounter between "theater" (bound by the constraints of representation) and "performance."

Meyerhold established himself as a revolutionary director by imploding theatrical representation. For a role to change, the performer of the role needed to change. *A List of Good Deeds* struck many of its viewers as the start of something new in Meyerhold's career (*OM* 523). Far from wanting his productions to represent something specific, he wanted his productions to represent representation. He decided that he could parody himself; he could quote from *Hamlet*, a play that he adored, in a manner that asked if *Hamlet* had any meaning at all—and then leave the question unresolved. Without proclaiming ambiguity as a goal, Meyerhold was reshaping his theater into a Globe Music Hall—a place where an Ulalume can enrapture every audience member, even (or perhaps especially) if that means having to demonstrate that he, too, is a kind of Hamlet.

OLESHA AS AN AUTHOR: THE AFTEREFFECTS OF PERFORMANCE

How did the paradigm of performance and self-understanding enacted in Meyerhold's production resonate with the self-staging project initiated in Olesha's diaries? As we saw, Olesha's attempts to write a nonfictional book about himself mutated into plans for an account of Meyerhold directing *A List of Good Deeds*.⁹⁸ I connected this transformation to Olesha's initial interest in the theater as an alternative arena for resolving the narrative crisis encountered in the diary, and argued that Olesha's experiment in staging the self was ultimately undermined by the efforts to continue writing that self.⁹⁹ At the core of Olesha's attempts to document the Meyerhold production, then, is the question of whether his diaries, which had originally catalyzed his self-staging experiment, could be used to account for, and derive meaning from, the experience of being staged by Meyerhold.

The effort to shift the emphasis away from a direct examination of his idiosyncrasies (emotional and writerly) so as to reposition himself within the narrative is especially pronounced in Olesha's account of the company meeting at the Meyerhold Theater, during which he read what he thought was the final version of the playscript of *A List of Good Deeds*.¹⁰⁰ Reading to the actors, he also, in a familiar ritual, transferred authority to them. By separating a description of his experiences from his reflections on them in his diaries, Olesha situates himself both inside and outside the narrative, metaphorically restaging the scene he is describing. His status as an outsider is underscored in his description of the setting. The reading takes place on the theater's stage, and the glare of stage lights blinds Olesha, limiting his perception of those around him and de-familiarizing the experience of reading the playscript.[101] Finding himself (literally) in the spotlight, Olesha is more acutely aware that he is in fact performing: "I read well, deriving pleasure from presenting to my audience the fruit of my labors. And, feeling pleasure, I felt in complete control of my intonation and caused everyone to fall completely silent whenever I needed it" (*KP* 29/13–14). This is Olesha's most important theatrical act to date, and yet in reporting it he is wholly consumed with the side *a*ffects of the experience. The focus of his diary narrative, however, is not on the performer but on the audience—or, rather, on one principal spectator, Meyerhold.[102]

Meyerhold's twofold function as a consumer of Olesha's performed text and an object of Olesha's scrutiny is reflected in the diary: backlit, "the Master" appears both as a recognizable version of himself and as an amalgamation of surreal metaphors. Under Olesha's gaze, he is transformed into a magician, a doctor, and an "auntie from a fairy tale" (*KP* 30/14). In the middle of a description of Meyerhold, the narrative seems to take on a momentum of its own:

> "I've come off a horse," [Meyerhold] says about himself. And sometimes I imagine a dream . . . I'm out walking somewhere, the ground is damp; it's springtime, there's lots of potholes, maybe up by the Petrovskii highway . . . or maybe some other place . . . and I'm running, skipping along . . . I have no idea where to. I mean, it's just a dream, my imagination, maybe a fragment from a future piece of prose . . . So I'm running and I stumble upon a horse's skull lying in a rut. I pick it up . . . The bone is weightless, hollowed out by the wind, the empty eye socket creating a draft. And in the shimmering light of the setting sun a little cobweb lights up in the eye socket—and it glitters just like a rainbow. A tiny little rainbow appears on the circumference of the eye . . . And I think to myself: "This is Meyerhold's head." (*KP* 30/14)

This fantasy is twice removed, as it were, from any immediate experience—Olesha is *imagining* a *dream*. His insistence upon this double remove indirectly points to the larger conceit of the passage. Olesha's self-conscious reflection on the act of scrutinizing Meyerhold is reenacted in Hamlet's discovery of Yorick's skull. The principal trope of the dream sequence, then, returns the narrative to the symbolic language of *A List of Good Deeds*.[103]

The description of the dream plays upon *Hamlet*, rehearsing metaphorically one of the central devices of Olesha's play.

The metaphors that precede the dream passage have a similar genealogy. An "auntie from a fairy tale" really comes from a fairy tale, as does the magician-doctor. Doctor Gaspar Arneri, who has the reputation of a magician, and Auntie Ganymede, his housekeeper, are characters from Olesha's fairy tale *Three Fat Men*—his previous play. The fanciful image of Meyerhold that emerges from Olesha's description, then, is a synthesis of Olesha's theatrical fantasies. It's a product of his diaries and concludes Olesha's effort to interpret the self and its circumstances. The categories that give meaning to Olesha's experience as he describes himself describing Meyerhold from across the brightly lit stage, and even the strategies for devising those categories, are from Olesha's plays. These plays, in turn, are products of Olesha's experiments with the symbolic and institutional resources of theater—experiments that had been conceived and justified in his diaries. And the scene in which Olesha finally *acts* on stage is seen as a reenactment of the Lelia-Ulalume encounter, with Meyerhold the mysterious, multi-faced performance artist who is just "being himself." At that moment he derives the authority of his position not from the blinding light of the stage but from how Olesha, the author who takes a turn as an actor, invests emotional experience with a specifically theatrical meaning.

Once again, the narrative seems to double up on itself: this entry represents Olesha's final attempt to document Meyerhold's staging of *A List of Good Deeds*. But this time the diary is halted for reasons not linked to the self-censure of Olesha's other diaries. Olesha's description of Meyerhold signals that the project of staging the self, and specifically the self being staged by Meyerhold, has become so thoroughly implicated in the dramatic structure of Olesha's play that it can now acquire full meaning only in performance. That conviction is embodied in Meyerhold's production. In the richly meta-theatrical context of the Globe Music Hall, the act of defining and affirming the protagonist's Soviet incarnation is linked to the recognition of the fundamentally transformative nature of performance.

The theater's appeal for Olesha as an aesthetic, cultural, and social institution was conditioned by his efforts, in his diaries, to purge those aspects of his personality—his identity—that did not fit the model of a genuine Soviet writer. Theater gave Olesha cultural authority; without it he would have considered himself deficient as a Stalinist "man of letters." Meyerhold's production of *A List of Good Deeds* circumvented the contradictions of Olesha's diaries when it comes to self-definition.

The critical responses to *A List of Good Deeds* indicate that, in Meyerhold's staging, Lelia's death at the end of the play was not interpreted as the execution of the paradigmatic pre-revolutionary *intelligent*. Her death did not fit the narrative, rehearsed in many earlier literary and dramatic works of the Soviet 1920s, of a wayward intellectual's conversion that happened too late to earn the forgiveness of the proletariat.

I began this chapter with Zinaida Raikh's comment, in her note to Olesha, that when she played Lelia in *A List of Good Deeds* she was in fact playing him, and now wanted a chance to play herself. The Margerette-Ulalume-Lelia encounter offers a model of the self that is constituted in, and by, the actual performance, deriving its authority from manipulations of the audience. At the First Congress of Soviet Writers in 1934, several months after *A List of Good Deeds* closed,[104] Olesha was lauded as a playwright. By the time he returned to Moscow in 1944 from wartime evacuation in Central Asia, he was but a marginal figure, recognized neither for his playscripts nor his screenplays (he became interested in cinema in the late 1930s) and barely acknowledged as a writer at all. For several years after the war, he neither kept a journal nor any sort of notebook for his creative ideas. When he returned to diary-writing in the 1950s, it was in a much different context, and for different reasons, than before.

Olesha's case has been held up in the past, sometimes to considerable polemical effect, as emblematic of the experiences of the *intelligent* writer under Stalin.[105] The readings in this chapter of Olesha's situation treat the "writer" and "*intelligent*" not as personal constructions but as transhistorical ones, not specific to Moscow in the 1930s. Jochen Hellbeck notes that "ambiguity and indeterminacy may be sought-after qualities in a liberal society that valorizes individual self-determination, but they neither fit the historical time inhabited by Olesha, nor his intellectual and aesthetic disposition."[106] The counter-argument holds that this "ambiguity and indeterminacy" is part of his context. His involvement in the theater was central to his shaping as a Soviet citizen.

Chapter Three

New Soviet Drama: Performing (for) Stalin

HOW DID SOVIET THEATER represent power? Yuri Olesha's quest suggests that theatrical power lay in the interaction among, and the fundamental interdependence of, different kinds of performers. Performers succeed when they cross the boundary between *en*acting (an actor who owns a role) and acting-as-being (a professional performer *for* whom the concept of a role has no meaning, does not exist). The two modes of performance are not alternatives to one another; they are, rather, doubles. Recall the interplay of identities in Olesha's *A List of Good Deeds*. A genuine Soviet self cannot be acquired, exchanged, or faked. It must be earned through an exchange of words and emotions that can only exist when every performer is, at the core, a travesty actor: always fully someone else, always fully oneself, always divided, yet neither a Hamlet nor a Don Quixote. The actors become their roles while also becoming one another's audiences. But what of the spectators in the audience? And what if, as Stanislavsky suggested, there is no other actor on stage, and all one sees is the terrifying darkness beyond the "curtain of light"?

The presence (often silent) and perception of the audience thus emerges as a source of theatrical power, engaging audiences as much real as imagined. Olesha's playscripts represent him trying to reshape himself; his diaries were exercises in becoming someone else based on his experiences in the theater. To whom was the rhetorical energy of plays of the 1930s directed, and what were the stakes of that engagement?

Addressing this two-pronged question requires revisiting a major event in Soviet culture before the purges: the 1934 First All-Union Congress of Soviet Writers, and two kindred remarks made in the middle of it. The authors of those remarks were from opposite sides of the cultural-political spectrum and had competing rhetorical aims. The first remark is a plea: "Write us plays, the shorter and merrier the better!" (*"Napishite dlia nas p'esy pokoroche i poveselee!"*) The second is a directive: "Write plays!" (*"Pishite p'esy!"*).

Chapter Three

The plea came from a certain Chuprunenko, a *komsomolka* and shock worker from the machine tractor station in the village of Troitskaya, in what is now the Slov'ians'kii region of Ukraine. She addressed the First Congress of Soviet Writers on the morning of August 27, 1934, on behalf of peasant-workers who had, she said, a vested interest in artistic matters.[1] Chuprunenko seems to have been an ideal spokesperson for the *narod* (down to her peculiar partial anonymity; no first name or patronymic is recorded in the Congress's detailed transcript). Her taste was the prevailing taste of the day, which wasn't particularly sophisticated. Out with the freewheeling, vibrant experimentation of the 1920s, she implies, and in with short and sweet fun!

The accuracy of this trajectory can be challenged. The standard to which Soviet writers and filmmakers as Socialist Realists were held evolved over time and was never entirely clear; their creations were the products of complex negotiations with sometimes unpredictable consequences. Transparency, clarity, accessibility: these terms were amorphous and repeatedly redefined. In a 2008 book about theater in the 1920s and first half of the 1930s, Violetta Gudkova compiled a list of character types, plot devices, and themes, with quotes from reviews and eyewitnesses.[2] The stress falls on Bulgakov (in whose plays Gudkova specializes) and several forgotten productions of the period. Chuprunenko's claim that "there are some good plays, but they are long, we can't handle them yet" is a kind of fulcrum of this book.[3] The repertoire was forced into simplicity: the glum, sometimes grim plays of the 1920s surrendered to mandated joyfulness.

The elaborate transcript of the First Congress of Soviet Writers explains this surrender. The Party wanted writers to stress everything and anything positive about the forced march toward communism, suppressing introspection and basking in the "giddy" successes (actual, invented, exaggerated) of the Soviet state. How to turn this celebration into compelling theater posed challenges that no one at the Congress wanted to address, never mind solve. Arguments intensified, as did the criticism of ideological deficiencies in the repertoire, but no consensus emerged about the path forward.

SEEKING A FORMULA

Maxim Gorky's plays were front and center in the drama about the future of drama, but Gorky himself stayed out of the fray. Stalin's favorite writer was experiencing a dip in his fortunes. Gorky had unquestionable talent and a major reputation, but his 1932 play *Yegor Bulychov and Company* (*Egor Bulychov i drugie*) wasn't as great a success as he wanted it to be. The three major productions of the play—in September 1932 at the Vakhtangov Theater in

Moscow and in October at Leningrad's Bolshoi Dramatic Theater, and then a February 1934 performance at MAT—were supplemented by dozens of regional productions. The reviews were fair and Gorky received hundreds of letters respectfully complimenting him on his play, which concerned a businessman coming to the gradual realization that his days were numbered after Tsar Nicholas II abdicates and revolutionaries fill the streets. But compared to *The Days of the Turbins* in the mid-1920s and Nikolai Volkov's adaptation of *Anna Karenina* in the mid-1930s, not to mention Vishnevskii's *An Optimistic Tragedy*, *Yegor Bulychov and Company* fell noticeably flat. Chagrined, Gorky distanced himself from the efforts to establish a template for Soviet playwriting.[4]

Another challenge was institutional. Before the massive Union of Soviet Writers was established in April 1932, the most important organization for writers was the Russian Association of Proletarian Writers (RAPP). Established in January 1925, it became increasingly intolerant and repressive. Its leadership included Vladimir Kirshon, Aleksandr Afinogenov, and Osaf Litovskii. In 1931, these three firebrands put out a manifesto for the new theater (the so-called "Theatrical Document"). Its first postulate was that only a proletarian playwright—that is, a playwright of the working class who was fully steeped in Marxist-Leninist dialectical materialism—could write genuine Soviet plays. Its second postulate was fuzzier: creating a classless society, while realizing the promise of the Revolution, required different forms of thinking and different kinds of people—who would be classless but not homogenized (like the spiritual ideal of *sobornost'*). Soviet drama needed to focus on the inner world of the human being (*vnutrennyi mir cheloveka*) and the coming-into-being of consciousness. That consciousness is at once individual and collective.[5]

This claim became known, reductively, as the theory of the living human being (*teoriia zhivogo cheloveka*), to which RAPP attached a slogan: "The [entire] world is the human being" ("*Mir—eto chelovek*").[6] The theory had a sociological basis; it rejected Symbolism and Expressionism, the mysticism and neurosis of the Russian Silver Age, and the degenerate psychosexual obsessions of the West. Ironically, however, RAPP's new theatrical aesthetic was remarkably consonant with the theater whose productions in the 1920s the RAPP leadership had most often attacked and ridiculed: the Moscow Art Theater. The new focus on the living human being, the nuances of individual psychology, the creation of complex characters, the insistence that "individuality is not individualism," the belief that a genuine Soviet person cannot be created until a new Soviet actor appears on the Soviet stage—none of this was foreign to MAT. And so the inevitable denouement: six months after the "Theatrical Document" became public, both Afinogenov and Kirshon had plays in rehearsal at MAT.

Chapter Three

The war that RAPP was waging did not subside, however. Their targets shifted to so-called epic playwrights who produced dramas about the history of the Russian Revolution and Civil War, industrialization, and the life of Lenin. The war continued even after RAPP was disbanded in 1932, despite the efforts of leading figures in the Soviet literary world to negotiate a truce. At the First Congress of Soviet Writers, from August 17 to September 1, 1934, the prominent children's author Samuil Marshak delivered a keynote address about children's literature moving forward. Karl Radek considered the relationship between Soviet and international progressive literature, and Nikolai Bukharin talked about poetry and poetics. Each style and genre of writing had its advocates, with the laborers in attendance urging writers to produce novels that romanticized their chores. There was no consensus about playwriting, just a series of conflicting reports summarized by presenters who clearly hated each other.

One of them was Kirshon. Fresh from travels in Europe, he began his hours-long presentation with a description of the German theater scene, including plot summaries from plays he saw and those he knew to be of relevance to the National Socialists and Hitler, who had recently seized power (*SSP* 397–401). He didn't like what he saw and trotted out the usual RAPP points about the alienating effects of formalism, the decadence of the bourgeois stage, the morbid interest in perverse sexuality and—above all—the cowardly, unseemly yearning for death as salvation from the world's imperfections. The darkness embraced by modernist plays, Kirshon argued, was Europe's in general, whereas Soviet playwrights embraced the light, meaning powerful purpose and progress and the aspirations of the new generation. Yet rather than going into detail about this sunny newness, Kirshon skipped back in time to the nineteenth-century imperial Russian classics, highlighting their psychological depth and evocative language, while also taking cheap shots at the "documentalism" of Nikolai Pogodin's and Vishnevskii's plays and the heroic, pathos-laden dramas he claimed to despise. After a scornful overview of older and newer plays, quotations from playscripts and critical articles, Kirshon concluded his presentation with a rehash of the RAPP recipe for successful theater. Slightly updating the "Theatrical Document" of 1931, he emphasized the need for fully fleshed-out characters and a focus on individual problems. He rejected plays of grand Russian/Soviet sweep, as well as those that indulged neuroses and mysticism and other bad habits of the bourgeois stage. Unsurprisingly, the future of Soviet theater rested in the kind of plays that Kirshon himself had been writing: ones about communist character development—the formation of personality or *stanovlenie lichnosti*—and the coming-into-being of consciousness; the conflict between old and new values in the Soviet workplace; and (in *Bread*) trouble in the kolkhozes.

Arguing against Kirshon, Pogodin defended plays of grand sweep. Recently back from a trip to observe the slave-labor construction of the White Sea Canal, he devoted half of his talk to the challenge of staging epic events on small stages and the encumbrances of conventional sets (*SSP* 385–89). He was at once defending his work to date and at the same time previewing his own coming attractions, including a comedy called *The Aristocrats* (1934), about the enlightenment through labor of bandits, thieves, prostitutes, imperialists, intellectuals, and kulaks working on the canal. The convicts are reeducated under the leadership of their wise but firm Chekist handlers, the aristocrats of the title. The play was staged by Nikolai Okhlopkov at the Moscow Realistic Theater using a series of highly conventional, expressionistic devices, including the stock characters and stylized movement of the commedia dell'arte but privileging the new, not-quite-formed language of the Soviet generation.[7] The production proved extremely popular and became a film, which dispensed with Okhlopkov's stage effects. After advertising the techniques used in *The Aristocrats*, Pogodin pivoted in his speech at the Congress to his enemies Kirshon and Afinogenov, taking them to task for their clichéd plot devices and template emotional situations (390–91). Afinogenov defended his position in a follow-up speech, as did Vishnevskii. In this spirited mix of egos and ideology, there was no possibility for a meeting of minds, save for the repeated references to Olesha, whose plays displeased all of them.

There were two other presentations on drama. The last slot—and so, in some sense, the last word—was given to Aleksei Tolstoy, a member of the pre-revolutionary intelligentsia who became a leading Soviet writer, embracing Socialist Realism and, like Gorky, advising other artists of his generation to do the same. Tolstoy had fled the Bolsheviks with his family to live in Paris and Berlin, but then received permission, in 1922, to return home. He demonstrated an impressive range in multiple genres, including science fiction and horror-fantasy (the screenplay for the 1924 film *Aelita*; the libretto for the unfinished Dmitri Shostakovich opera *Orango*), biography, fairy tales, and later on, a historical novel about Peter the Great. Playwriting wasn't Aleksei Tolstoy's creative focus, but his plays proved quite popular and entered the repertoires of provincial theaters. His speech at the Congress was diffuse, disinterested, perfunctory, and rather unoriginal. He followed the lead of other speakers by quoting from the classics—Aleksandr Griboedov's *Woe from Wit* (*Gore ot uma*) and Nikolai Gogol's *The Inspector General* (*Revizor*)—and then summarized recent achievements (*SSP* 416–20). Tolstoy raised (without answering) crucial questions: How should we write? And what should we write about? (418–19).

His remarks didn't land anywhere, and it seemed that he had either detached himself from the factional bickering in Moscow (Tolstoy lived in Leningrad) or wanted to remain neutral.

Chapter Three

The other presenter, Valery Kirpotin, was a puzzling choice. A graduate of the Institute of Red Professors and the Institute of Literature and Language of the Communist Academy, he wasn't well known, and he wasn't much of a writer. He dabbled in criticism and edited the journal *Problemy Marksizma*, published by the Leningrad Research Institute of Marxism and Leninism; later he wrote a book anachronistically aligning Pushkin's "progressive morals" and "worldview" with the rise of communism.[8] Kirpotin's role in the Congress could be compared to those of Nikolai Bukharin and Karl Radek, prominent politicians who had worked as journalists. Kirpotin was an employee of the Central Committee of the Communist Party, working as chief of the fiction section in the Department of Propaganda and Agitation. He had served on the organizing committee for the Union of Soviet Writers, but when Gorky began to take a more active role in the organization, Kirpotin was demoted. It is remarkable, then, that he delivered the longest and most detailed speech on playwriting at the Congress and that the other speakers, for all their disagreements, repeatedly returned to Kirpotin's simple and alarming declaration about Soviet playwriting. According to him, there existed no formula for success. Writing a good, true Soviet play was a theoretical and practical impossibility.

Kirpotin believed that Soviet playwriting had failed to meet its many obligations. Language, images, themes, narrative conventions, the nature of the conflicts—everything was unsatisfactory. Rather than seeking to reconcile the factions, Kirpotin in his address complained that each of them lacked insight and acumen. He upbraided Pogodin and Vishnevskii for their "arbitrary rationalizing form, taken whole hog from Meyerhold and Mayakovsky and no longer acceptable [*priyomlema*] in the theater." Kirshon's and Afinogenov's "living person" ("*zhivoi chelovek*") dramas derived unimaginatively from Chekhov or Ostrovskii and failed to serve the audiences of the present (*SSP* 377–81). There was an existential aspect to Kirpotin's remarks. The proletarian revolution had given people the chance to master fate, rather than succumb to it, and Soviet drama needed to reflect this development. It hadn't done so thus far, Kirpotin concluded, and it remained unclear if it could, given the focus on existential crises in the plays of Pogodin and others (383–85).

This was not to say that every Soviet play had been a terrible failure. Even Kirpotin conceded that some of them showed promise, but showing promise wasn't the same as setting a standard or providing guidance for the next generation of writers. Kirshon's account of the situation was unsparingly contemptuous: success in the Soviet theater, popularity with audiences in the major cities and the provinces, was a matter of good luck and good timing. The author's hopes for success rested on the actors and director and theater. It also depended on the audience seeing something in the performance that he himself couldn't see. As Kirshon explained,

> Sometimes it comes to pass that while someone is delivering a report, a beloved leader [*liubimyi vozhd'*] enters and takes his place on the dais behind the speaker's back with other leaders. Everyone in the hall bursts out in applause. The speaker assumes that the applause was provoked by a particularly clever remark of his, which makes him very happy, and a self-satisfied grin appears on his face. (*Applause [in Kirshon's audience]*). It's terribly tempting to say to such a speaker: "Turn around, you doofus!" ["*Chudak, povernis'!*"].[9]

In this timely Soviet reworking of Plato's allegory of the cave, the turn from fate to freedom, to the "living human being" of the future Soviet world, becomes a turn to the face of the Leader, *Vozhd'*, the solver of all problems.

STALIN IN PERFORMANCE

The draft of Kirshon's report was vetted and edited by Gorky (as was the case with Kirpotin and to a lesser degree Pogodin). It was Gorky who became the guiding force in Soviet literature in October 1932 as the host of several writers' meetings in Moscow. During these meetings, the principles of Socialist Realism were explained and the catchphrase "writers are the engineers of human souls" was introduced.

Two such meetings took place that month at the former Riabushinskii mansion on Malaia Nikitskaia Street, where Gorky lived after returning to the Soviet Union from Sorrento. On October 20, writers who were members of the Party were invited; on October 26, the audience of about fifty people included unaffiliated writers as well. Gorky organized the meetings in his capacity as chair of the organizing committee of the Union of Soviet Writers, and he made sure to extend an invitation to Stalin, who accepted. Formally, the occasion was the upcoming plenary session of the organizing committee on October 29, a public forum allowing writers to offer their thoughts on Soviet literature since the dissolution of RAPP and other writers' groups. Kirpotin, the supervisor of the organizing committee's staff, took detailed notes at both meetings.[10] There are two other accounts: Feoktist Berezovskii's description of the first meeting, including what he claimed was a near-verbatim transcript of Stalin's fiery speech to the writers;[11] and Kornelii Zelinskii's distant recollections of the second meeting, of which there are several versions.[12] All three note-takers sought permission from Party officials to publish their accounts. These requests were denied, although, to

Chapter Three

be sure, Stalin's supposed remarks were widely distributed and frequently quoted. The surviving accounts of what he supposedly said are idiosyncratic.

The two meetings followed the same pattern. Writers and Communist Party leaders were seated around a large U-shaped table in the main room of the house. Gorky presided; Stalin, Viacheslav Molotov, Kliment Voroshilov, and other top functionaries flanked him. As the writers spoke, Stalin frequently got up and walked around the room, smoking his pipe and playing with a mother-of-pearl penknife suspended on a watch chain from his jacket. He moved along the outside perimeter of the table, sometimes stepping out of the room to attend to some matter or other but often standing behind the writers' backs. The same agenda items—personnel, ideology, and budget—were discussed in the same order at the two meetings. And the same promises were made: the disgraced former leaders of RAPP would be permitted a prominent role in the new Writers' Union, despite vocal objections from the fellow travelers; and the government would do something to address the severe shortages of printing paper and increase the print run for works of fiction. At the end of the Congress, a new, luxurious writers' colony would be constructed in the suburbs. And the results were identical, or almost identical, formulations of the official writers' method. Stalin used the phrase "*revolutionary* Socialist Realism" to describe the writing of the future, along with "revolutionary *romanticism*," but the same points held about accessibility, populist themes, Marxist-Leninist principles, and Party-mindedness.

Kirpotin, who was present at both meetings, remembered the bawdy folk songs performed by Aleksandr Fadeev mutating into an all-night party. And even Zelinskii, who attended only the second meeting, felt that he was participating in a reenactment: he notes moments when Communist Party participants prompted Stalin to rehearse scenes from the original conversation for the benefit of those who missed them. "Fadeev," Zelinskii related,

> was asking Stalin to repeat the stories he told about Lenin at the meeting of the Party-member writers . . . which took place a week ago, also at Gorky's. Pavlenko (and then after him Fadeev) told me that Stalin proved an amazing storyteller. He related rare, intimate details from Lenin's life, things no one knows about.
>
> "Lenin understood that he was dying," Stalin said, "and asked me once, when he and I were alone, to bring him some potassium cyanide. 'You are the cruelest [*samyi zhestokii*] man in the Party,' Lenin said then, 'you can do it.' I at first promised him I would, but then didn't dare. How could I just give poison to Ilyich. You've got to have some pity for the man. And then again, how could I know what course the disease would take. So this one time we all went to see Ilyich, and he points at me and says: 'He deceived me, he's wavering!' No one could understand what that meant then. Everyone was surprised.

New Soviet Drama: Performing (for) Stalin

> Only I knew what he was talking about: I had reported Lenin's plea to the Politburo when he first asked me. Of course everyone turned that request down. Gronskii here knows about this."
>
> Today, with non-Party-members in attendance, Stalin does not want to repeat the exchange.[13]

Kirpotin's account of this scene slightly differs from Zelinskii's and includes these details about Lenin's death.

> After a brief pause, Stalin began to tell us about Lenin's illness. While doing this, he got up and firmly grabbed Bukharin's goatee. And while holding him in this way he continued to speak. Occasionally he would look into his eyes and ask: "Right?" And Bukharin would nod.
>
> "Comrade Lenin took being ill very badly. I met him on the staircase once. Comrade Lenin was crying. He made me give him my word of honor that when his condition worsened and there was no longer any hope of recovery, I would give him poison. The moment came when recovery was no longer possible. Comrade Lenin, the eagle of the Revolution, could fly no longer. He said to me, 'You gave me your word, give me poison!'
>
> "I could not dishonor my promise. So I raised the question at a Politburo meeting. And the Party freed me from the obligation to give Lenin poison. There is a passage to that effect in the minutes. And there's a record of a resolution to release comrade Stalin from fulfilling an impossible promise."
>
> As he spoke, Stalin continued to hold Bukharin by his beard. "Remember?" he said. And Bukharin nodded in response:—yes, I do. Or maybe Stalin helped him nod by pulling firmly down on his beard.[14]

The clutching of Bukharin's beard emblematizes the predicament of the audience—Stalin's audience at Gorky's residence and the audience reading about these events long after the fact. What are we to make of this jarringly strange scene? The personalities of the two mythical Stalins in the competing versions of the poison story do not align neatly: "the cruelest man in the Party" is somehow also fond of transparently Gorky-like revolutionary-romantic avian tropes as he bemoans the demise of the "eagle of the revolution." The conflicts he describes between duty and feeling, honor and compassion, fate and freedom (recall Kirshon's speech), as well as the deus ex machina resolution of the moral conundrum by the collective wisdom of the Party's elders—these details are consistent.

Kirpotin's notes establish that Stalin's audience received substantial guidance during the October 20 meeting. Two moments in particular stand out. At one point during the rambling after-dinner conversation in Gorky's library, Stalin plucked a book of Gorky's prose off a bookshelf and read aloud all or part of the 1899 short story "Kirilka." Gorky didn't seem that surprised, as though Stalin had put on similar impromptu performances on other occasions. Stalin's reading of "Kirilka" was followed by an analysis of sorts of the short story and some additional comments about the place of this minor, early text in Gorky's career. Stalin's approach to literary criticism, Kirpotin noted, was solidly class-conscious, and he was less impressed by Stalin's oratory than by his description of the different ways that a story, any story, can be interpreted.[15] (Or misinterpreted: "Kirilka" is about an elderly, unkempt, somewhat tongue-tied peasant who, waiting for a ferry, shares the "crust of bread" he had tucked into his sheepskin coat with famished fellow passengers. Gorky stresses the naturalness of Kirilka's act of generosity with people much better off than he was himself. Stalin added an entire section about Kirilka's involvement in a peasant uprising and struggles with class enemies.)[16]

The other key event in the meeting, and probably the best-known one, was Stalin's speech to the writers about the future of Soviet literature, which he would repeat at the October 26 meeting. Stalin blasted the leadership of RAPP, declaring that the organization should have been disbanded earlier than it had, given all the squabbling and mudslinging that defined its existence—not to mention its "lack of understanding [of the needs of Soviet society], as well as its factionalism, isolation, love of red tape [its "administrative-ness"], and inertia. And if you don't get over these ailments, we can say in advance: you won't succeed. We will only have victory on the literary front when you've cured yourselves." For Stalin, which meant for everyone, the future belonged to "revolutionary Socialist Realism" and the internalization of dialectical materialism. "Kirilka" bolstered Stalin's arguments.[17]

The anecdote about Lenin and Bukharin's beard, according to Kirpotin, is of a piece with the staged reading of Gorky's story and Stalin's set of instructions on the kind of literature the Soviet people need:

> What should we be writing about? Poetry is good. Novels are even better. But plays are what's needed most of all now [*No p'esy nam seichas nuzhnee vsego*] . . . We have to realize that drama, theater—it has an utterly unique type of artistic influence upon a human being [*sovsem osobyi vid khudozhestvennogo vozdeistviia na cheloveka*]. Neither novels nor novellas nor short stories nor sketches can influence a reader the way a play, produced in a theater, can . . . After all, it is in our interest to have a good work of art, one that aids in the construction of socialism, the reconstruction of human psychology in the direction of socialism, be accessible to millions of working men and women . . . A book cannot yet serve all those millions. But a play, the theater can. There are no limitations to the theater's possibilities.[18]

New Soviet Drama: Performing (for) Stalin

Stalin's emphasis on theater in shaping the masses is surprising given his love of film. One and the same celluloid blockbuster could reach millions of people. And his description of theater's mass appeal seems more typical of the cinema:

> Workers from Tula buy out all the seats in a theater for a period of thirty days; then groups of them come to Moscow over the course of that month; they come with wives, with children; whole families come, so that all can watch this play. And civil servants in Moscow do the same thing: they buy out a whole theater for a month.[19]

Stalin notes the success of Afinogenov's *Fear*; it had been performed all over the Soviet Union, in over a hundred theaters, and seen by all sorts of people (he emphasized as always that workers were the most dutiful attendees at the shows).[20] The differences in acting styles, pacing, and decor were significant enough to make the trip from one theater to another worthwhile. *Fear* had more than one ideological point to make. And so the Leader issued his command—"Write plays!"—with the aim of offering theatergoers different perspectives on the Soviet experiment.

As a guest at Gorky's residence, then, Stalin demonstrated not the "how" or "what" but the "aha!" of the new Soviet theater—the side *a*ffects that could be so central to the audience's experience. Stalin issued his command having already been shaped, as an audience member, by a particular way of making texts acquire force on stage—and then he extends it, by raising the stakes for all those present.

During these meetings, Stalin certainly talked about poison, Lenin, and Bukharin: we have three different testimonies as confirmation. Certainly, too, some of the details of his meetings with the writers were embellished or made up. Recall Zelinskii's claim that he heard what happened at the first meeting from Fadeev, and Kirpotin's counterclaim that Fadeev never talked about the meeting—the proceedings were confidential. Whatever happened at Gorky's place, Stalin's anecdote about Lenin took on a life of its own and became a kind of urban myth. The writers attending the meetings never forgot the performance that had been put on for them, even if the details became fuzzy. What mattered was its impact—the insights it offered into the workings of the theater and what a theatrical performance could be like.

When Kirshon, at the podium of the First Congress of Soviet Writers, urged the imaginary "doofus" of a speaker to turn around to see that the applause was directed not at him but at the "dear leader" behind him, he cast that speaker in the role of a performer who didn't—couldn't—understand the power of the performance of which he is a part. Stalin performed before the writers, and their task, it had become clear, was to re-create the power of that event—not the details of the event, but the experience of it—on stage.

In the immediate aftermath of the 1932 meetings with Gorky and Stalin, the organizing committee of the Writers' Congress (still at this point under Kirpotin's control) convened a special conference devoted to the problems of playwriting. An All-Union competition for the best play was announced. The initial agenda of the Congress specified a single keynote lecture about Soviet playwriting, not the four competing lectures that ended up being delivered. The lectures settled nothing, and the playwriting competition came and went without a first prize being awarded. Instead, there were two second prizes: one given to Kirshon, for a play, *The Magnificent Alloy* (*Chudesnyi splav*), that he asked Stalin to read and approve before publication.[21] The action of this comedy takes place in the research facility of the Soviet aviation industry. The facility's leading designers, who come from different places in the Soviet Union, struggle to refine materials to improve the performance of Soviet fighters. As they work to perfect the greatest alloy ever invented, they themselves become a human alloy, fused as a collective, and living better, merrier, more seamless lives. In the ludicrous final scene, the main character rushes out to shake the hand of the director of the plant, forgetting that he doesn't have his pants on. His comrades come to the rescue.[22] The other second prize went to Boris Romashov for *Fighters* (*Boitsy*), which concerned, straightforwardly, the conversion of peasant-worker leaders and tsarist officers to the Soviet cause.[23] Both plays succeeded on stage, though they had nothing in common, no shared dramaturgical formula beyond militarism. The adjudicators of the playscripts decided they had potential, and the actors gamely proved them right.

Stalin and other "dear leaders" attended productions at Moscow's theaters in the 1930s, and those who saw them were wonderstruck. It was amazing to be in the presence of the powers that be. Bulgakov's wife Elena Sergeyevna recorded her impressions of these chance encounters in her diaries:

> We sat in the administration's box, right by the proscenium. The box was just packed with people. Right before the beginning of the second act, in the government box—across from us—there appeared Stalin, Molotov, and Ordzhonikidze. After it was over, all the performers gathered on stage and started an ovation in Stalin's honor. Then the entire theater took part in it. Stalin greeted the actors by waving his hand, applauded.[24]

Stalin could appear in the theater at any moment, which added to the excitement and trepidation in the house on first nights. His appearances had precedent in the Romanov era. The tsar or tsarina often took a seat in the tsar's loge along with family members and visiting dignitaries. St. Petersburg noblemen fashioned their attendance and behavior in the boxes with Alexander II or Alexander III's gaze in mind.

The end of the nineteenth century witnessed the introduction of electric lighting on the stage and dimming of the lights in the audience. The experience became much more immersive, at the expense of the social side of theatergoing. As Wolfgang Schivelbusch writes of the era before electricity, "the display of wealth through clothing, the assertion of rank and class through their location in the house, the deployment of the erotic gaze (flirting), as well as the conduct of other social and economic relations. All of these had to be done with the lights on."[25] Looking at the sovereign, presenting oneself to him, was very different than trying to catch a glimpse of Stalin and trying to discern his reaction to the performance. Soviet theatergoing wasn't a fashion show, and the light came not from overhead, from an enormous chandelier, but from the stage. Stanislavsky writes of the curtain of electric light striking terror into the heart of the actor. It turned the stalls and boxes into a dark and frightful realm and gave him stage fright. Stalin might or might not be out there, but Stalin was always in view, deciding how everyone, actors and viewers alike, should perform their parts.

Chapter Four

Aleksandr Afinogenov's Acceptable Ambiguities

IN 1920 ALEKSANDR AFINOGENOV held sixteen different jobs. Among other things, he edited a newspaper in the provincial town of Skopin (south of Moscow near Ryazan), ran the local publishing firm, served as the district military censor, and, as a member of the school board, turned up at his former elementary school wearing a revolver to intimidate the teachers. He was sixteen years old.

He boasted of these adolescent activities in an autobiographical sketch for a brochure published by the Kharkiv Theater of Russian Drama in November 1933.[1] This Ukrainian SSR theater had just been established; its first production was the premiere of Afinogenov's play *The Lie*. The brochure offered an ideological guide to the play, explaining what it was trying to achieve, and featured both the playwright's directorial instructions and an "Open Letter to My Future Directors" in which he discussed everything from lighting design to acting technique.[2] The seriousness of the effort to guide the audience's interpretation was unusual; most brochures, irrespective of the significance of the production, avoided heavy-handed explanations. They might include pictures of rehearsals, chronicles of the genesis of the production, and the names of the actors and production team. Sharing the autobiographical sketch in the brochure accompanying *The Lie* suggested that to understand the play, the audience needed to imagine its author parading around a provincial school building with a pistol in his hand. A politically conscious teenager who aspired in equal measure to bring the Revolution to the masses and to succeed in the writing business—here was another piece of theater.

It didn't much matter how accurate the tale was, though subsequent biographical sketches of Afinogenov insist on its truth. What mattered was its contribution to the show. Awarded a lengthy standing ovation on its opening night and a warm reception by local Party authorities, *The Lie* seemed to be on its way to a success as great as Afinogenov's previous play *Fear*.[3] In Stalin's infamous October 1932 meeting with writers, he singled out *Fear* as a model

Soviet play with a broad reach; in his own account, it had been seen by millions of Soviet citizens in just a few months.[4] *The Lie* was designed to go just as far—with help from the production booklet, Afinogenov's guidance, and the implied connections between lives real and represented.

Yet less than two weeks after that triumphant first night, Afinogenov was forced to withdraw *The Lie* from the Kharkiv theater and all the other Soviet theaters where it was being rehearsed, including the First and the Second Moscow Art Theaters. What happened?

Theater was meant to establish Afinogenov's credentials as a genuine Soviet person, and the purity of his ideological commitments would justify his artistic choices as a playwright. But like other travesty actors, Afinogenov appealed to the disjunction between what was shown, or not shown, and what was seen on the Soviet stage. The kind of theater he helped make possible paradoxically depended—aesthetically and ideologically—on what the playscript could not, would not, represent. Legibility depended on illegibility and uncertainty. Ideological cliché and complexity were co-dependent. To understand the paradoxical workings of this travesty act requires reconstructing the terms of the theatrical, literary, and cultural arrangements that made questions of legibility so meaningful and so urgent for Afinogenov's audiences—that is, the measures taken by the theatrical productions' many coauthors to "legitimate a certain kind of experience for the audience as significant."[5]

For all the controversies about the future of the Soviet theater, the plays championed by the various opponents in these debates had much in common. Vishnevskii's *An Optimistic Tragedy* and Kirshon's *Bread* borrowed from classical melodrama. Both pitted the community of ideological doubters against the greater mass of true believers. This conflict was represented both on the Stalinist stage and in the Moscow show trials: the courtroom that had been set up in the Hall of Columns of the House of Unions.[6] What distinguished the plays from each other was their hold on their audiences, their visceral impact. Whereas reinterpretations of the classics like Gogol's comedies or Leo Tolstoy's novels relied on extra-textual meanings, Soviet plays, in contrast, exploited a divide between the written text and the performed act.

The case of *The Lie* reveals the tensions in theater during the 1930s between form, theme, idea, and performance. *The Lie* failed where *Fear* had succeeded, and the consequences of these two reception histories proved far-reaching. Afinogenov's diaries of 1937–38 chronicle his efforts to fashion, for the stage, a genuine Soviet person, together with declarations of his "admiration for Stalin!"[7] The diaries also furnish the opposite: an up-close, in-the-moment account of Afinogenov's humiliation and his craven efforts to restore himself to favor in official circles.

Chapter Four

"REAL" *FEAR*

Afinogenov enjoyed his first major hit at age twenty-five with the Second Moscow Art Theater's production of *The Eccentric* (1929). In 1931, when *Fear* went into rehearsal, he was sitting on the boards of the most important playwrights' and writers' organizations and was also editing the most influential Soviet theater magazine.[8] *Fear* built on the success of *The Eccentric* by addressing the challenges of constructing the new Soviet society, the detritus of the past, and preparations for the next major phase of class struggle. The decision to address the experience of fear, to structure his exploration of the concerns of the day around a single emotion, was a provocative move on Afinogenov's part. The stakes were raised when it was announced that the premiere would be at the First Moscow Art Theater, the center of the Soviet theater world.

Under Stanislavsky and Nemirovich-Danchenko, MAT was associated with realism. The "system," or "method," of realistic acting bearing Stanislavsky's name became *the* technique for training stage and screen actors on both sides of the Atlantic. In part because "realistic" acting is so ubiquitous, its purpose seems self-evident: the fashioning of lifelike characters who behave in believable ways.[9] Settings need to look real, and audiences needed to feel the emotions expressed by the characters. To achieve these goals, Stanislavsky relied on uniquely theatrical techniques. He asked his actors to lengthen pauses, manipulate intonations, and alter gestures, gaits, and other nonverbal elements of the performance. Fashioning a convincingly complex character required fulfilling several smaller objectives, chief among them identifying and highlighting each line's "subtext." Ostensibly, the point is to reveal the meaning already contained within the text and make that meaning more palpable. In practice, however, finding the subtext meant enriching the playscript with additional meanings, by adding nonverbal narratives altogether absent from the performance's text as written. Subtext as performed often achieved the effects of realism by seeming to violate or contradict the spoken language. Noting the subversive potential of such "realistic" method acting, Osip Mandelstam associated Stanislavsky's offerings with a fundamental "mistrust of the word."[10]

Cultivating the nonverbal, resisting the text even as the text was being articulated, became the essence of MAT's productions of Chekhov and Gorky. The same method was also applied to melodrama. Though melodrama was denigrated in the 1920s for its reactionary conservativism, MAT returned to it in the 1930s, with poetic realism as preached and practiced by Stanislavsky part of the reemphasis. It was neither revolutionary nor experimental, but effectively cultivated ideologically productive tensions between

Konstantin Stanislavsky and Vladimir Nemirovich-Danchenko, 1910s. Private collection. Credit: Heritage Image Partnership Ltd / Alamy Stock Photo.

the written word and physical action. In this sense, realism as championed by MAT stood at odds with the stated goal of 1930s theater: limiting and homogenizing the range of interpretive responses to a production.

The decision to produce *Fear* was also counterintuitive. As one of the officials of the ideologically militant Russian Association of Proletarian Writers, Afinogenov had often berated MAT and both of its directors.[11] But here was the chance to perform, realistically, an ideologically sound, aesthetically exemplary Soviet drama. And *Fear* was a triumph. Stalin and senior officials attended, taking the time to compliment the playwright and the creative team on their success. Gorky was spotted weeping during one of the performances.[12] The play had even deeper, personal resonances with audiences, whose own fears belonged to the play's subtext.

> A conversation overheard in the theater: "So how do you like it?"—"How do I like it? You can say whatever you want about the Art Theater's production before the show and after the show. But during the show you find yourself entirely in the power of a marvelous spectacle [*tselikom popadaesh' vo vlast' izumitel'nogo zrelishcha*]."[13]

Chapter Four

There are several questions here. What does it mean to be "in the power" of a Stalinist spectacle? How was that power manufactured? Was the power of *Fear* about fear in a general sense or something specific to the plot? How was the emotion rhetorically exploited? What did the performance hope to accomplish?

Afinogenov's playscript claims to be "about" an emotion but is chiefly concerned with intentions and hidden meanings. It is also meta-theatrical, anxious about how it might be interpreted. The first productions of *Fear*, in Moscow and Leningrad, exposed ideological fault lines in their efforts to generate, but also control, the ambiguities of the text, the subtext, and theatrical realism.

FEAR AND ANXIETY

Fear chronicles a few months in the life of the fictional professor Ivan Ilich Borodin, an internationally renowned scientist and leading researcher at the Institute of Physiological Stimuli. Borodin's world is falling apart. His favorite student has been denied promotion and permission to attend a conference in Berlin. His colleagues are being purged from their jobs and arrested. The institute's key positions are being taken over by the boorish recipients of the government's class-conscious promotion policies. One of the people promoted (*vydvizhentsy*) is Borodin's new assistant Elena Makarova. The professor isn't opposed to the Soviet system and acknowledges the financial support his research has received since the Revolution. But he wants to stay out of politics and focus his efforts on testing the hypothesis that all behavior is governed by four unconditioned stimuli: love, hunger, anger, and fear. Makarova, on the other hand, believes that politics has the power to remake human beings and insists that Borodin is moving too slowly. Arguing that science can be harnessed to eliminate petty, obsolete feelings such as jealousy, malice, and fear, she demands that the institute open a laboratory with human subjects. Infuriated by what he perceives as an attack on his scholarly and personal authority, Borodin plots to turn Makarova's proposal against her; he will use the resources of the new lab to demonstrate the flaws of "the Soviet system of people management."

There's a snag. Borodin's other assistant, a soft-spoken but principled scientist, signals to Makarova that she is walking into a trap. After a series of complicated maneuvers involving shifts in romantic alliances among the institute's employees, Makarova succeeds in submitting an article condemning Borodin's methods to a scholarly journal. To forestall the attack, Borodin decides to announce the preliminary conclusions of his study at a public lecture to which he invites the foreign press. Borodin's findings vindicate his behaviorist theory. Eighty percent of the Soviet population, he announces during the lecture, is animated by the same impulse: fear.

> The milkmaid is afraid that her cow will be confiscated; the peasant is afraid of compulsory collectivization; the Soviet worker is afraid of the endless purges; the Party worker is afraid that he will be accused of deviating from the Party line; the scholar is afraid that he will be accused of idealism; the technical worker is afraid that he will be accused of sabotage. We live in a time of great fear. Fear compels talented members of the intelligentsia to renounce their mothers, to falsify their social origin, to wiggle their way into high positions . . . Oh yes . . . The fear of being exposed is not so great when you're in a high place. Fear stalks everyone. People become suspicious, aloof, dishonest, sloppy and unprincipled . . . The rabbit who has seen a boa constrictor is unable to move from the spot. His muscles petrify. He waits, submissively, until the rings of the boa constrictor squeeze him and crush him. All of us are rabbits. (S 451/229–30)[14]

The other twenty percent of the population, according to Borodin, are those who benefit from the government's policies, like Makarova—people who have nothing to fear, since the Soviet Union belongs to them. Yet they, too, are victims of a debilitating anxiety; they might never "catch up to and overcome" those who are smarter and better educated.

The lone response to Borodin's speech is delivered by Klara Spasova (Klara the Savior), an Old Bolshevik who represents the factory that is maneuvering to supervise Borodin's institute. Klara uses the story of her own son, brutally put to death by the tsarist regime, to make the point that true revolutionaries have always been, and remain, fearless. Fear, she claims, is the curse of those who have been defeated and those who continue to bear ill will toward the Soviet authorities. In Klara's world, fear has no place. It is a sign of ideological inadequacy.[15]

After the lecture Borodin is arrested and, at the OGPU investigator's office, confronted by his closest colleagues. One after another they accuse Borodin of harboring virulently anti-Soviet sentiments and actively conspiring to undermine the authorities. The investigator gives Borodin the chance to defend himself and his theory. Shocked by his friends' disloyalty, the professor is at a loss for words. In the play's final scene Makarova assumes directorship of the institute, and Borodin turns up to give her the keys to his former office. It's not clear if he's been to prison, but he has aged and looks defeated.[16] But then Makarova offers him a job at the institute. He accepts it and vows to work productively with the Bolshevik researchers.

In terms of the plot, *Fear* offers a "brief course" in Stalinism. The disaster befalling Professor Borodin recapitulates the familiar intelligentsia-conversion narrative of the late 1920s. He is betrayed by his friends; he must overcome humiliation and submit to his humiliator's guidance. Much here is in keeping with melodrama,[17] which accounts for what is likely to strike today's reader as the most unexpected aspect of the play: its explicit engagement with the experience of fear. Borodin's eloquent portrayal of Soviet society as terrorized and spitefully insecure hardly aligns with official discourse and its cheerfully confident sentiments. Throughout the first three acts, and especially in the monologue Borodin delivers during his confrontation with the Old Bolshevik, *Fear* clearly goes beyond any acceptable criticism of the Soviet system. Borodin is not, after all, opposed to the Soviet regime and he's not unsympathetic, which makes his comments about the pervasiveness of fear so compelling and potentially scandalous. The play seemed to risk causing panic in the audience.

But for a melodrama, this was not a problem. The genre courts hysteria; the stakes have to be raised as high as possible for the idea of a "spectacular reversal" to work. Borodin's conversion had the desired effect on the audience only because his arguments are taken seriously before he is shown to have erred. In turn, the conversion (theoretically) renders his social critique harmless, no matter how articulate and persuasive it might have seemed earlier. He is in the wrong, and his rhetoric is hysterical. Purging emotions, as the play does, is equivalent to ideological purging. But can we assume that this equivalence is complete and sufficient? Might the character's conversion not allow the audience to enjoy with impunity the critical comments offered by the character, perhaps even identify with them? For that matter, can this critical impulse ever be completely purged from the minds of the spectators? The relationship between conversion as an ideological or even theological transformation, on the one hand, and theatrical purging (catharsis) as an aesthetic category, on the other, is the question at center stage.

Motivations are questioned at several levels in *Fear*. The ideological allegiances and intentions of each character are questioned by the others. What is Borodin out to prove with his study? What does his assistant really have in mind when he offers his support to the old professor's opponents? Why, later in the play, does Makarova's ex-husband protect the professor? For a play that overtly claims fear as its central theme, the characters aren't often afraid. But when they are, their fear is linked to discovering the horrible truth about the insincerity of someone's motivations. In the most explicit instance, ten-year-old Natasha, a loyal and vigilant Young Pioneer, overhears her father admitting to forging documents to conceal his bourgeois social origins from Party authorities. Seconds before the curtain falls to end act 2, Natasha is alone on stage screaming with fear [*ot strakha*] (according to the stage direction): "Papa! Papa! Where are you going?! You've deceived the working class!" (S 431/215). Fear is caused by those whose motivations are unclear and therefore liable to be misinterpreted. The melodrama requires that evil speak evil, and that when evil lies, the lie must be made transparent to the audience. To say "no" and mean "maybe" or "yes" or "sometimes"—that is, to "play a subtext"—is not an option in melodrama but a trademark gesture of the realistic stage.

Professor Borodin's academic pursuits, the audience is repeatedly reminded, are about the fundamental impulses of human behavior. His alignment of certain stimuli with certain actions causes the greatest anxiety among his opponents. During one confrontation, Makarova, an exceedingly earnest communist, accuses the professor of fabricating evidence to support his theories about the physiological inspirations of the Bolshevik Revolution (anger) and Stalin's First Five-Year Plan (sex and hunger) (S 434/217–18). Such an alignment is not especially unusual in the 1930s.[18] The danger resides in the framing of physiological impulses as counterintuitive subtexts for ideologically significant actions.

Borodin's daughter Valya, an aspiring artist, attempts to apply her father's teachings to an entry in a sculpture competition. She seeks to represent collectivism as the sum of fundamental stimuli: rage, love, suffering, and victory. When she reveals her creation, a "huge impressionistic mound of muscles, bodies, and faces," to a member of the competition's jury, Valya receives a stern lecture about the fallacy of trying to embody an abstract idea and about the virtues of simplicity:

> Ever been out in the fields on a summer evening? Grass fresh as ever, clouds looking like they've just been washed, mist rising from the river, the earth still warm, time passing inaudibly. Everything's simple, right?—the birch trees, the meadow, the clearings in the forest, the rye . . . But this simplicity makes the thoughts and the feelings more pure, more profound. And that's exactly how it is here, too. (S 405/194)

The scolding jurist is Klara Spasova, the Old Bolshevik from the factory. In act 3 she delivers the rebuttal to Borodin's lecture about the omnipresence of fear, bringing together the play's concerns with aesthetics, science, and politics. Her sublimity anticipates essential features of Socialist Realism: namely, the glorification of transparency and the mistrust of formal experimentation. Valya's complex and overly clever attempts to represent the underlying meaning (a kind of "subtext") of human behavior are, for Klara, as profoundly suspect as Borodin's theories.

At the end of the play Valya destroys the newest version of her sculpture, the version she had been trying to make heeding Klara's advice (S 464/240). Her failure to represent a topical, complicated subject speaks to questions of motivation and problems of interpretation and performance.

Chapter Four

On the one hand the play insists on the complexity of human motivations, while on the other it insists on transparency in representation.

Fear's most unambiguously positive characters, Makarova and Klara, are suspicious of attempts to ascribe physiological "subtexts" to human behavior (whether those subtexts are revealed through laboratory research or built into a sculpture). According to the ideal model of artistic creation and reception outlined in Klara's conversation with Valya, art should strive for the utmost simplicity. Abstract formalism is aberrant. Transparency and accessibility will purge incorrect thoughts and feelings. Correct, unambiguous meaning becomes transparent on its own, precluding the need for theories or interpretations. At issue in Afinogenov's play is the need to keep extra-textual meanings in check but also using those extra-textual meanings—those subtexts—to sustain the illusion. The burden of finding an effective theatrical solution to this problem defined the staging of *Fear* at the Moscow Art Theater. Ambiguity is central to the plot, but the production needed to avoid it.

FEAR IN LENINGRAD

In October 1931, Stanislavsky was getting nervous. *Fear* had been scheduled to open at MAT the previous spring, but the premiere had been repeatedly delayed. The director feared *Fear* "losing its edge."[19] As it happened, the tribulations of the fictional professor echoed those of actual scientists accused of masterminding a counterrevolutionary organization (the so-called Industrial Party).[20] Borodin was also likened to the physiologist Ivan Pavlov, whose studies of physical reflexes and skepticism about the Soviet worldview were well known.[21] *Fear* was plenty topical, and MAT was in competition with the Leningrad State Academic Drama Theater (Gosdrama, the former Aleksandrinskii Theater) to be the first to perform the play. Stanislavsky lost that competition by several months and had to respond to the ideological infelicities of the Leningrad production, which opened on May 31, 1931. (The production almost fell through during the final dress rehearsal, but the highest-ranking Party official in Leningrad, Sergei Kirov, allowed it to proceed.) Afinogenov's RAPP associates insisted that Stanislavsky move forward with the Moscow production, but he was anxious to avoid pitfalls. Moscow's censors were less tolerant than Leningrad's.[22]

The Leningrad crisis originated in the play's casting. Gosdrama's director, Nikolai Petrov, wanted Ekaterina Korchagina-Aleksandrovskaia in the role of Klara Spasova. A representative of the company's older generation, Korchagina had made a name for herself as a comic actress. Petrov admired her heartfelt approach and believed she would bring strength of feeling to an otherwise somber part. The problem was Klara's act 3 monologue: her rebuttal to Borodin's indictment of the Soviet system and her description of her son's execution. To accommodate Korchagina, Petrov asked Afinogenov to rewrite part of the scene, making Klara's exchange with Borodin less academic, more emotional.[23] At a public discussion of the Leningrad production in June 1931, Petrov justified his thinking as follows:

> There have been many attacks on Klara for her monologue, for not refuting Professor Borodin's report in a sufficiently scholarly manner . . . Two pages of Karl Marx delivered by Klara at this point in the play would have been less convincing than the emotional charge which the audience receives through simple but moving words. What's important here is winning: organizing the audience by artistic means so that our intentions are aimed in the direction we need them to go.[24]

Petrov didn't want to stereotype Afinogenov's characters. And he didn't want to make "who was right and who was left" obvious, at least not in the first act (*OS* 18). Klara's monologue had to catalyze and validate the viewers' crucial realization. Korchagina, Petrov insisted, wasn't being asked to approach the role in a way that resisted or "deformed" the explicit meaning of her lines. The complaint was that she hadn't proven the point about fear having no place in the lives of genuine Soviet people. Petrov strove for something much subtler: Klara would avoid quoting from Marx but would expose the rhetorical inefficacy of Borodin's claims through her demeanor. She wouldn't force the point, she would instead "draw the spectator into the experience of the stage [literally 'the situation of the scene,' '*stsenicheskaia situatsiia*']" (21).

At Gosdrama that experience was defined by Nikolai Akimov's striking designs, which became the production's most controversial feature. Akimov centered most of the action on a wide platform that sloped downward toward the audience at a ten-degree angle, extending a few feet past the edge of the stage. This prominent perpendicular axis also determined the placement of the major set pieces. Rows of bookshelves in the library of the institute, a conference table extending almost the entire length of the platform, the line of Valya's unfinished sculptures, doors in the hallway of Makarova's communal apartment—all seemed to stretch into infinity upstage. The illusion was accentuated by a shifting panel that defined the vertical boundary of the principal acting area. This panel, whose lower edge outlined the cross-section of a slightly curved ceiling, could be raised and lowered. Akimov essentially created a smaller, flexible proscenium arch inside Gosdrama's old-fashioned portico. Every time the edge of the vertical panel moved toward the floorboards or away from them, the relationship

Chapter Four

between the actors and the audience changed. By separating performers on an illuminated stage from spectators immersed in darkness, modern proscenium theater reinforces the dramatic illusion of the "fourth wall." The separation enhances the audience's voyeuristic experience.[25] Soviet theater of the 1920s, in contrast, often tried to eliminate boundaries, exploring ways to physically connect the audience and the spectacle through lighting and set design. When Petrov discussed the relationship between the audience and the "situation of the scene," he was referring to how the *scenic* design of *Fear*—Akimov's mobile set—repositioned the audience with respect to the action.

The feeling of infinite depth and constraint in the design perfectly captures the tension in the play between the illusion of freedom and the need to conform. Though Petrov allowed for interpretive ambiguities ("who is left and who is right") in act 1, he ensured a single, unambiguous response to the crucial confrontation scene—a response even more powerful for not being imposed by force. Korchagina ensured that the "situation of the scene" elicited the correct emotional response in the audience. The set enhanced the rhetoric: a huge panel hung over the stage like a guillotine, pushing the actors and action closer to the spectators when it descended, becoming in effect a "fourth wall."

In scale and structure, then, Akimov's set resisted realism—the stage representation's claim to verisimilitude. At a public discussion of the production, cast members expressed their discomfort with the set, complaining that it limited their range as actors. Illarion Pevtsov, the Gosdrama actor in the role of Professor Borodin, recalled having to invent a "realistic" justification for the sloping platform. He convinced himself that Borodin lived in a building designed by an eccentric architect fond of slanted floors (*OS* 75).[26] Other actors borrowed from the play's title to describe Akimov's set as a cause of stress—fear—for them (68). Could the production possibly convince its spectators that they had nothing to fear when the actors themselves were so uncomfortable?

The audience at the penultimate rehearsal audibly gasped at the forcefulness of Borodin's monologue.[27] Encouraged by this reaction, Pevtsov pressed on, finishing the monologue with confident intensity. As soon as Korchagina moved to the podium to deliver Klara's rebuttal, it was clear that things had not gone as planned. Korchagina hesitated, skipped several words, then a line, went back, and stumbled again; Klara's arguments sounded tentative, and the tale of her son's execution didn't elicit much of a reaction from the audience. There was no applause at the end of act 3, and things got worse in act 4. The scene in the investigator's office, which Afinogenov added during the rehearsal process, was supposed to mark the beginning of Borodin's conversion by exposing his colleagues as traitors. But Pevtsov's "victory" over Korchagina in the performance conveyed the wrong message. Borodin's encounter with the authorities became an object lesson in the destructive power of the state. And rather than being exposed as traitors, Borodin's colleagues seemed pitiful, unjustly treated. The play's final scene, at Klara's apartment, meant to represent Bolshevik "fearlessness," instead depicted the humiliation of a courageous old man. *Fear* faced an immediate and permanent ban.

Leningrad's chief theater censor, a friend of Afinogenov's and Petrov's, convinced Kirov, the Leningrad Party chief, that despite this unfortunate performative lapse the play should be given a chance. The final dress rehearsal, which under normal circumstances would have been attended by a dozen or so people, played to a full house: hundreds of Party functionaries and theater personalities had heard about the debacle at the previous runthrough. Pevtsov's monologue remained confident and effective. Korchagina changed her response to it, beginning tentatively, as she had before, then becoming more severe and precise in her delivery. As she described the execution of her son, Afinogenov and Petrov saw audience members wiping their tears—something that would become a kind of ritual in later performances and often described in the reviews. Korchagina's achievement was even more remarkable for its restraint: it excluded the overblown gestures typical of melodrama.

The tears ensured Kirov's endorsement of the play, though Korchagina fretted over her ability to reproduce the effect.[28] Her initial failure to move the audience to Klara's side attested, perversely, to the power of her realistic acting. Pevtsov as Borodin shocked the audience, and she reached for another level, exploiting, in the final dress rehearsal, emotions "discovered in the moment" and responding to Borodin as if she, not merely her character, was dealing with him. That last rehearsal also benefited from the actors appearing in full costume, which hadn't been the case earlier, and from the production being run without pausing, with full use of the set.[29] Korchagina's enforced awareness of the "scenic situation" prompted her to enact and project her character's—and her own—refusal to be defeated by fear. "It's interesting," a doctor who saw the play recalled,

> that it's not just the audience reacting to the performance—the performers are also not acting like they usually do. Don't you have a sense that *Fear* is being performed in a way no other show is? Are the actors just acting? Oh, no! They've performed a ton of different plays since the revolution, but try conducting psychological analysis of how they act in *Fear*. Words sound like actions. The ideological import of the production is so strong that no actor can possibly undermine it. The theater has turned this production into a play of steel. This play, like the original theory about conditioning reflexes,

is something profound yet at the same time simple. No, no, we've never seen a play like this one before. Everybody says that—the audience, the theater professionals. (*OS* 46)

"Not just acting" is a far-reaching statement. The doctor might be referring to the actors' worries about the set, or their efforts, despite the set, to fashion a perfect illusion. Describing *Fear* as a "production of steel" might be a reference to the "man of steel" Stalin. Calling it "profound yet simple" recalls Klara's conversation with Valya Borodina about transcendent art: "simplicity makes thoughts and feelings more pure, more profound." The actor cannot undercut the ideological import of the production because the cast collectively "speaks in actions" so simply and profoundly that their logic is inviolable.

Another audience member focused on the interrogation scene and its correction of the flaws in Klara's response to Borodin.

It made a much greater impression on me personally than Klara's speech. From a scholarly point of view, Klara did not really prove the professor wrong. Her argument led me to conclude that a revolutionary hero is also ultimately motivated by fear. Our GPU is excellent at finding the right moment and impressing things upon all kinds of people in fitting ways. Professor Borodin looks at a glass of water and contemplates the life of the paramecia. Then he draws conclusions about human psychology based upon those observations. And they found an excellent remedy for him at the GPU—transferring him into a laboratory of living, breathing human beings. (*OS* 73)

An obvious connection is made between culture and the state, MAT and the OGPU. It's not that the secret police were theatrical, their actions disingenuous and suspect, but that the performance was a kind of "laboratory of living human beings" that derives legitimacy from methods not entirely unlike the OGPU's. The dramatic authenticity (the "simplicity") of the interrogation episode convinces an audience member to discard the "politically incorrect" conclusion drawn from Klara's monologue. The interrogation is retroactive motivation for the confrontation between Klara and Borodin—not because it justifies the characters' actions, but because it reveals the production's meta-theatrical logic to the viewer.

Petrov's production relied on realistic acting to emphasize the ambiguity of the characters' motivations. The OGPU scene cleared up the ambiguity: the play could not be misread as a warning about growing fears in Soviet society. This effect was not achieved by obscuring the rhetorical strategies of the performance from the audience. Akimov's decor led the actors, willingly or unwillingly, to refine their methods. It recast the theatrical experience to enhance the already familiar narrative of renewal and conversion. Soon after the Leningrad opening, Gosdrama began sending touring "brigades" to the provinces. Their task was to convince local theater companies reluctant to stage *Fear* that it was not, in fact, subversive, so long as acts 3 and 4 were handled "correctly." Most provincial theaters found the brigades' performances compelling. *Fear* continued to spread.[30]

STANISLAVSKY'S *FEAR*: "ACCEPTABLE DISTORTIONS"

For the Moscow Art Theater, where Afinogenov's play finally opened on December 24, 1931 (seven months after its Leningrad premiere), replicating the Gosdrama production was not an option. MAT strove for contrast, and reviewers responded accordingly, summarizing the pluses and minuses of the new interpretation.[31] The most fascinating response came from Osaf Litovskii, the chairman of the central censorship board (Glavrepertkom). Through complicated bureaucratic maneuvering, MAT circumvented the standard procedure for gaining official approval, but Litovskii insisted on stating his objections in a formal letter to the theater's administration. Most of his complaints concerned individual characters; just one addressed the staging of a specific scene. "The OGPU interrogation scene is done in an entirely unacceptable fashion," Litovskii wrote:

> A windowless room with dirty walls, with black doors upholstered with black felt and oilcloth, which open without a sound—all this creates an unacceptably distorted representation of the way in which the interrogations actually take place. The dreary, muffled feel of the setting is furthermore emphasized by the utterly persecuted look on the face of [Borodin's favorite student Hermann] Kastalskii.[32]

Formulating his grievance in terms of "unacceptably distorted representation" suggests that Litovskii had firsthand experience with OGPU interrogations, and if so, it was prudent to lighten their grim effect. He wanted MAT to represent that experience "accurately," irrespective of the nuances of Afinogenov's playscript.

The MAT set, by Nisson Shifrin, did not strive for precise photographic verisimilitude. The bookshelves in Borodin's apartment and the institute library—the most prominent feature of the set—stretched toward the rafters, hyperbolizing the "scholarly" setting for the study of rats and rabbits. The set complemented and accentuated the actors' movements as a comfortable, impediment-free space suited to a traditional, "realistic" performance.[33]

Chapter Four

The production was directed by Ilya Sudakov and supervised first by Vladimir Nemirovich-Danchenko, and then (after Nemirovich-Danchenko fell ill and traveled abroad to recuperate) by Stanislavsky himself. When Stanislavsky took over, most of *Fear* had already been staged. But even under pressure from Afinogenov and his RAPP associates, Stanislavsky insisted on continuing rehearsals for several more weeks.[34] The problem that appeared to preoccupy him was, as in Leningrad, the problem of Klara. At MAT the part was performed by Olga Knipper-Chekhova, one of the troupe's most senior members and the widow of Anton Chekhov. Knipper was a dramatic actress from an earlier generation trying to perfect a role that, as her colleagues constantly reminded her, had no grounding in her personal experiences. Stanislavsky scheduled several additional one-on-one rehearsals with her but the role, she reluctantly acknowledged, wasn't coming together for her. Time was running out; barely a week remained until the opening.[35]

In the crucial confrontation scene, Knipper was paired up with Leonid Leonidov as Borodin. A great tragic actor whose repertoire ranged from Dmitri Karamazov and Othello to Yegor Bulychov,[36] Leonidov had appeared

Maquette for the MAT production of Aleksandr Afinogenov's *Fear* (1931). Photograph by the author.

opposite Knipper before—most memorably in the original production of Chekhov's *The Cherry Orchard*. In 1904 Knipper, as Ranevskaia, unsuccessfully defended the orchard she owned and the way of life it denoted from the onslaught of modernity represented by Leonidov's passionately ruthless Lopakhin. In 1931 in *Fear*, she had to convince the audience of the superiority of the present (embodied by Klara) over the past (embodied by Leonidov/Borodin). But unfortunately, the dynamic between them in *The Cherry Orchard* persisted in *Fear*. Leonidov's character was not only more forceful but also more visibly powerful than Knipper's.[37]

In one respect, Leonidov's task was less complicated than Knipper's. He was playing a member of the intelligentsia, a paradigmatic MAT character. Yet while reports from the rehearsals repeatedly pointed to Leonidov's performance as the production's strongest, the actor struggled with the role of Borodin and even asked Stanislavsky to find a replacement for him. During one lengthy conversation at Stanislavsky's apartment, Leonidov complained that his performance had failed to interest the few chance observers of the first rehearsals because his character was so obviously unsympathetic.

> *Leonidov*. But look, there's just nothing positive about Borodin! He's a reactionary—until he gets kicked in the head. You yourself said that he should be arrested!
>
> *Stanislavsky*. The author has proved to me that I was mistaken, that the Borodins should be re-educated rather than arrested. And I think that I was wrong and Afinogenov is right . . .
>
> *Leonidov*. So how would you play Borodin? You, from your position as Stanislavsky the scholar and master of the theatrical craft?
>
> *Stanislavsky*. I would constantly check myself: Am I right or wrong in my views on science, on politics, on people in these new, changed life conditions?
>
> *Leonidov*. Yes, but that would be quite a subtext for the entire role! The author's written text quite literally says something entirely different![38]

Arguing from the perspective of someone who had contemplated playing Borodin himself, Stanislavsky insisted that Afinogenov's inexperience as a playwright sanctioned the actors—himself and Leonidov—to compensate for the apparent lack of an explicit justification for this reading in the text.[39] Stanislavsky suggested a way of "resisting" the text in the opening scenes: convincing the audience, through intonation shifts and understated movement, that Borodin's disciple Kastalskii was overstating the anti-Soviet case.[40]

Chapter Four

Stanislavsky adhered to the logic of stage realism, according to which any character can hold the interest of the audience if they invest that character with sufficient complexity. Stanislavsky's Borodin would not merely suggest motivations "left out" of the playscript; he had to acknowledge his awareness of the motivations of others. The professor's "re-education" happens in a world where enemies become allies and allies become enemies. Permanent mutual suspicion is the subtext. MAT's staging of *Fear* cultivated a kind of interpretive paranoia among its performers but stood little chance of causing panic (a fear of fear) among its audiences because it avoided excessive hysteria, excessive melodrama.

Stanislavsky's strategy had important implications for the play's dramatic structure. The OGPU scene had to represent the final stage in a process of transformation. It could not be a sudden and complete revelation; rather, it represented Borodin's growing suspicion that he had erred in his views on science and choice of friends. In the act 3 scene with Klara, Stanislavsky expected Leonidov to treat Borodin's lecture like the professor's other scholarly endeavors—with a degree of detachment that signaled slowly growing self-doubts.[41] But the step toward rebirth (*pererozhdenie*) had to happen during, and be palpably motivated by, Klara's response. This meant that even as Leonidov's performance acquired a new subtext, the stakes were raised higher than ever for Knipper. At the same time, the range of strategies available to her shrank. She was no longer Borodin's opponent and could not merely reclaim moral authority by revealing her character's vulnerability, as she did in her confrontation with Leonidov in *The Cherry Orchard*. Klara had to serve as Borodin's future mentor; she needed to persuade the audience that she had convinced him. This added "objective" (a Stanislavskian term) meant avoiding an overly emotional reading of Klara's monologue, moving away from melodrama.

At one of the last rehearsals before he asked Knipper to relinquish the role, Stanislavsky attempted an experiment. The audience that day included members of a special "workers' brigade" appointed as ideological supervisors of the production. Stanislavsky had run through the confrontation scene twice, first with Knipper and then with her understudy, Nina Sokolovskaia. The director asked the actors and students present at the rehearsal but not taking part in the scene to enter the stage and then instructed Leonidov and Knipper to repeat the scene. He told most of the chorus he had gathered onstage to express their support for Klara's rebuttal; the rest backed Borodin. The "workers' brigade" responded in kind, responding to Knipper's delivery of the monologue with enthusiastic applause.[42]

The tenacious ideological and aesthetic problem of "defeating" Borodin on stage seemed to have been resolved. And yet Stanislavsky chose not to use this device in the production. Knipper was replaced with Nina Sokolovskaia, who had joined MAT in 1917.[43] She wasn't as famous or experienced, but she didn't have Knipper's baggage. Though Sokolovskaia struggled with the part of Klara, she didn't require a chorus of extras to produce the desired effect. To include the chorus in the Klara-Borodin scene was to dictate how the audience should respond to it. Such a theatrical effect might have been appropriate in a production trying to mobilize its viewers for immediate action (as the agitprop spectacles of the 1920s had done), but Stanislavsky sought to avoid excess. Instead, he wanted to build tension slowly, through the addition of layers of amorphous meaning. Borodin's research centered on the reproduction of stimuli; Stanislavsky didn't want his play to do the same thing. The chorus would have jeopardized the entire production.

Just as he had with Leonidov, Stanislavsky encouraged the minor actors to bring out the subtexts in their parts. No one secured the playwright's advance permission for these changes, yet Afinogenov, who observed rehearsals regularly, seemed pleased with the result. "I experienced the most joy at those rehearsals," he wrote in a retrospective account of his experiences at MAT, "during which I witnessed the performers moving further and further away from the characters I had originally devised."[44] Significant though these modifications may have been, the playwright delighted in them. There were risks, however. Through the months of rehearsals, the characters became more nuanced, with dozens of details added to the playscript—some potentially distorting the play's ideological message. Judging from the initial responses to the production, the concerns were unfounded. Leonidov's forceful delivery of Borodin's lecture about the omnipresence of fear was singled out by critics, even those most hostile to MAT, as a remarkable achievement.[45] The reviews suggested that Klara's rebuttal, even as performed by Sokolovskaia, fell short of "defeating Borodin's scholarly argument." The "fine shades, half-tones and subtleties" noted in the production were lauded.[46] It was not the "play of steel" seen in Leningrad, but neither the "subtleties" of the individual performances nor questions about the meaning of the confrontation scene (questions that almost scuttled the Gosdrama production) caused Stanislavsky trouble. The play's message was delivered.

Still, one detail rankled. Each time Borodin receives a piece of bad news he says, "What's happening to people?" And each time Leonidov delivered the line, the audience chuckled. "What's so funny?" one reviewer asked.[47] On the streets outside MAT, people were changing, but nothing was funny.

As instructed by Stanislavsky, Leonidov was to indicate, with silent gestures, Borodin's frustration with his devious protégé right at the start of the play, long before he's identified as a villain. Leonidov's gestures made his motivation transparent, but they were played as though only the audience could see them, not the other characters. The meaning of the play, its interpretation wasn't dictated to the audience. Instead, the audience was placed in a position of authority; deeply invested in the outcome of stage action, the spectator was privy to the (hidden) motivations of fictional characters. "What's happening to people?" was not a funny line, but it provoked the laughter of those who felt that they, unlike the old professor portrayed by Leonidov, knew what was happening, and had every (theatrical) reason to believe that *it*—whatever it was—would not happen to them, at least not without them noticing.

This carefully constructed theatrical illusion would not have worked if the stakes had been lower. The 1930s witnessed the show trials and purges and brought heated rhetoric about traitors, saboteurs, and "double-dealers" ("*dvurushiniki*") into the consciousness of all Soviet citizens. Some of those watching *Fear* experienced that emotion acutely. The MAT had been the theater of the intelligentsia before 1917 and continued to function as such in the 1920s; its audiences included people like Borodin. But Afinogenov's play was written to appeal to as broad and generic an audience as possible: people of different generations, genders, professions, political alignments, and ethnicities could find a character or a situation germane to their own lives. The production treated them all as equals in imagining and experiencing fear. Such was its "stimulus." Whether or not to accept the terms of this "theatrical offering" (to laugh or not to laugh at Leonidov-Borodin's line, for instance) was up to the spectator.

Several weeks after *Fear* opened in Moscow, the newspaper *Vecherniaia Moskva* invited playwrights, actors, and directors to share their opinions of the production. Yuri Olesha drafted several versions of his response, some harshly critical of Afinogenov's playscript. The statement he submitted to the newspaper ended up being short and polite. He praised the actors and talked, generally, about the audience:

> While I was watching *Fear* and was observing the spectators' reactions, I came to realize that there indeed exists a Soviet audience, and that its tastes, sympathies, and traditions are now being established. *Fear* has revealed to us the Soviet audience in a broad sense. And that is an enviable accomplishment.[48]

For audiences of *Fear* in Moscow and Leningrad, the experience of "being in the power" of a Stalinist spectacle meant basking in the sights and sounds as well as possessing them. The meaning of the events unfolding on stage could not, however, be exhaustively, "objectively" captured in words, could not be quoted, and therefore left room for reinterpretation and misinterpretation. There were different takeaways.

In between the Moscow and Leningrad premieres, *Fear* opened in the provinces. Workers at a power plant south of Moscow in Kashira debated the local performance and sent Afinogenov their reactions to it (the summary of their post-performance discussion): "What's good about your play is that it doesn't show the saboteurs and class enemies already exposed [literally 'stripped naked'—*obnazhennye*]. The audience must identify them, uncover [them] and draw the appropriate conclusions. That is something truly innovative about your play."[49] *Fear* taught audiences that something always lay beyond the text, that all was not as simple as it seemed, and that not even the OGPU could reveal everything to them during the performance.

BETWEEN WORDS AND DEEDS: *THE LIE*

Thus, Afinogenov reached the professional and political zenith. After the Moscow opening of *Fear* and the avalanche of positive reviews, journalists and colleagues began to refer to him as the leading Soviet playwright and an established authority in the field. The young author didn't rest; he immediately moved on, with Stakhanovite speed, to his next project. Barely a month after *Fear* opened at MAT, Afinogenov penned a polite, enthusiastic letter to Stanislavsky asking to collaborate again.[50] The playwright's interest in "solidifying the creative connection with the theater," as he put it, was driven by two related considerations. It would showcase and further develop the dramatic and theatrical "devices" (*"priyomy"*) he had tested in *Fear*, to the benefit of MAT, which was seeking to expand its repertoire. The new collaboration would also be of personal benefit to Afinogenov, who talked about his experience at MAT as a period of self-improvement (*"vremia bol'shoi vnutrennei raboty nad soboi,"* or "time of major internal work upon the self"). His play would conclude his development into a model Soviet writer. His letter is highly rhetorical and full of clichéd Soviet-speak. Still, the difficult history of his next play, alternately known as *The Lie* and *The Ivanov Family* (*Sem'ia Ivanovykh*), suggests that we can take Afinogenov at his word.

The Lie picks up where *Fear* left off. The plot is set in motion by an argument over the interpretation of a single sentence—that, is, over the subtext of a single line of dialogue. The protagonist of *The Lie*, a 21-year-old factory worker named Nina Ivanova, causes a stir when she announces, during a meeting of the factory's Party cell, that she wants "not to believe in socialism."[51] Rumors spread. Some of Nina's colleagues, including the leaders of the Party cell, cite this remark as evidence of waywardness and call for her expulsion from the Party. But as the play gradually makes clear, Nina's declaration has been taken out of context by her rivals. Eager to ascribe the most sinister intentions to her, they recast her claim as the ideologically suspect "I don't want to believe in socialism."[52] A crucial piece of evidence is contained in Nina's private diary, which one of her adversaries steals in the hopes of finding even more compromising statements. To his dismay, the diary establishes that Nina, in fact, wants not *merely* to believe in socialism but to understand fully what she is fighting for and why.[53] This will to knowledge, her desire to serve the Truth with certainty, precipitates Nina's conflict with her coworkers and her family. Everyone, she gradually realizes, is lying about something. Even her husband, a factory administrator, has lied to her, denying that he's been embezzling state funds. Nina records her distress in her diary; once that diary has been made public by her foes, she pours out her soul to one of her few remaining friends:

> The whole country is covered with dust from limestone and cement. From construction. And this dust clouds our eyes and obscures real life from us. We don't notice that people are growing up to be monsters [*urody*], speechless and apathetic to everything. Only maybe if a streetcar runs over a woman—then we'll react by cursing the delay. It's a double life [*dvoinaia zhizn'*]. And we reassure ourselves—this is just the kind of life we need, we are all new, we are all good, we praise ourselves, we write fancy words, draw portraits, confer awards—and it is all just a show . . . And all our slogans—people applaud them during meetings, and then they get home and have their own things, very different things, to say about it all. That's why there are no strong convictions anymore—yesterday there was a leader, people were falling over themselves to please him, and then tomorrow comes—and he's been fired and no one will shake his hand . . . We are growing up without thinking or feeling. For how many years now we've been going to the parades and celebrations, we've been putting our faith in you—but none of this is unshakable. And we'll give you up with the same ease with which we sang your praises, because that's how we've been brought up. We've got no one to compare you to—but we are never given the chance to compare anything anyway. And we never know what the general line is going to be tomorrow—today's general line might be tomorrow's "deviation." And the newspapers never tell the whole truth either.[54]

The friend to whom she addresses these remarks (the "you" of the final sentences) is a much older and wiser Bolshevik named Aleksandr Riadovoi, the deputy *narkom* (minister) in charge of Nina's factory. Riadovoi suspects that Nina's doubts are fed and amplified by her conversations with her other mentor and confidant—the director of the factory, an old-timer who has been reprimanded for siding with the opposition in the past. In the third act of the play, Riadovoi discovers that the director has not freed himself of his oppositionist past and is spearheading a counterrevolutionary conspiracy. Riadovoi warns Nina that she is being manipulated by the director. She suspects duplicity on Riadovoi's part, however, and seeking to protect the director, points a revolver at the deputy minister. She fires. Although seriously wounded, Riadovoi tries to protect Nina; when others arrive on the scene, he claims that he shot himself by accident. Moved by his loyalty and courage, Nina realizes that her uncompromising pursuit of the Truth has been tainted by her connection to the evil director. Just when she resolves to end this association and admit that she was the one who shot Riadovoi, the news arrives that Riadovoi has died in the hospital.

In focusing so explicitly on the tension between words and deeds, *The Lie* echoes the central concerns of *Fear*. But the ideological battle in *The Lie* is waged not over the fate of the old intelligentsia, as in the earlier play, but over the soul of the younger generation: Nina is roughly Afinogenov's age and experienced the Revolution as a teenager. For her, the process of becoming a genuine Soviet person is a matter of deciphering hidden intentions—subtexts—in the behavior of those around her. This is the only way to avoid being unduly influenced by counterrevolutionary factory directors.

Early on, Nina declares that a genuine Soviet person is true to his word. This wholesome conviction lies at the root of her problems. As Riadovoi explains to her, a genuine Soviet citizen has no use for a fixed, transparent definition of the truth. Trusting what you're told means giving equal weight to what the Party says and what its critics say. In Afinogenov's play, being a good communist means, above all, navigating the murky realm between actions and words. As in *Fear*, the possibility that someone's malicious intentions will go unrecognized is a source of anxiety. But *The Lie* is preoccupied with another, no less dangerous proposition: misattributing evil intentions to someone who is trying to do good. In an early scene, one of the leaders of the factory Party cell announces that his goal is to bring to light "not what [Nina] said, but what she wanted to say." The motivation he proposes, however, clearly goes against the facts to which the audience has already been made privy.[55] This deliberate misreading of a subtext, more than any other action undertaken by the character in question, attests to that character's corruption.

There are few conversions in *The Lie* but a lot of confessions, especially within the context of the family (namely Nina's in-laws, the Ivanovs). Nina's husband comes clean about his financial schemes, for example, and Nina's mother-in-law admits to cheating on her husband. At the end of *The Lie*, Nina's confession—her description of what happened between her and Riadovoi—signals to the audience that she has stood up to the factory director. "Truth" emerges through the examination of the impulses of one's own actions as well as others'—whether in a private conversation or public performance.

In April 1933, just days after finishing the first draft of *The Lie*, Afinogenov sent the manuscript to Gorky in Sorrento. Gorky had taken him under his wing following the successes of *The Eccentric* and *Fear*, offering him professional and personal advice and recommending his writing to others.[56] In the letter that accompanied the manuscript, Afinogenov claimed that he had poured his heart's blood into the play. It allowed him to confess "painful thoughts, doubts and unresolved questions."[57] Gorky penned a lengthy, grumpy review of the play that took Afinogenov to task for making it too much about himself and for pandering to the various "sons of bitches of the past" ("*sukiny deti proshlogo*") who "have been exiled from the ruined paradise of bourgeois existence."[58] Gorky made a list of the most contentious passages that would rankle or, because of their ambiguousness, confuse the audience. He resisted assigning sharply critical statements to benign characters and making the characters associated with the Party—deputy minister Riadovoi and the local Party boss Seroshtanov—seem dull if not dim-witted.

Significant, from this perspective, is that Gorky's final judgment ("*The Lie* is . . . a fantasy, and not a very good one at that") is based on assumptions anticipated by, and challenged in, the play. One of the least attractive characters, a jealous spinster working as a Party activist, tells Nina: "You bring up things no one is supposed to talk about, and people listen to you . . . They listen and keep quiet. They keep quiet, but they are thinking! And when a person is thinking in silence . . . Ooooh . . . Who can tell what he is thinking about?"[59] The spinster's notion that Nina's words might breed discontent among rank-and-file Party members is shown to be misguided. Afinogenov thematizes the importance of unspoken, intended meanings. At the same time, he anticipates the counterweight of meanings of the performance and how these will guide his audience to the conclusion that "thinking in silence" is beneficial, not harmful, to the well-being of the Soviet man and the future of the Soviet state. Gorky's gravest concern is whether the play does enough to train its audience to look for that reading—that subtext—in performance.

Gorky's reaction was equal parts irritation at Afinogenov's ideological carelessness and contempt for insufficiently Soviet audiences. Gorky's attacks on the latter were much more forceful than his paternalistic condemnation of Afinogenov's supposed ideological weaknesses. Afinogenov's offer of a "confession" was never brought up, and his status as a genuine Soviet writer never questioned. But the verdict of the play's other famous reviewer and editor—Stalin—was less equivocal.

Afinogenov's cover letter to Stalin says nothing about painful questions or the need to confess private doubts. He reminds Stalin that they had discussed the play several months before, making it seem that the play had received Stalin's provisional approval.[60] The pages of Afinogenov's manuscript, preserved at RGALI, are covered with Stalin's handwritten comments. They range from check marks to sardonic marginalia ("Ha-ha-ha!" "Vulgar!" "What is this nonsense?!") and extensive editorial intrusions—passages crossed out, lines of dialogue inserted or drastically rewritten. At the end of the playscript, Stalin offered general comments and instructions that merit quoting in full:

Com. Afinogenov!

The idea for the play is a rich one, but the way it has shaped up is not so rich [*Ideia p'esy bogatia, no oformlenie vyshlo nebogatoe*]. For some reason you've got all Party members looking like freaks [*urody*], physical, moral or political freaks (Gorchakova, Viktor, Kulik, Seroshtanov). Even Riadovoi at times looks like he lacks something, like he's some kind of retard [*nedonosok*]. The only person who pursues a consistent and fully conscious tactic (of hypocrisy [*dvurushinchestvo*]) is Nakatov. He's the most "solid" character.

What did you need Nina's shot for? It only confuses matters and puts it all out of whack.

It would be good [*nado by*], in counterpoint to Kulik, to have a different, honest worker, <u>one who is selflessly and wholeheartedly devoted to the Cause</u> (open your eyes and you'll see that we do have workers like that in the Party).

It would be good to feature in the play a workers' meeting where Viktor is unmasked, Gorchakova is overthrown, and truth is restored. This is all the more necessary because you've got no <u>actions</u> in this play, you just have <u>talk</u> (that's if you don't count Nina's shot, which is senseless and needless).

Where you've succeeded, I think, is with the characters of <u>the father</u>, <u>the mother</u>, <u>Nina</u>. But none of them have been fully developed; it's as if they lack a dimension [*ne vpolne skul'pturny*].

Almost every character has a (conversational) style of his own. But these styles have not been fully developed; they are stilted, rendered carelessly. Seems like you were in a hurry to get the play done.

Why does Seroshtanov look like such a freak physically? Do you maybe think that only physical freaks can be devoted Party members?

The play can't run like this.

Let's talk, if you like.

Cheers [*Privet!*],
I. Stalin.

P.S. You shouldn't go on and on about "the leader" [*vozhd'*]. That's not good, and maybe even inappropriate. What matters is not "the leader" but the collective leadership—the Central Committee of the Party.

I. St.[61]

Though Stalin often expressed his opinions on Soviet culture, from Gorky's allegorical poems to Eisenstein's films, *The Lie* is one of the few instances in which he served not merely as a critic but as a hands-on editor. It was much more common for Stalin to express his overall thoughts on a book or play, or haggle about specific elements in a letter or during a conversation with the author(s). Another strategy involved culling a writer's collected works, but even in such instances Stalin didn't change the texts. *The Lie* is unique in the history of Stalin's engagement with Soviet literature. His description of the "improvements" he expected to see in Afinogenov's play includes expressions taken from his speeches.⁶² Stalin's red pencil turned the first version of *The Lie* into a play of his own creation.

Some of Stalin's complaints about the play echoed Gorky's. He proposed minute alterations aiming to reduce the pathos of Afinogenov's characters. During Nina's first conversation with Riadovoi, when she tells him that she seeks to match her actions to her words, Afinogenov had the wise deputy minister warn her: "You'll make enemies, you'll lose friends, you'll break up with your loved one. Living with lies is cozier." Gorky objected to this passage in his letter.⁶³ In Stalin's revision, Riadovoi would first commend Nina's intention to live truthfully, and then deliver a kinder, gentler warning: "*That's good. But keep in mind that* you'll make enemies, lose friends, break up with the loved one. *Will you be able to stand it? They say that* living with lies is *calmer and* cozier."⁶⁴ Likewise, Stalin's final note points to a special concern that Gorky shared: too many Bolshevik characters have unseemly physical characteristics and questionable moral traits. Unlike Gorky, Stalin doesn't only reprimand; he also investigates and accuses. His analysis of the play's plot and characters builds to an indictment of the author. Gorky declines to speculate about the cause of Afinogenov's failure, whereas Stalin makes his thoughts explicit.⁶⁵ To portray a communist as a physical freak (*urod*), he writes, is to defame the entire Party.

Afinogenov was an exemplary communist, and yet here he's accused of slandering the Party in a lamentably typical example of Stalin's "criminalized hyperbole."⁶⁶ But Stalin wasn't altogether unjustified in his critique. His interpretation is of a piece with the paranoia and suspicion built into the playscript.

Stalin reserves his harshest criticism for the scene at the end of act 3 where Nina shoots Riadovoi. Crossing out the entire page, he proposes that the scene be dropped, the rest of the play rewritten to reflect the cut.⁶⁷ He returns to the scene at the end of his critique, reiterating that the shot and Riadovoi's subsequent death are unnecessary, unmotivated, unjustified. His reaction perhaps tells us something about his personality, his obsessions and fears. Did he reject it because he was afraid that it might encourage assassination attempts? *Fear*, we saw, turned ambiguity into a virtue; *The Lie* much less so. Nina's shot was not a shot in the dark. It was not the rash action of a misguided but decent young woman. It was a threat to the state.

Afinogenov had no choice but to rewrite the playscript.[68] He changed the names of some of the characters along with their personalities. He also changed settings, rewrote monologues, and, when he could, incorporated Stalin's editorial suggestions verbatim. In the second version of *The Lie* the Bolshevik characters are less severe, and Nina's declarations (in the act 3 monologue and elsewhere) less categorical. And yet—this is the crucial point—he ignored Stalin's advice when he came to the gunshot. Rather than cutting it from the play, he changed its context. Nina tries to shoot *herself*, not Riadovoi, in her moment of despair. Riadovoi is wounded by accident trying to prevent her from taking her life, and the end of the play makes clear that he will live. Afinogenov clearly thought that he could get away with the gunshot, that he could rely on the actors and the rhetorical force of their performances to correct the ideological problems.[69]

Afinogenov expected *The Lie* to succeed, to do even better than *Fear* and *The Eccentric*. As many as 320 theaters announced plans to produce the play,[70] and there were to be two simultaneous Moscow premieres: at the First Moscow Art Theater, where *Fear* was still running in 1933, and at the Second Moscow Art Theater, which had premiered *The Eccentric*.[71] Director Nikolai Petrov and designer Nikolai Akimov, who had made *Fear* such a success in Leningrad, were enlisted for the official premiere of *The Lie* in Kharkiv.[72]

Afinogenov's "Open Letter" to "Future Directors" of *The Lie* reflects Gorky's and Stalin's criticism. He gives as an example Nina and Riadovoi's discussion of the meaning of truth in act 1. In the first version of the playscript Riadovoi, after listening to Nina swear to be truthful in everything she does, philosophizes: "For capitalists, honesty is like an icon. Or a toothpick . . . Their teeth are all rotten, you see. No toothpick can help them. Whereas we don't worship truth and don't pick our teeth with it either."[73] Stalin added the line: "For us, it [the truth] is struggle, life, existence itself." The ideological maneuver is transparent: in Afinogenov's original formulation, the description of truth is practical to the point of sounding utilitarian and even cynical; Stalin's terse, easy-to-remember pronouncement lent mythical gravitas to the discussion and, by extension, to Riadovoi's persona. In the second version of the play Afinogenov omitted the references to capitalists and their rotten teeth and got straight to the point:

Riadovoi . . . Because for us truth is not an icon. We don't worship it and we expect no miracles. For us "truth" is struggle, life, existence.

Nina. Struggle, life, existence . . . That's good . . . It's not for nothing that [Nakatov] always says that you are smart, approachable . . . and that you've got a big heart.[74]

Chapter Four

Nina's response to Riadovoi guides the audience to the correct ideological interpretation of events, something that Stanislavsky had avoided doing in his staging of *Fear*. But Soviet theater, as a reflection of Soviet politics, could no longer indulge in ambiguities. "The events in the play," Afinogenov writes in his letter,

> lead to questioning the kind of understanding of the concept of truth according to which truth is turned into a fetish devoid of specific class meaning. For us truth is struggle, life, existence. These words, which belong to one of the play's characters, Riadovoi, are what this play was written for [*est' to, radi chego p'esa napisana*]. That is why I used them as the epigraph. They contain the key to understanding all the events that unfold in the play.[75]

He quotes directly from Stalin, though without quotation marks, making Stalin's words his own. Of course, few of Afinogenov's "future directors" were privy to the details of the play's editorial history, but few could fail to appreciate the extraordinary significance attached to the line by Afinogenov.

For the play to succeed, certain passages had to have indisputable ideological authority. Yet Afinogenov cautions against interpreting the monologues and dialogues too literally and encourages directors to "infuse life" into the characterizations by emphasizing less obvious elements. The long-suffering Party activist Seroshtanov, whose dull name—Gray Pants—and homely appearance provoked Gorky's and Stalin's particular displeasure, ought to be played as a thoughtful and generous friend—not because he is a Bolshevik, but to allow the actor to capitalize on the tension between Seroshtanov's appearance and his personality. This dictum and its corollary—that the play's negative characters should never be played as heartless villains—reprise the principles of the realistic stage that were so liberally in evidence in productions of *Fear*. Afinogenov's use of them in *The Lie* is interesting not for the originality of his insight, but for his conviction that theater's function is to repeatedly challenge the audience, constructing additional meanings that more effectively promote a fundamentally Soviet worldview.

There is, then, an important tension between the twin objectives of Afinogenov's letter. He is trying to steer the play's putative future directors and designers away from certain assumptions and interpretations. He describes the atmosphere which the set and light design need to evoke; he discourages actors from using superficial, excessively stylized stage techniques. He asserts the theater's ability to solve the problems in the playscript through nonverbal means, which contradicts his presentation of Stalin's slogan about the proper meaning of truth, writing that "it would be incorrect, in working on this play, to cling only to these words, looking for them in places where they don't belong and emphasizing them stubbornly in the production concept and individual actors' performances."[76]

The biggest change in the playscript, following Stalin's instructions, is the scene in which embezzlers and hypocrites are exposed at a workers' meeting and social justice is restored. In the rewrite, the meeting occupies the entire second act but goes unseen. It happens in an outdoor theater, and the audience sees only a door from which characters emerge to report on the discussion inside. Both Afinogenov, in his letter, and Nikolai Petrov, in his Kharkiv production notes, were interested in the meta-theatrical possibilities of the scene. To "disclose" ("*raskryt'*") the meaning of the scene, the action needed to be concealed and the audience relocated, as it were, backstage.

After the triumphant opening of *The Lie* in Kharkiv in November 1933, Afinogenov returned to Moscow to assist with the productions at MAT I and II.[77] A few days later he cabled all the theaters rehearsing *The Lie*, telling them that he was withdrawing it. He had learned from his colleague, Vladimir Kirshon, that Stalin disliked the second version. On November 9, Afinogenov wrote to Stalin asking him to withhold his final judgment until he had seen the play at MAT I or II in December. The following day he received Stalin's curt and unambiguous reply: he "considered the second redaction of *The Lie* unsuccessful [*neudachnaia*]."[78]

Stalin could have put an end to Afinogenov's career as a playwright or at least forced him to rethink his approach to the theater. But Afinogenov continued to write plays without noticeably altering his theatrical philosophy, and for several years the plays continued to be staged (some to greater acclaim than others).[79]

DIARIES AS A FORM OF THEATER

The disaster came for Afinogenov three and a half years after the premiere, and withdrawal, of *The Lie*. His diaries provide the details.[80] Having "reworked" the selves of his fictional characters, he now had to rework his own life—everything that he had expected his career to be, everything that he had believed in.

In 1937 the head of the NKVD, Genrikh Yagoda, was arrested and charged with espionage in one of the last of the show trials. All the former leaders of RAPP who had been associated him came under attack, including Afinogenov, who was expelled both from the Communist Party and the Union of Soviet Writers. He spent nine months at his dacha in the writers' enclave of Peredelkino expecting arrest. He was spared, however, reinstated in the Party, and encouraged to return to writing. Afinogenov's 1940 play

Mashen'ka was a hit; a comedy in three acts, it is still occasionally performed. The intervening period, especially those nine months expecting arrest, were, according to his diaries, deeply scarring, a painful ordeal that wrecked his mental and physical health. He writes poetry, rather poorly,[81] ruminates on spiritual matters, imagines interrogations,[82] and speaks of his cleansing and conversion. He tries repeatedly to understand what he had done wrong, what his crimes were, and then sorts through different confessions. Even as he did this, he gave the NKVD and Stalin a near-mystical ability to see into his soul and so discover that he is innocent.

His diaries also contain book reports, summaries of and commentaries on what he was reading in his seclusion. He quoted from texts, reflected on their narrative organization, the craft and the ideology of the author, and the tricks of the writerly trade he wanted to borrow. The play he had begun to write, tentatively titled *Moscow, Kremlin*, was put on hold after the first draft failed to satisfy him, and he turned his attention to writing a large-scale, quasi-autobiographical novel. He read both Russian and non-Russian novels and scavenged them for tropes, ideas, and devices for his own project. At his lowest moments, he read ancient Greek and Roman tragedies. These allowed him to abandon, in his own words, the "petty" preoccupations of the present and future for the "real, full, meaningful" task of immersing himself in the classics.[83] In November and December 1937, Afinogenov devoted dozens of pages of his diaries to passages from Sophocles, Seneca, and Aeschylus.

His usual procedure was to comment piece by piece on a scene, emphasizing its structure and particularly striking details. Where possible, he contrasted the ancients' handling of similar stories:

> November 11 . . . After a stroll—Sophocles and Seneca. They both wrote about Oedipus—but what a difference. Sophocles is a true playwright, with peripeties, an intrigue, a powerful hidden tragedy of human passions. All Seneca has is reflections and aphorisms, endless choruses and the static presence of two people on stage. You'd almost think that Seneca lived hundreds of years before Sophocles, not vice versa.[84]

Afinogenov remains with this point, offering additional examples of Sophocles's superiority. He also offers his own reading of Sophocles's tragedy, focusing on what Sophocles omits or leaves to the side (or in the background). Regarding the opening scene between King Oedipus and the blind prophet Teiresias, for instance, Afinogenov commends Sophocles for focusing not on the bloody pagan ritual of soothsaying, as Seneca does, but on the powerful yet vulnerable ruler's conversation with a wise man.

And since this scene is done without prophesying and incantation, without the blood and livers of oxen and calves—it's only natural that Oedipus here suspects a conspiracy to take over his throne, led by Creon, the very person who sent Teiresias. And that is why Oedipus's wrath is justified: Do you imagine you can always talk like this, and live to laugh at it thereafter? and then, as if a thought suddenly strikes him: Was this your own design or Creon's?[85]

Afinogenov gives a detailed, occasionally line-by-line, analysis of *Oedipus the King* (and later *Oedipus at Colonus*, *Antigone*, and Aeschylus's *Oresteia*). He moves between speculating about the reasons why the playwright has his characters say certain things and treating those characters like actual people with complicated emotional lives, terrible secrets, and tragic fates. Afinogenov is obviously able to distinguish fact from fiction, but he regards these ancient texts as guides to life, keys to understanding his own predicament. Though he dislikes Seneca's tragedy, he admires the playwright's thoughts on the nature of political power:

Oedipus.
There is the power-seeker's surest card!
To cry up moderation, to extol
Peace and contentment! The pretense of peace
Is the sharp practice of the malcontent.
—that's the Roman definition of two-facedness [*dvurushinchestvo*], and also the following line—
Through loyalty lies the traitor's way to mischief.
What a precise expression; it could even serve us today in identifying the tactics of our enemies.[86]

Afinogenov is acutely attentive to motifs of insincerity, treachery, and undisclosed motivations—the subtexts of individual actions. He reads Seneca's lines as if they were a description of the Stalinist purges, and he seeks to tease them out, make them relevant to his contemporaries. His study of Sophocles, on the contrary, is informed by his interest in the characters' more ambivalent motives. He reads both plays less as a playwright would than as a director at MAT would, seeking a realistic treatment of the subject matter. His diary becomes a mental exercise: How might he stage the Greek and Roman classics? How might Stanislavsky?

Afinogenov is trying to come to terms with the approaching end of his career in theater. He tells his diary that he can recover from the blow; he boasts that he's been able to overcome his ego and that he's not as jealous of the successes of other playwrights as he used to be. He's reconciled to the disappearance of his plays from the playbills. But he's also considering the plight of the Soviet artist in general. He uses the third-person singular, speculates about Stalin's thoughts and feelings as he initials lists of names of people to be arrested, and he imagines, at length, visiting the Leader's office—responding to the implicit accusations of disloyalty and Stalin's critique of the first version of the play *The Lie*. Afinogenov describes symbolic death and resurrection, losing and regaining his eyesight. These latter aspects of the diary acquire power and poignancy when read in the context of Afinogenov's Stanislavskian reconstructions of *Oedipus* and other ancient tragedies.

In his speech at the First Congress of Soviet Writers, in 1934, Afinogenov had called for a rethinking of the Soviet trope of the positive hero.[87] His diary is also another sort of character study. It's an experiment in finding meaning in events beyond his control, expressing that which is hidden and concealing the obvious, coming up with a strategy that will demonstrate to the NKVD and to Stalin personally his commitment to the Cause. He wants to bare his soul; he just doesn't know how. This struggle was also Soviet theater's struggle. The plays produced at MAT and other venues narrated journeys toward self-understanding.

Chapter Five

Remarkable Lives and Soviet Stage Deaths

AS MALCOLM MUGGERIDGE set out to find "the real Russia" in the summer of 1933, the flagship Soviet theater monthly *Teatr i dramaturgiia (Theater and Playwriting)* invited Moscow's literary luminaries to share their views on the future of Soviet drama. Preparations for the First Congress of Soviet Writers were underway, and the organizing committee of the Writers' Union had held its first plenary session. It sanctioned an all-Union competition for the best play on a contemporary theme (which, as we saw above, would result in no one receiving the first prize) and instructed its playwriting division to prepare special "discussion volumes" (*diskussionnye sborniki*) intended to devise an ideal model for Soviet drama. The appeal from "our dear leader" Joseph Stalin to write plays was still in force, and the task of creating a master plan for Soviet theater did not seem too daunting. (The fractious 1934 Congress would considerably raise the stakes.) This was a time to weigh in and make one's voice heard if one wanted to have a bright future as a playwright.

One of the first to respond to the journal's invitation was Yuri Olesha. *A List of Good Deeds* was still running at the Meyerhold Theater, and he had started work on another play commissioned (some five years earlier) by the Moscow Art Theater. His activities were chronicled in the literary and theatrical press, which regularly carried updates on and excerpts from Olesha's new project. He now broached a subject no one had ever mentioned before, at least not in public:

> I am interested in the question of the physical annihilation of characters in a play . . . A drama is constructed around the sufferings of one character or another. Ultimately, it all comes to either this character killing someone, or getting killed, or killing himself. Every drama possesses a certain sheen of criminality [*imeet nekotoruiu vneshniuiu ugolovshchinu*] . . . In our plays, though, if a character pulls out a revolver, the question immediately comes up: Where did he get it from? . . . The right to bear firearms has been placed under strict control, and this right is granted precisely to those people who are the least

Chapter Five

likely to fire a shot for personal reasons . . . Life itself experiences certain problems in this regard [*Sama zhizn' ispytyvaet v etom otnoshenii nekotorye zatrudneniia*].[1]

Olesha transforms a technical problem into an existential dilemma. Life, he reminds us, is in permanent struggle with death. He also raised a simpler question about the right to bear firearms: Who has it? It is bound up, oddly, with a creative matter: how best, in a play, to kill a character. The possibilities include poison, pickaxes, chairs, and even an ink blotter, but Olesha doesn't think any of these methods would be convincing in the Soviet context. No, the character needed to be dispatched with a gun, and that gun must first be stolen—by implication, from a representative of the government or the Party.

The play Olesha wrote for the Moscow Art Theater was *The Death of Zand* (*Smert' Zanda*, 1932). The protagonist, Modest Zand, is an ambitious, cynical communist functionary who gets his just deserts in the final scene. The murder is arranged by a young outcast whose appearance, behavior, and language bear a clear resemblance to Olesha's most articulate, if pathetic protagonist: Nikolai Kavalerov from the play *A Conspiracy of Feelings*, who is doomed to a bad end for his refusal to accept communist values. After the formal presentation of *The Death of Zand* to MAT, the repertoire committee asked Olesha to revise several scenes. Instead, he rubbished the draft and decided to start over with a new plot. Zand would still die, but Olesha had to figure out how.[2]

Thus, the problem: how to stage death in a genuine Soviet manner. Should it be a heroic death, as in the Meyerhold Theater's production of Vsevolod Vishnevskii's *The Ultimate Battle* (*Poslednii reshitel'nyi*, 1931)? Vishnevskii's deaths almost always happen on the battlefield (and he was fond enough of battlefield scenes to involve himself in the making of Sergei Eisenstein's 1938 film *Alexander Nevsky*). Commissars and soldiers are martyred to the strains of the "Internationale." Or should it be a Romantic death, as in Meyerhold's controversial 1934 production of Alexandre Dumas fils's 1848 *The Lady of the Camellias*? That production was excoriated by critics for its bourgeois excesses—particularly Marguerite's protracted swooning—but was popular with audiences. Then there is the so-called ambiguous death, as in *A List of Good Deeds*. Olesha's protagonist, a brilliant actress and a committed *intelligentka* in search of a meaningful future, is shot just as she joins a proletarian uprising. Perhaps the Soviet theater should approach the "art of dying" in the spirit of the Renaissance: *ars moriendi*. The death scenes I list here belong to non-Stalinist contexts: the Russian Civil War, Paris in the nineteenth century (the age of tuberculosis and cholera), and Paris in the turbulent 1930s. It merits adding that Meyerhold and Stanislavsky each

Remarkable Lives and Soviet Stage Deaths

Vsevolod Vishnevskii speaking before a group of soldiers from the Central Asian military district (1934). Credit: Russian State Archive of Literature and Art f. 1038, op. 1, ed. khr. 4738, l. 16.

lobbied to produce Nikolai Erdman's *The Suicide* (*Samoubiitsa*, 1928), which would have had an explicitly Stalinist context. Their petitions reached Stalin himself, who rejected the possibility of a production owing to its subversive content (centering on the rewriting of an unemployed man's suicide note).[3] Olesha, dissatisfied with these options, suggests that death as a stage event needed rethinking.

Just as Olesha's article was going to press, a member of the editorial board of *Teatr i dramaturgiia* and its future editor-in-chief, Aleksandr Afinogenov, was himself puzzling over death as a theme. As mentioned earlier, Afinogenov had shown an early draft of his play *The Lie* to Stalin in April 1933. Stalin expressed doubts about a scene in which the heroine (Nina) shoots a leading Bolshevik. Afinogenov conceded that pulling the trigger and either hitting or missing the target just before the curtain falls was a theatrical cliché. (Chekhov agreed: in *Uncle Vanya*, from 1897, the title character throws down his gun in disgust after missing his target.) Excessive naturalism, like excessive melodrama, had no place on the Soviet stage. Following Gorky, Stalin specifically faulted Afinogenov for failing to justify Nina's gunshot. The episode lacked meaning, a problem Afinogenov tried to solve not by eliminating the gunshot but by changing its context. Still, in the eyes

Chapter Five

Vishnevskii with Sergei Eisenstein during the filming of *Alexander Nevsky* (1938). Credit: Russian State Archive of Literature and Art f. 1038, op. 1, ed. khr. 4734, l. 2.

of officialdom, he had failed to dispatch a Soviet character the right way, with proper ideological justification. Four years later, in 1937, Afinogenov suffered the consequences of his creative decision when his career cratered. Meantime, one of his rivals, Mikhail Bulgakov, was struggling with the same problem of how to avoid cliché and represent the right kind of death.

Bulgakov worked in 1936 and 1937 on his autobiographical novel *A Dead Man's Memoir*, alternately known as *A Theatrical Novel*. A satirical take on Soviet theatrical life reflecting Bulgakov's ups and downs as a playwright, the *Memoir/Theatrical Novel* remained unfinished. Though it is obviously not a play, it merits discussion here for its consideration of theatrical misfires—pun intended—and, more generally, its relationship to Stanislavsky's 1938 *An Actor's Work Upon the Self*.

MISFIRES

The *Memoir/Theatrical Novel* is chockablock with references to stagecraft, behind-the-scenes intrigues, and playwriting. Bulgakov is a fan of concealment, ensuring that what is most significant is downplayed. Understatement is the greatest statement. A death occurs, but it is upstaged by something else, made to seem incidental, like something that doesn't belong in the scene, a failed performance.

The novel's protagonist, Sergei Maksudov, is an aspiring playwright. His most recent play is about to be staged by a famous institution, the Independent Theater. As Maksudov dictates the handwritten draft of the play to a typist, he finds himself changing it, improvising new lines of dialogue and reshaping key passages. There are also interruptions from the theater's administrators, from the mail (the theater's director has sent a letter from India), from the actors, and from various stagehands. The phone keeps ringing; people from out of town are looking for tickets. The conversation between the actress and the typist is, for Maksudov, an irritating distraction. He has been trying to figure out the directions for a scene in which one of the characters is wounded from a gunshot in a failed suicide attempt. Maksudov considers this failure his play's most important scene.

The typing continues despite the distractions, and the typist manages to anticipate Maksudov's changes, mysteriously adding them to the playscript before the author even thinks of them.

> In the heat of the day, when I was tearing my hair and trying to think how to express myself more precisely how a man would fall . . . drop his revolver . . . blood flowing—but *would* it be flowing or not? . . .—in came a young, modestly dressed actress and cried, "Dear Polikhena Vasilievna [Toropetzskaia, the typist]—how are you? Look, I've brought you some flowers!"
>
> She kissed Polikhena and put four yellow asters on the desk.
>
> "Is there anything for me from India?"
>
> Polikhena replied that there was and took out a thick envelope from under the desk. The actress showed great excitement.
>
> "'Tell Veshniakova,'" Toropetzkaia read out, "'that I have solved the problem of the role of Xenia . . .'"
>
> "Ah, yes, yes . . !" cried Veshniakova.

Chapter Five

"'I was standing with Praskovia Fyodorovna on the bank of the Ganges and it came to me: the answer is that Veshniakova should not enter through the big double doors center stage, but from the side, near the piano. She shouldn't forget that she has recently lost her husband and in her state of mind nothing would induce her to come in through the center doors. She should walk like a nun, looking down at the floor and holding a little bunch of daisies—so appropriate for a widow . . .'"

"God, how true! How profound!" cried Veshniakova. "It's true! Somehow I felt wrong coming through the big doors . . ."

"Wait a moment," Toropetzkaia went on, "there's some more," and she read on: "'However, let Veshniakova use whatever entrance she likes. When I return I will explain exactly what I mean and then it will all be quite clear.'" (ZP 86–87/93)[4]

The scene is deeply satirical. Everything that transpires—from the actress's gift of daises to the contents of the letter to the secretary's Hellenic-sounding first name and the reference to the shores of the Ganges—is in equal part bemusing and ridiculous. Bulgakov mocks the histrionics of theater people—the earnestness with which the actress and the typist take in the fake-profound, nonsensical instructions from India. He also tackles institutions and specific personalities. That the Independent Theater is MAT is obvious. The director in India is Nemirovich-Danchenko, MAT's cofounder and co-director, who sent a pile of letters to Moscow during his two and a half years in the United States in the 1920s (ZP 195). The typist is a stand-in for Nemirovich-Danchenko's faithful confidante, Olga Bokshanskaia, who was also Bulgakov's sister-in-law (194). The prototypes for the other characters, including the actress Veshniakova, have been cataloged, though there remain some disagreements as to who represents whom in the Soviet theatrical world. Bulgakov talked about his sources of inspiration, but the recollections of what he said conflict.[5] Bulgakov's widow claimed that the commentary on theatrical life is as much affectionate as critical, but others have argued the opposite: it's a caustic, savage recollection.[6]

The *Memoir/Theatrical Novel* is about a theater—MAT—but it is also a meditation on cultural authority and creativity. The lines between satire and parody and irony crisscross in the *Memoir/Theatrical Novel*. Bulgakov is an ambiguous writer: one point of reference, one target of satire, shifts imperceptibly into another. He deliberately confuses names and places. Despite these devices (or because of them), his *Memoir/Theatrical Novel* provides invaluable insight into his experiences in 1930s theater.

Bulgakov began the *Memoir/Theatrical Novel* twice, in 1929 and in 1936, at low points in his career when his prospects seemed bleakest. In the summer and fall of 1929, his three plays running at the time were yanked from the stage, and in the fall of 1936 he severed his relationship with MAT, resigning his position as assistant director after a decade with the organization. His first crack at the *Memoir/Theatrical Novel*, a partial draft called *To a Secret Friend* (*Tainomu drugu*), opens with an account of the narrator's failure as a fiction writer and ends in mid-sentence with him on the cusp of joining the theater world. The narrator refers to the year he became a writer as "the year of the catastrophe" (ZP 355). Returning to the project in 1936, Bulgakov pushed the plot in a grim direction: the narrator speaks from beyond the grave, having committed suicide because of his career choices.[7]

Bulgakov thus aligns art with death, and the *Memoir/Theatrical Novel* traffics in suicide. First there is Maksudov's leap into the Dnieper River from a bridge in Kyiv, about which the novel's reader learns from the introduction (ZP 170–71/18–19). Maksudov had tried to kill himself once before, in despair at his failure to get his writing published. Bulgakov describes Maksudov's first suicide attempt in detail, focusing on the revolver he obtains from a friend who works for the police (24–25/32–33). (Recall Olesha's 1933 comment about gun restrictions: killing oneself in the Soviet Union wasn't easy.) He was saved, however, by a mysterious journal editor who turns up in his apartment with a last-minute publication offer.

Then there is the suicide that Maksudov writes about, the suicide at the heart of his new play. "Again those same people," the text reads, "again that distant city, the side of a grand piano, the sound of shots and again someone falling in the snow" (ZP 50–51/58). The title of the play, *Black Snow* (*Chyornyi sneg*), is revealed in one of Maksudov's internal monologues (162/172), and it becomes clear that the suicide that takes place within it was to have been—and will be—Maksudov's own. We're in a hall of mirrors.

After Maksudov and the typist finish the newest version of the playscript, he is invited to read *Black Snow* for the Independent Theater's founding artistic director, the illustrious Ivan Vasilievich. It cannot be staged without the director's approval, and he is displeased with it, especially the blood-in-the-snow scene. Chapter 12, in which Maksudov visits Ivan Vasilievich's house, is probably the most often cited chapter in Bulgakov's novel, for it is here that the two layers of his satiric mode—the particular and the general—come closest together.

Before going to Ivan Vasilievich's house, Maksudov's mentor Bombardov makes it clear that the success of the meeting will depend on Maksudov's ability to exercise forbearance. He needs to perform a certain way. Bombardov has a lot of advice for him, and Maksudov blanches at it, especially the recommendation that he "not read that bit in the third act where there's a shot [*tam vystrel v tret'em akte, tak vy ego ne chitaite*]" (ZP 103/110). The reference is obviously to the blood-in-the-snow scene. Nevertheless, Maksudov heeds Bombardov's advice, and the conversation is pleasant enough at

Chapter Five

first—until Ivan Vasilievich starts asking about Maksudov's father, the deputy governor of a province, whom Maksudov shouldn't be talking about. Things completely fall apart when, later in the afternoon, Maksudov reads the scene in the play with the gunshot:

Bakhtin (to Petrov). Farewell. You will follow me soon, very soon . . .

Petrov. What are you doing?!

Bakhtin shoots himself in the temple, falls.

From afar comes the sound of an accordi . . .

"Now *that* is uncalled for [*Vot eto naprasno*]!" exclaimed Ivan Vasilievich. "What is that for? It has to be crossed out without a second's delay. Why in the world must there be shooting?" (ZP 110/117)

The director wants to eliminate the episode and offers several alternatives to it. He first proposes having the character stab himself with a dagger rather than shooting himself (ZP 110/117), but when he realizes that other gunshots are heard in the play ("My God! Shots! More shots! What a disaster!"), he decides that the scene needs to be scrapped altogether (110/118). When Maksudov insists that the suicide is central to the play, Ivan Vasilievich suggests having it happen offstage. The other characters would recall it; no gunshot would be heard. The climactic crowd scene that follows the suicide in Maksudov's playscript—Maksudov describes it as the "clash between the two opposing sides"—receives from Ivan Vasilievich an even harsher rebuke: "*That*," he declares, "must not be seen under any circumstances" (111/118).

Ivan Vasilievich describes what happened at a recent production at the Independent Theater: the crowd scene in that production was done with such excessive naturalism that the staged gunfire, yelling, and screaming on stage could be heard outside on the street, nearly scaring his horse to death as he approached the theater. The scene was subsequently eliminated (ZP 111/118). Maksudov considers this tale absurd. The most ridiculous part of Ivan Vasilievich's story about the frightened horse, from Maksudov's perspective, is how he concludes it: "So I said [to my assistant]: 'What were you thinking? Do you want me personally to end up in front of the firing squad? What if the theater burns down? That won't go over well, will it?' . . . And now you—with these gunshots! Do you realize what the repercussions could be—for these shots?" (111/119). Somehow, fake gunfire was a greater threat than real gunfire, the theater burning down, or the director getting arrested.

Ivan Vasilievich's aunt makes an appearance to warn Maksudov that "they" (an ambiguous pronoun that seems to mean the entire staff of the Independent Theater) do not want to pick a quarrel with the authorities about the gunfire scene: "*My protiv vlastei ne buntuem*" ("We're not rioting against the authorities") (ZP 109/116). Maksudov assures her that he, too, has no intention of "rebelling" against the government but gives Ivan Vasilievich new reasons to worry about a potential fracas—"*bunt v teatre*"—caused by the inclusion of gunshots in the playscript. He and Ivan Vasilievich continue their squabbling about the inclusion, or exclusion, of the gunshot scene through the novel's final, unfinished chapter. Maksudov insists that without the traumatic blood-in-the-snow scene "his play would cease to exist. And it had to exist, because I knew that it contained the truth [*v nei istina*]" (161/172).

But what, really, was so risky?

An explanation of sorts can be found in Bulgakov's biography. Just before *The Days of the Turbins* premiered, Stanislavsky ordered the scene of the murder of an unnamed Jew by Ukrainian nationalists cut from the second act, claiming that the censors wanted it gone.[8] The play called for gunfire in several other scenes, but those were left intact. Another explanation is ideological, related to Stalin's reaction to Afinogenov's 1933 play *The Lie* and its "unneeded" ("*nenuzhnaia*") shooting scene. Bulgakov probably knew of Stalin's aversion to shooting scenes, given that most of what the Leader said about the theater reached his ear. Playwrights should not be playing with gunfire, no matter at whom it was directed. Insisting on the right of his character to commit suicide, insisting on sticking with the playscript, becomes a potential death sentence for the author.

The theories of theatrical representation advanced by Ivan Vasilievich have ancient histories, dating back to Greek tragedy as reimagined in Renaissance Europe. In both contexts, deaths and other violent acts are only described; they're not shown, and never physically embodied.[9] Such is Ivan Vasilievich's conception of an effective and powerful performance, but it is not what Maksudov has in mind. He wants a spectacle with fake bullets and fake blood, not a description of one, not a recollection of something that happened elsewhere. Maksudov wants the death he wrote up to become an act. And he wants to be part of it. Ivan Vasilievich earns Maksudov's respect when he hops up on stage to demonstrate how a scene should go, when he puts himself on the line, takes the show over. The director is obsessed, however, with alternative theatrical possibilities, and none of them matches what Maksudov had in mind. The performance as he imagined it will never take place. Maksudov is an idealist: he considers his text absolute, something that contains a transcendent truth, but in rehearsal that truth is violated, and Maksudov realizes that there is no room for him as the author of the play in the play itself. He insists on his character committing suicide, and in this sense insists on being one of the performers. But he is not, in fact, one of the performers. The Stalinist playwright finds himself in a paradoxical position, responsible for a show that he cannot control.

Maksudov's suicide stems from his failure to do what Ivan Vasilievich wanted him to do, to perform as required. The theater Maksudov covets is one in which the performers displace or subsume the meaning of the performance. The protagonist's death has nothing to do with the words spoken or the events seen or the sets and props. It resides with the performer and his or her experiences as a genuine Soviet person, a subject of the state.

LIVES AND DEATH

Maksudov isn't a real author, of course. Like Ivan Vasilievich, he is Bulgakov's invention, an instrument of his imagination and a means to think about signs and signification, matters physical and metaphysical, and the problem of asserting agency in a world that has withheld it. Bulgakov made his ruminations part of the plays he wrote. Biographical and autobiographical writing dominated during the 1930s and 1940s, but the involvement of theaters in this cultural project was modest. A major event was the 1933 revival of a pre-1917 series of popular (non-specialist) biographies of famous figures, *The Lives of Remarkable People* (*Zhizn' zamechatel'nykh liudei*). The revival was Gorky's idea, and he served as editor-in-chief. Bulgakov contributed a biography of Molière to the series, though it didn't get published until after his death. There followed a string of biopics of remarkable people: from Vasily Petrov's *Peter the First* (1938) and Sergei Eisenstein's *Alexander Nevsky* (1938) to lavish color films like Vsevolod Pudovkin's *Zhukovskii* (1950) and Grigory Aleksandrov's *Glinka the Composer* (1952). Earlier, the People's Commissar of Enlightenment under Lenin, Anatoly Lunacharsky, had himself contributed to the genre, with plays about Cromwell (1920) and Campanella (1922).

The fractious First Congress of Soviet Writers in 1934 encouraged the writing of plays about remarkable people, but in the end fewer than a dozen reached the stage in Moscow and Leningrad. The 1937–53 repertoire included plays about Ivan the Terrible by Aleksei Tolstoy and Vladimir Soloviev; plays about Pushkin by Mikhail Bulgakov and Leonid Liubashevskii; a play about Peter the Great by Aleksei Tolstoy, revised several times but much less successful than the novel on which it was based and the film with which it competed; plus an assortment of dramas about wartime heroes: Ivan Bekhterev's *Commander Suvorov* (1940), Vladimir Soloviev's *Field Marshal*

Kutuzov (1940), Igor Kukovskii's *Admiral Nakhimov* (1938), and more unusual entries like Ilya Selvinskii's *General Brusilov* (1944).

Cinematic representations of remarkable lives underwent a different sort of transformation. Stories of formative experiences and coming-into-consciousness narratives were abandoned. What took their place were epics, tales of famous folk like Alexander Nevsky born into heroic roles. Nothing shaped them. From the start, they possessed an uncanny ability to intuit historical necessity.[10]

The most successful Soviet biographical drama, at least in terms of the length of its run, was Bulgakov's 1934–36 play about Pushkin. It is perhaps best known for what it lacks: Pushkin himself. The play is structured as a chronicle of the weeks before and after Pushkin's death, and there are many references to the poet's appearance and behavior, but he himself is not there. A door can be heard slamming behind him as he walks around the house, and a body can be seen from afar after the fatal duel, but his presence is otherwise spectral. One of his poems, "Winter Evening," is quoted, mumbled and sung in the play, though nothing is said about how it was written. Pushkin is absent, as is the bulk of his output, yet the play advertised itself as being about both. Nevertheless, it was praised by critics and audience members alike.

The decision to have Pushkin *not* appear had, I think, provocative implications for audiences at the time. Beyond a desire to avoid a failure—since no representation of Russia's greatest poet could possibly satisfy the guardians of his legacy—Bulgakov makes a statement about the past versus the present. Pushkin is *left* offstage, as opposed to *kept* offstage. He is spared the realm of theatrical illusion, removed from the space where he could function as a sign, and yet he remains an agent of everything that happens on stage. There is no place for Pushkin in the Stalinist present; he belongs to history and its invisible force, which Stalinism sought to deny, or to reshape in its own image, but could not.

Bert States characterizes the theater as "the paradigmatic place for the display of the drama of presence and absence," producing

> its effect precisely through a deliberate collaboration between its frontside ("on" stage) and its backside ("off") whereby anticipation is created through acts of entrance and exit (the recoil of the world beyond), and finally between the frontside illusion (character and scene) and the backside reality (the actor, the unseen stage brace that "props" up the illusion).[11]

As we will see in the next chapter, alternations between revelation and concealment, onstage and offstage action underpin Bulgakov's dramatic efforts in the 1930s, especially the biographical works: the play about Molière, which was banned after a short run; the play about Pushkin, which didn't reach the stage until April 10, 1943, after Bulgakov's death; and the play about Stalin—*Batum*—which was also banned (despite being an overwhelmingly positive portrayal of the ruler's youth). The bioplays have many of the same features of 1940s biopics insofar as they are episodic, monumental, and awkwardly stylized in their dialogues. The absent protagonist becomes the subject of the other characters' "backstage" discussions (or conspiracies).

ANNA'S SUICIDE

In the spring of 1937, when Bulgakov was drafting his *Memoir/Theatrical Novel* and Afinogenov faced expulsion from the Writer's Union and the Communist Party, MAT staged a spectacular suicide. I refer to the terrible final scene of Nemirovich-Danchenko's production of *Anna Karenina*. As Anna Muza argues in her discussion of this production, the image of a life-size train rolling downstage over the body of the heroine and, by allegorical extension, into the audience evoked not pity, but fear. Anna's anguished cry of "For what [*Zachem*]?"—which even shocked listeners of the radio broadcast of the production—made the scene seem less like a private act of suicide than a public execution. The stage became the state, which pretended to protect the Soviet people but in fact terrorized them.[12]

Anna's suicide could not serve as a model for death scenes in new Soviet plays. The allegory was too explicit, too easy to interpret as an act of dissidence, which Stalinism could not and did not permit. The success of the theatrical adaptation of Leo Tolstoy's great novel only increased the uncertainty about how to dispatch a Soviet character. Yet this is, perhaps, the point. Killing a contemporary Soviet character in the Soviet context on the Soviet stage invested death, and the symbolic shorthand of the gunshot, with too much direct meaning. Death on the stage had to be approached differently than death in movies or novels. It needed to overwhelm the medium, otherwise the death would not mean enough. For modernist visionaries of theater like Antonin Artaud, death and performance were mutually implicated, and reciprocally useful, because the destruction of old forms, of imitation and representation, was the only theatrical practice that could liberate the stage. Death became performance—flattered it, befitted it, made it matter anew.[13]

Philippe Ariès has famously described the changing attitudes toward death in Western cultures as a movement from "tame" death, omnipresent as late as the Middle Ages—"death that is both familiar and near, evoking no great fear or awe" as "the collective destiny of the species"—into "invisible" death—"death that is so frightful that we dare not utter its name," no longer public, no longer physically evident except for the briefest of moments. As he examines this "denial of death," Ariès highlights two modes of dying: *la mort de soi*, which, beginning in the twelfth century, gives primary importance to one's own demise—and *la mort de toi*, concern for the death of the other, whose loss and memory inspired from the eighteenth century onward the fashioning of tombs and cemeteries and a Romantic, rhetorical treatment of death.[14]

To use (or misuse) this classic taxonomy, the death that Olesha, Afinogenov, and Bulgakov respectively envisioned for their characters was too imminent, too proximate—in effect, too much like "one's own death." The ending of Olesha's *The Death of Zand*, in the version submitted to MAT, sees Zand shot accidentally by a trigger-happy security guard suffering from post-traumatic stress disorder. Just before the killing, Zand signs a bizarre contract with the play's acerbic, Kavalerov- and Olesha-like lyrical hero. The two characters become each other's alter ego, their identities and names flipped around.[15] The death of Zand, then, is only possible through the death of the lyrical hero—*la mort de soi*. After Olesha received back this draft of the play for mandated revision, he changed the plot altogether. Rather than a Bolshevik official, Zand becomes a talented writer struggling to complete a play. Even more remarkably, Olesha went on to publish several articles in which he voices his concerns about the future of Soviet literature. These include a semi-fictional avatar, a fellow traveler named Zand ("Koe-chto iz sekretnykh zapisei poputchika Zanda").[16] Killing Zand, in other words, is not about the right plot twist. It is the fictional equivalent of the death of one's own self, without which another self, a genuine Soviet self, cannot come into being.

In his 1933 article, Olesha posited the ontological superiority of the drama he and his fellow engineers of human souls were to manufacture: "Only in our drama can there be plays where annihilation is carried out by the apparatus of logic. Instead of a physical annihilation you have a logical one. The person becomes not a corpse, but a zero."[17] As Anne Nesbet has written, "logical" rather than physical annihilation was an important theme in the Soviet cinema of the 1930s. The kulak foe is killed through the sheer collective ecstasy of the masses in Aleksandr Dovzhenko's *Earth* (*Zemlia*, 1930) and through laughter in Sergei Eisenstein's *Bezhin Meadow* (*Bezhin lug*, 1937).[18] But, as Olesha's own experience suggests, on stage the "logical" obliteration of a genuine Soviet character is, in a way, even less possible to accomplish than his physical obliteration.

In 1934 Olesha decided to republish, in slightly edited guise, his first play, *Playing Execution*.[19] Reintroducing this work to the public tacitly acknowledged what he had been unable to achieve with *The Death of Zand*.

Chapter Five

Late in 1937, around the time Bulgakov ceased working on his *Memoir/Theatrical Novel*, Olesha quietly put *The Death of Zand* to rest. In the hundreds of fragments of the play Olesha left behind, Zand changes professions, lovers, mannerisms, and ideological convictions. But the all-important death scene failed. Olesha was unable to kill Zand, or have Zand kill himself, in an ideologically instructive way.

Chapter Six

Mikhail Bulgakov's Theatrical Everyday

THE PLAY IS NEARLY OVER. Fanfares sound in the distance. A military fighter pilot returns victorious from the battle to end all battles. He addresses a disheveled, confused man—a brilliant and eccentric inventor: "Ah, Professor, Professor! . . . you [*ty*] will never understand those who work to organize humankind. Oh well. At least your genius will serve us. Come! The Secretary-General wants to see you [*tebia*]."[1] Curtain.

The characters, setting, and events in this four-act play, from 1931, would have been familiar to Soviet audiences. The inevitable global triumph of communism and the recruitment of pre-revolutionary intellectuals to "serve" Soviet power is a subject explored by playwrights of competing backgrounds, Olesha and Afinogenov included. This particular apocalyptic example of the agitprop trend, *Adam and Eve*, merits mention less for its recycled subject matter than for its enigmatic, endlessly fascinating author: Mikhail Bulgakov.

More has been written about Bulgakov, it seems, than any other Russian-language writer of the 1930s. Unlike Olesha and Afinogenov, Bulgakov is regarded as a heavyweight, a modern/modernist "classic," everywhere serious books are sold. Most of his work was published after he died (and, no less importantly, after Stalin died), making his relationship to his immediate historical context a matter of animated, often fierce, debate. He wasn't a Soviet lackey, not even close. His writings of the 1920s; his journal entries; the feuilletons he wrote for *Gudok* (alongside Olesha); his published novellas; the plays that reached the stage; and the huge mass of unpublished material in the archives—all of this comes across as sharply critical of the Soviet system under Stalin. His protagonists resent the new political order and ridicule those in charge of it. As a theater writer he came under attack less for the works that flopped than for those that succeeded: *The Days of the Turbins*, the NEP-era drama *Zoyka's Apartment* (*Zoykina kvartira*), and the political satire *The Crimson Island* (*Bagrovyi ostrov*). He seemed like a fellow traveler but turned out to be much "worse" than one, in the ironic formulation of a minor eyewitness.[2]

Chapter Six

Readers familiar with Bulgakov's writings, both published and unpublished, tend to focus on his subversiveness, if not his dissidence.[3] *Adam and Eve*, a dystopian drama about chemical warfare and survival in the wilderness, is emblematic of his borderline anti-Sovietism. The ominous figures who arrive in suits without invitation, paying too much attention to the other characters, are obviously OGPU (precursor to the NKVD) operatives. In the final scene, the protagonist—a prominent scientist who saves humankind through his development of an antidote to poison gas—petitions to leave the Soviet Union for a quiet retirement in Switzerland. Bulgakov was here describing a wish of his own. The OGPU authorized a search of his home in 1926, and he wrote several times to the government for permission to leave Russia because, he claimed, he had no future in his homeland.

Ideological conformity was not the be-all and end-all in theatrical life. Subversiveness was tolerated, so long as it was placed in properly critical, heuristic, context. The censors permitted constructive criticism of the Soviet system (consider *Fear*) and more ambivalent representations of brilliant but alienated intellectuals than those encountered in *Adam and Eve*. Even in the most repressive of circumstances, the later 1930s, ideological lines could be blurred, with positive and negative Soviet characters aligned. The emphasis fell on the ideological correctness of final scenes: apotheoses. In *Adam and Eve*, the aviator (occupying the role of the magical "helper" of fairy tales) encourages the intellectual to embrace the global communist government. Unlike Afinogenov's Professor Borodin, however, Bulgakov's absentminded professor resists conversion. Still, grace is extended to him in the final scene in the form of a meeting with the character standing in for Joseph Stalin: the "Secretary-General." How this episode is staged determines the play's ideological message. What exactly does the summons to the ruler mean?

In the late 1980s, when Bulgakov's plays finally appeared in print and bolstered his reputation as an iconoclast, the answer to this question seemed obvious: nothing good could possibly come out of a one-on-one meeting with the Secretary-General, real or imagined.[4] But for Bulgakov in 1931, the thought of meeting Stalin filled him with optimism. He anticipated a new beginning, a clearing of the road that, for him, had become extremely rocky.[5] Earlier, in the spring of 1930, Stalin had telephoned Bulgakov's apartment and, after a brief chat, suggested a formal meeting at some later date. Much of the rest of the decade passed in anticipation of this meeting, but it never happened.[6] *Adam and Eve* was written when Bulgakov's hopes of a resumption of his conversation with Stalin were high. His protagonist's summons to the Secretary-General promises, farcically, answers to all questions and solutions to all problems. In 1931, Bulgakov fully expected *Adam and Eve* to be staged, and he was confident that it would succeed with the public. But like most of the plays he wrote in the 1930s, *Adam and Eve* was consigned to oblivion, a development that darkened Bulgakov's perception of Soviet theater and literature for the rest of his life.

This darkening is the focus of this chapter. I will detail the fate of Bulgakov's later plays and consider the paradox of a writer insisting on his own independence from, and even opposition to, the cultural establishment, while also seeking to reach the zenith of that establishment.[7]

In 1929, Bulgakov's play *The Days of the Turbins* was running at the Moscow Art Theater. *Zoyka's Apartment* could be seen at the Vakhtangov Theater and *The Crimson Island* at Aleksandr Tairov's Kamerny Theater. Within two square miles, the Soviet public had access to a lot of his playwriting. And a fourth piece, the Civil War drama *Flight, or On the Run (Beg)*, was under consideration at MAT. Then the tide turned against him; he was attacked in the press and his plays pulled from the stage. The proposed production of *Flight* was halted. Most of the invective came from RAPP critics, Bulgakov's old foes from the mid-1920s; *Flight*, however, was subject to Central Committee debate before being scuttled as anti-Soviet.[8] Seeking to regroup, Bulgakov began a new play about the great French writer Molière and a pseudo-autobiographical novel titled *To a Secret Friend*. Low on funds, unable to collect royalties on the canceled plays, Bulgakov took a part-time job at TRAM, the Workers' Youth Theater. He wrote a series of letters to government officials declaring that he had been unceremoniously deprived of the means to support himself and asked permission to leave Russia. Then came the rescue: the call from Stalin in April 1930.[9] Bulgakov received an offer to join MAT as an assistant director. He resigned from his grunt work at TRAM. Then, almost unbelievably, *The Days of the Turbins* went back into production on Stalin's instructions, bringing an end to Bulgakov's first crisis.

The years ahead were remarkably productive but also planted the seeds for additional crises. Bulgakov adapted Gogol's *Dead Souls* for MAT, rehearsed and performed in an adaptation of Charles Dickens's first novel, *The Pickwick Papers*, and in 1932 participated in the rehearsals for his Molière play. He also completed a theatrical adaptation of Leo Tolstoy's *War and Peace*. And that wasn't all. In addition to *Adam and Eve*, commissioned by Leningrad's Red Theater and set in a future version of that city, he produced a play about time-travel called *Bliss (Blazhenstvo*, 1934) for Moscow's Satire Theater. It was revised a year later as *Ivan Vasilievich*. These works were followed by *Alexander Pushkin*, an account of the poet's final days written for the 1937 Pushkin centennial. Meanwhile there was promising talk of staging *Flight* along with a revised version of *Zoyka's Apartment*; nothing came of it, however. The rehearsals of *Molière* at MAT were interrupted and resumed and the production reconceived. New actors were brought in, and in the spring of 1935 Stanislavsky assumed control of the rehearsals, Bulgakov rejected Stanislavsky's requests for rewrites, and Nemirovich-Danchenko

Chapter Six

took over. But cultural freedom was now everywhere increasingly restricted. *Molière* ran just seven nights in February and March 1936 before being canceled. There followed the cancellation of *Ivan Vasilievich* in the middle of dress rehearsals. The play narrating Pushkin's end was dropped. In September 1936, Bulgakov felt he had no choice but to resign from MAT.

He worked for hire for the Bolshoi Theater, writing the libretto for an opera about Russia's Time of Troubles, *Minin and Pozharskii*, and becoming a repertoire consultant. He completed three more libretti: *Black Sea* (*Chyornoe more*, 1937, set during the Civil War), *Peter the Great* (1937), and the anti-German drama *Rachel* (aka *Mademoiselle Fifi*, 1939, based on a short story by Guy de Maupassant). Bulgakov also served as the "script doctor" for revivals of tsarist operas and ballets. Boris Asafyev wrote music for *Minin and Pozharskii*, but the production never reached the stage. The lone play Bulgakov produced in the late 1930s was an adaptation of Miguel de Cervantes's *Don Quixote* for the Vakhtangov Theater. Work on his novel *The Master and Margarita* began to take precedence over his *Memoir/Theatrical Novel*, which Bulgakov left incomplete. In the fall of 1938, the Moscow Art Theater commissioned *Batum*, a drama about Stalin's youth. Bulgakov had pitched the project two and a half years earlier, during the rehearsals for *Molière*. Things looked promising for *Batum*: the draft was reviewed in the Kremlin and MAT had committed to it. Bulgakov made plans to travel to Georgia for further research into Stalin's youth. Just hours before he was to leave Moscow, however, he was told not to bother: the trip was off. Production of *Batum* had been suspended on order of the Central Committee.

Bulgakov was diagnosed with a severe form of hereditary kidney disease and died just a few months later.

It's a sad story, a tale, according to the academic consensus, of frequent setbacks and panicky appeals to the government. It's also the tale of a subversive playwright's indefatigable efforts to achieve success in impossible circumstances. The regime persecuted him even after giving him second and third and fourth chances to correct his mistakes, to atone for daring to challenge the new order and its promises of a bright future.[10] The cancellation of *Batum* broke Bulgakov's spirit and, it is said, hastened his death. There are other, more nuanced interpretations of the final years of his career, however, and these undercut the reading of his career as a series of painful compromises coming to naught.[11] These alternative readings, including the one I will introduce here, highlight the profound ambivalences in Bulgakov's work in, and for, the theater. His letters and his wife's journal explain how he functioned as an artist after it seemed that he was no longer functioning, after he had been forced to silence himself.

Bulgakov was not a writer's writer. He belonged instead to the theatrical elite, more at home with Soviet actors, directors, designers, composers, and administrators than with fellow writers. As guests at his apartment, at meetings in the creative unions, and in public—at restaurants, receptions, and banquets, at MAT and the Bolshoi—these people were his support network. In her diaries, Elena Sergeyevna Bulgakova describes in minute detail their responses to the readings he organized of his plays.[12] Cultural officials were not part of these gatherings, nor were his peers. His relationship with Gorky cooled as his interactions with Nemirovich-Danchenko and Stanislavsky increased. He maintained contact with them even after leaving MAT.[13]

He complained that his administrative jobs at MAT, TRAM, and the Bolshoi kept him away from his desk, but these jobs gave him a position of authority in the Stalinist cultural establishment that writing alone could not. The Union of Soviet Writers was a cauldron of intrigue and invective; he happily avoided drowning in it. He co-directed rehearsals of several MAT productions, all successes, and earned the respect of the theater's old guard, who imagined him becoming a director in his own right. He consulted on, and shaped, the most significant Bolshoi productions of the 1930s, including the lavish 1939 staging of *Ivan Susanin*, a monumental rethinking of Mikhail Glinka's *A Life for the Tsar* (*Zhizn' za tsaria*, 1836) that set the standard for the Stalinist equivalent of French grand opera. The success of that production interrupted the scheduling for his own super-ambitious opera about the Time of Troubles (*smutnoe vremia*), *Minin and Pozharskii*. Though he constantly advocated for it, the opera didn't reach the stage. Still, he felt at home in the Bolshoi. The principal conductor, Samuil Samosud, was deeply impressed by his work, and told a mutual friend that Bulgakov "felt the epoch like no one else," he was "the most Soviet of all the writers [*samyi sovetskii iz vsekh pisatelei*]."[14]

Meantime, *The Days of the Turbins* was revived at MAT and well received. It was a favorite of government officials, right up to Stalin, and foreign diplomats also took it in. Bulgakov reacted ambivalently to the attendance of the US ambassador to the Soviet Union, William Bullitt, at one of the performances, but, as we will see, he developed a relationship with Bullitt.[15] Most of his plays lasted only one or two seasons at best, but *Turbins* outlasted him and fared even better than *Anna Karenina*, a big hit of the 1930s.

Theater was his bread and butter, the source of most of his income. Perks included proper housing for his family (Elena Bulgakova and her son) at a time when housing was in desperately short supply. Moscow's population had increased rapidly in the 1930s, when forced collectivization and the subsequent Red Famine caused an exodus from the countryside. The "apartment question" bedeviled Bulgakov. His, Elena's, and her son's first apartment together was impossibly cramped and unbearably noisy. He counted on using his name to secure another apartment in a building allocated to the Union of Soviet Writers—on Lavrushinskii Lane, opposite the Tretiakov Gallery—but the arrangement unexpectedly fell through. It must have galled him that "lesser writers"—Yuri Olesha, Vsevolod Ivanov, Boris Pasternak, Viktor Shklovsky, and Mikhail Prishvin—received apartments in that coveted building while he did not. The Moscow Art Theater came to the rescue, guaranteeing housing for him should he accept the commission for *Batum*.[16]

Besides this logistical hassle, Bulgakov had to deal with NKVD interlocutors and operatives. He and his wife suspected several of his friends and acquaintances of spying on him, reporting to the NKVD on his home life, his activities in the theater, and, crucially, his interactions with foreigners. The NKVD agent responsible for "escorting" a delegation of American actors around Moscow insinuated himself into Bulgakov's home. The NKVD kept tabs on him through other means: an actor regularly informed on him, as did the relative of a friend being considered for the position of managing director at the theater.[17] It's a banal truism to say that Bulgakov's novel *The Master and Margarita* highlights the omnipresence of the secret police, which spied on everyone and everything.

The Soviet government operated behind the scenes, and Bulgakov made the backstage a symbol for his professional life and the fate of his work. What happened there expanded to include all manner of events. In *The Last Days of Pushkin*, he moved the "life of a remarkable person" from the spotlight into the shadows, profiling him enigmatically in backstage space rather than placing him at the center. *Molière*, the only Bulgakov play staged in the 1930s, and only briefly, likewise exploits the relationship between the seen and unseen. The backstage is the place of secret negotiations, conflicts, and resolutions that determine the fate of the artist. It is also, more broadly, a metaphor for the subject in history: how one's standing—one's posthumous reputation—is determined by one's connection to hidden mechanisms of power.

Here I must return to Bulgakov's *Memoir/Theatrical Novel* and his account of failed performances in the Soviet theater. I will revisit the production of *Molière* at MAT and its emphasis on the everyday (*byt*). As with Olesha and Afinogenov, the discussion will involve diaries, in this case not the writer's diaries but those of his wife Elena Sergeyevna. These describe Bulgakov's ambivalent relationship to power: the power of theater, culture, and the overbearing state. The diaries describe Bulgakov's public efforts to conform, his struggles to maintain a place of prominence within the Stalinist matrix. But Bulgakov didn't think of himself as cowed and humiliated. His true self—his behind-the-scenes self—existed in opposition to the ruler. This self is not fraught, not a hypocrite, not masked or a trickster, but just the real self, the stage and its audience be damned.

Mikhail Bulgakov's Theatrical Everyday

THE DEAD MAN'S THEATRICAL EDUCATION

In 1965, when the *Memoir/Theatrical Novel* fragment was published, Bulgakov's widow said that she was disappointed with those readers who found the book "merely funny." She was also dismayed at the effort to identify the biographical subtexts in the book and the prototypes for Bulgakov's characters. The *Memoir/Theatrical Novel* instead had a conceptual basis, rooted in Bulgakov's interest in the antagonistic relationship between the artist and the powers that be: *Vlast'*. The language Elena Bulgakova uses in her corrective is multilayered. The *Memoir/Theatrical Novel* is not concerned with "that"—"*ne pro to*"—and so, she alerts the reader, it must be concerned with "this," "*pro eto*" (ZP 9). The phrase is also translated as "about that," and serves as the title of a famous love poem by Vladimir Mayakovsky from 1923. Love isn't named in the poem, since doing so cheapens the feeling. For Bulgakova, who is channeling the intentions of her dead husband, the artist's relationship to power is amorphous. And so the protagonist (Maksudov) of the *Memoir/Theatrical Novel* contemplates this relationship, trying to decide if the artist's power is real, or *theatrical*, merely performative.

Maksudov's experiences at the Independent Theater are initially positive. The theater is a new world for him, and he's eager to join it because his other world, the community of litterateurs, has alienated him. He's attuned to the absurdities of the theater business, but he remains enamored with it. "Nothing in his life before or since gave him greater pleasure [*naslazhdenie*] than being in the audience" (ZP 56/63). He can't say for sure if the plays he sees are good or bad, but he finds in all of them an "inexplicable charm [*prelest'*]." His experiences backstage, too, are strangely magical; he's fascinated by the stagehands, an eccentric bunch, and awed by the seemingly all-powerful house manager Tulumbasov.[18] Maksudov extols the latter's "perfect knowledge of human nature. I was moved by this discovery, and my heart trembled and went cold [*pokholodelo*]. Yes, here in front of me stood the greatest authority on the human heart [*serdtsevedets*]" (95/10).

The gunshot debate puts the relationship to the test. The future of Maksudov's play is at stake, but also, we learn, his sense of self, which his work with the director conditions. He's a weak person, he acknowledges, and he's emotionally fragile and prone to self-loathing (ZP 19, 26, 27, 32, 53). Bulgakov titles one of the first chapters of the book "An Attack of Nerves" ("*Pripadok nevrastenii*," 18/26), and he describes Maksudov "waking up in tears" after dreaming about the suicide ("blood in the snow") scene (50/58). "I feel certain that, having read this, many people are going to call me an *intelligent* and a neurotic," Maksudov adds. "The former I won't argue with, but as for the latter, I warn you quite seriously that you are wrong. There is not a trace of neurosis in me" (49/56).

Chapter Six

This denial is undercut by his other references to fear and obsession. Through them, Maksudov emerges as a stand-in for the weak-willed intellectual often encountered in Soviet fiction. Olesha's Lelia Goncharova and Afinogenov's Valya Borodina incorporate (and challenge) elements of this same character. The short stories of Bulgakov's early years are populated by lonely and helpless protagonists, and he is careful to portray frailty in a positive light. The intelligentsia represented in the NEP-era satire *Heart of a Dog* (*Sobach'e serdtse*, 1925) and in the play *Adam and Eve* comprises troubled but brilliant scientists and inventors. They are confident and successful despite their alienation from, and criticism of, Soviet power.

Maksudov's troubles evince his intellectual refinement and cultural superiority. Yet the novel's repeated references to Maksudov's unattractiveness, the descriptions of embarrassing situations (some imagined or dreamt: ZP 92, 98), and the repeated mention of his squalid home (18/26) suggest a different pedigree for the character. The first word of Bulgakov's title (the word for "memoir" in the original is *zapiski*, "notes") and his use of a first-person narrator calls to mind Dostoevsky's *Notes from Underground*. At the start of the *Memoir/Theatrical Novel*, after Maksudov finishes reading to a group of writers, one of them says that "there's a touch of Dostoevsky [*dostoevshchinka*]" in him (22/30). It's a meta-reference, establishing a connection between Bulgakov's protagonist and the Underground Man's 1920s reincarnation (Nikolai Kavalerov, the protagonist of Olesha's *Envy*).

Maksudov is a mixture of high and low; he is deeply capable, deeply neurotic, and at a turning point: his theatrical career rests on the outcome of his encounter with the fearsome Ivan Vasilievich.[19] Immersed in the everyday activity of the Independent Theater, he learns, as noted, not to be embarrassed about rethinking and rewriting his playscript in front of strangers (ZP 85/92). According to the confessional norms of the genuine Soviet person, there is no shame in self-doubt; in fact, self-doubt gives a person strength. Before meeting Ivan Vasilievich, Maksudov has already decided to be more assertive, to play a much more active role than originally planned.

Until this point in the *Memoir/Theatrical Novel*, everything happens *to* Maksudov rather than *by* him: he writes the novel and the play almost against his will. He is haunted by the ideas he has unwittingly turned into prose. Opportunities to publish his writing arise through no effort of his own. Now he has to have agency. Turning up at Ivan Vasilievich's house, he announces "*Naznacheno!*" (meaning "I have an appointment," but also something more impersonal, like "It's been arranged!"). Maksudov "revels in the power of this magic word" (ZP 104/111). The strength or force (*sila*) that he acquires contradicts the weakness (*slabost'*) that he has identified in himself and lamented earlier in the text (50/58). It comes from becoming an actor—becoming theatrical.

He is fascinated by the possibility of replicating on stage the three-dimensional images that he sees in his dreams, translating the "little box" of his mind's eye into an actual performance.[20] Maksudov's multiple accounts of the gunshot scene are illustrative. He focuses on the physical details of the "little box": the sound of the accordion and the depth of the snow and the flow of the blood. Elsewhere, Bulgakov has Maksudov describe his delight at one of his actors' performances. It embodies his conception of the part so perfectly that he wonders if the conception existed elsewhere, a priori, with Maksudov "miraculously divining" his existence (ZP 163/174).

The attempt to re-create life sensually—the *topos* that resurfaces in both Olesha's and Afinogenov's diaries—is invested, in the *Memoir/Theatrical Novel*, with an additional dimension. Maksudov's theatrical ideal is of a world that can reproduce a single author's vision like no other medium. His clash with Ivan Vasilievich is not a confrontation between a writer who wants to show the audience something forbidden and a director who wants to hide this material from the audience. The only audience member with whom Maksudov is ultimately concerned is Maksudov himself. He is the sole spectator to benefit from the theater's "magic." This is exactly Bulgakov's position in the 1930s.

The *Memoir/Theatrical Novel* follows both the conventions of a *Bildungsroman* and the "master plot" of Socialist Realist fiction. It traces the protagonist's progress from spontaneity to consciousness. He moves from being ignorant about the theater, understanding nothing about it, to imposing his will on it and, through that action, demystifying it. Bulgakov's manuscript ends as Maksudov is formulating his ideas about what makes good theater work. Before this passage, crucially, Maksudov speaks of finding the ultimate truth about the order of things. In chapter 13, titled "I Grasp the Truth" ("*Ia poznaiu istinu*"), Maksudov attends a disastrous meeting with Ivan Vasilievich and the theater's oldest actors, and then, convinced that his play will never be staged at the Independent Theater, ends up at an all-night dinner with another actor, Bombardov, talking about the big questions of life.

Thus, Bulgakov allegorizes his one-step-forward-two-step-backwards experience at the theater, and thus he "de-familiarizes" that experience. In passages with parallels to Dostoevsky's and Olesha's characters, Maksudov claims ignorance about the cause of the failure of his theater work. All he wants is to create a magical effect on the stage: What could possibly be wrong with that? His defeat becomes a revelation: he begins to discover and express the truth that he had been seeking from the moment he stepped into the theater. The director won't stage the play that he envisions, but Maksudov still finds himself "consumed with love" for the theater. No matter how upset he might be with the director and the treatment of his play, he can no longer see himself existing without him (ZP 169/180). He needs to be in this space; he needs to submit to its authority. The reason the director rejects the gunshot episode is because he too is submitting to another authority, one that operates in another space: the backstage of the Kremlin. For the Soviet citizen of the 1930s, understanding that authority is crucial to the shaping of the self. The playwright invests himself in his work; the director insists on changing it, and so the playwright is himself changed. To achieve agency, one needs to surrender agency, to acknowledge that a subject of the state has no subjectivity and to be grateful for this. The subject is in a state of grace, that is, he is ineluctably and multiply mediated.

MOLIÈRE AT THE ART THEATER: THE BOUNDARIES OF THE THEATRICAL EVERYDAY

Here I turn to Bulgakov's play about the actor and comic playwright Jean-Baptiste Poquelin (1622–1673), better known by his stage name Molière. Bulgakov's play has been subject to multiple allegorical readings combining the personal (Molière's sex life) and the political. According to legend, Molière made a fateful deal with Louis XIV: if he wrote plays that sufficiently flattered the Sun King, his career would flourish. Bulgakov imagines the bargain not turning out as Molière wanted, and he had a fateful bargain of his own to compare it to. The more one tries to please the ruler, Bulgakov cautions, the harsher the criticism from on high (the ruler and his minions). The relationship between the stage and backstage in *Molière* becomes a simulacrum of the relationship between the theater in general and theater in the Stalinist context.

Bulgakov wrote *Molière* in 1929–30, after the devastating prohibition of his other plays. He titled the draft *The League of Hypocrites* (*Kabala sviatosh*), which hardly endeared him to the hypocritical censors of Glavrepertkom, who rejected the play.[21] Eighteen months later, after Bulgakov had returned to official favor, Glavrepertkom sanctioned the play for performance so long as it was renamed *Molière*.[22] Under that title it was contracted for production at Leningrad's Bolshoi Dramatic Theater and the Moscow Art Theater. Rehearsals for the Leningrad production stalled, then halted. The Moscow production, which now lacked any "competition" from Leningrad, took more than four years to reach the stage. (Recall the situation with Afinogenov's *Fear*, which was also in rehearsal at MAT in 1931; the success of the competing Leningrad production prompted MAT to accelerate its rehearsal schedule.)

The version of *Molière* that reached the stage in the winter of 1936 bore little resemblance to the play of 1931. Actors, designers, and directors had come and gone. After nearly three years of intermittent rehearsals, in

Costume design for Mikhail Bulgakov's play *Moliére*. State Central A. Bakhrushin Theatre Museum, Moscow. Artist: Eduard Stepanovich Kochergin. Credit: Album / Alamy Stock Photo.

the fall of 1934 and then again in the spring of 1935, the production's primary director, Nikolai Gorchakov (whose previous MAT projects included *Three Fat Men*), finally had the cast perform the play in Stanislavsky's presence. Then, in his capacity as the production's artistic director, Stanislavsky took over the day-to-day rehearsal process for three controversial months.[23] His demands for changes angered Bulgakov, and Stanislavsky also lost the confidence of the actors, who complained about his technique and the glacial

Chapter Six

pace of the rehearsals. Gorchakov appealed to Nemirovich-Danchenko for an intervention. A firm date was set for the premiere and Stanislavsky was excluded from the remaining rehearsals. Stanislavsky did not attend the meeting where these decisions were made, but he read the transcript and disavowed *Molière*.

Halfway into the next season, Gorchakov arranged a run-through for Nemirovich-Danchenko. The latter agreed to take on a supervisory role until the play's opening night a month and a half later. The production was well received by the public during the dress rehearsals (the previews) and the first seven performances, but even before the official premiere it came under attack in the newspapers. In February 1936 the chairman of the all-powerful Committee on Arts Affairs, Platon Kerzhentsev, submitted a denunciation of *Molière* and MAT's production to the Politburo of the Central Committee. Stalin approved Kerzhentsev's proposal to publish a disparaging review in *Pravda*, which prompted MAT to annul the production. The review appeared on March 9, 1936, and got right to the point about Bulgakov's blunder: turning what might have been a heroic saga into melodrama.

> The Moscow Art Theater has been preparing Bulgakov's play *Molière* for production for a long time now: about four years. The audience had the right to expect a performance of exceptionally high quality. These expectations were not met. The audience saw not only a bad performance but also a clearly incorrect interpretation of a most interesting historical theme. Molière's life, his work, his struggle would seem to be a rewarding subject for a playwright. A brilliant writer of the seventeenth century, a progressive opponent of the clergy and aristocrats, a brilliant realist who championed materialism over religion and simplicity over perversion and affectation—such a biography would seem almost impossible to distort and vulgarize. However, this is exactly what Bulgakov did in his *Molière*. From this great theme the author managed to scrape out and peel away everything serious, truly dramatic, replacing great human feelings with cheap effects and piquant situations in the spirit of the worst works of Dumas or the plays of Scribe.[24]

That was that: *Molière* was removed from the stage the same day. Later that year, before Bulgakov quit his job at MAT, he was unofficially approached by Gorchakov and other members of the theater's management about making changes to the playscript in hopes of reviving the production, but he firmly refused: once burned, twice shy. No other attempts to stage *Molière* were made during Bulgakov's lifetime, and the playscript remained unpublished until 1962.

The play is easy, perhaps too easy, to interpret as a parable about the conflict between a brilliant playwright and the authorities, since just such a conflict is embedded in the plot. Even Kerzhentsev gleaned that. Bulgakov's Molière is willing and eager to serve his king with his art, but the king withdraws his support, and the playwright is destroyed by vain and vicious mediocrities. In most accounts of the drama surrounding Bulgakov's drama, the role of the "league of hypocrites" is assigned to the theater critics and those of Bulgakov's fellow playwrights—among them Afinogenov and Olesha—who condemned the production weeks before Stalin, the counterpart to Louis XIV, allowed Kerzhentsev to cancel the play.[25]

In the accounts interpreting Bulgakov's play through the prism of his characters, the attacks of the "league" and the behavior of the "king" are often complemented by another explanation—a set of factors over which Bulgakov had little or no control. The 1930 draft of the play ended with one of the characters announcing that the cause of Molière's downfall was not the league or the king. Rather, it was the work of fate.[26] Molière gets married to a young woman and, unbeknownst to him, she is his first wife's daughter (and so his own child). This act of incest is Molière's doom.

That the MAT production, when it finally opened, had problems, seems to be a point of general agreement among eyewitnesses, even those who wished Bulgakov well.[27] The play was confusing, the acting subpar; much of what Kerzhentsev complained about, in his caustic way, was justified. Most Soviet critics before the 1960s blame Bulgakov for its shortcomings; since then, researchers have looked at the archival documents and recognized Stanislavsky and the MAT directorate as the cause of the problems. Scholars seeking an evenhanded account of the writer's quarrel with the director point to the discrepancy between the bathetic image of Molière in Bulgakov's playscript and MAT's attempts to fashion a more heroic persona. This divergence is seen as the principal and in some sense inevitable—fatal—reason for the production's denunciation.

Stanislavsky was interested in staging a grand historical drama about a progressive, and therefore ideologically acceptable, writer, director, and performer. Gorchakov and Nemirovich-Danchenko clashed with Stanislavsky over the focus of the rehearsals and smaller details in the playscript, but didn't change the play's conception. Bulgakov, however, disagreed with the reimagining of Molière as a symbol of revolutionary action; the character he fashioned was too flawed to be any sort of role model. Still, the writer's clash with the theater was not merely, or even chiefly, about the representation of Molière. It concerned the play's relationship to its immediate social and ideological context. MAT wanted to be part of the cultural establishment's creation of a pantheon of "remarkable people." The reviews of the production agreed that the theater failed: the onstage Molière was insufficiently "great."[28] Whatever Bulgakov intended to communicate in his play (and multiple hypotheses have been offered), he was unwilling to turn

Molière into the kind of hero MAT or the times demanded. So MAT settled for "glitter" over "substance," as Kerzhentsev complained. Had the play been staged a few years earlier, the irreconcilable differences between the stance of the author and the theater on this issue might not have been so decisive. But in 1936 these differences ensured the production's failure.

The historical context—seventeenth-century France—makes it difficult to read the play as autobiographical allegory. Bulgakov finished the first draft of the playscript months before he had received his famous phone call from Stalin—before he had reason to claim for himself the symbolic role of the ruler's protégé and then project it onto his fictional character. In fact, the political risk-taking attributed to Bulgakov in Kerzhentsev's report to the Politburo became apparent only during the rehearsal period. The longer the wait for opening night, the greater the peril for the author and the theater.

The play's central themes of fate and incest could be read, then, as allegories of the play's reception: its fate on the Soviet stage, and the metaphorically incestuous relationships precipitating its demise. But the theme of incest was repeatedly suppressed—first by the censorship board (Glavrepertkom, which insisted on cutting a reference to fate in the final line) and then by the people involved in the MAT production, including Bulgakov's widow, who eliminated as many references to fate and incest as possible from the playscript when she prepared it for publication many years later.[29] This collective censorship effort succeeded: the symbolic meaning of the incest motif and its relationship to fate have been ignored in interpretations of *Molière*. Still, the motif allows us to rethink the parallel between Molière's fate in Bulgakov's play and Bulgakov's fate at MAT. To understand what was concealed *inside* the play, we need to consider what was being concealed—and revealed—*about* the play.

For more than a quarter of a century, the text of the play could not be studied. Between 1936, when MAT canceled the production, and 1962, when the expurgated version of the playscript was published through Elena Bulgakova's efforts, *Molière* existed only in the memories of those participating in the production, those who saw its previews, and those allowed to read a copy of the playscript by a member of the author's family. Public references to the play and its production were rare and brief. Since the play was a MAT project, it was listed in the repertoire catalog, but it might otherwise have been invisible.[30] The lengthiest, most detailed account of the production appeared in a late Stalinist (1950) book on Stanislavsky's directorial techniques by *Molière*'s director Nikolai Gorchakov, an established theatrical figure in his own right.[31] Gorchakov's book included what he claimed to be authentic accounts of the plays of the 1920s and 1930s, based on Gorchakov's own notes from rehearsals and directorial staff meetings led by Stanislavsky. A separate chapter was devoted to Bulgakov's *Molière*. For the plays with which his readers may have been unfamiliar, Gorchakov provided plot summaries. His page-long synopsis of the plot of *Molière* was the closest the play came to publication, and Gorchakov (because he had to) omitted mention of the act of incest, insisting that in the play Molière's bride, the actress Armande Béjar, was not in fact his daughter.[32] Paradoxically, as we will see, Gorchakov's insistence upon the motif's insignificance ended up affording it special prominence.

Gorchakov's chronicle of the rehearsals includes transcripts and a running commentary about how and why the production failed. Gorchakov blamed Bulgakov for not creating a "play about a genius," while also chiding himself for not being as strict with the playwright and the actors as Stanislavsky had wanted him to be.[33]

Gorchakov's description of the *Molière* production process received a crucial ideological endorsement: his book on Stanislavsky's acting system received a third-place Stalin Prize in 1952. Two more editions of the book and an English translation quickly followed.[34] The book became one of the most respected sources on Stanislavsky's later period; paradoxically, his production of *Molière* was canonized even before Stalin's death and more than a decade before the text of the play was published. It was not until the 1970s that Gorchakov's version of events was challenged in print, owing to discrepancies between what he claimed happened and what the transcripts in the MAT archive reveal.[35]

Inaccurate, too, is Gorchakov's account of the relationship between *Molière* and Bulgakov's previous meta-theatrical play, *The Crimson Island*, which was set during the final dress rehearsal of a new play in an unnamed theater, and which portrayed the torturous process by which a playwright and director seek to get a new play approved by a government censor, posing timely questions about the relationship between the writer, theater, and the state. The prologue of *The Crimson Island* is set in the office of the theater's managing director and the dressing rooms of its actors; the draft of *Molière*, completed a year after Tairov's production of *The Crimson Island* was canceled, has virtually the same setting. *Molière* begins with the sound of the spectators' distant laughter, and when the protagonist first appears, he is exiting the stage of the Palais Royal theater, separated from the implied audience of Bulgakov's play by an enormous curtain, and entering the backstage area.

This area is the setting of the opening scene, although Bulgakov's detailed stage directions also specify that the spectators should be able to see part of the stage proper (which Molière reenters at one point to perform for the king, Louis XIV), as well as a small section of the theater beyond the stage—the edge of the royal box, out of which Louis XIV is heard (but not seen) speaking to Molière. Curtains are raised and lowered, and the onstage theater expands and contracts. But the locus is backstage, and in this respect *Molière* is both a sequel to *The Crimson Island* and a prequel to the *Memoir/Theatrical Novel*—another fable about the workings of theater which, as we have seen, gradually leads its narrator and readers to the realization that the backstage is the seat of power.

Let us move back a decade before the stormy *Molière* scandals, to the earlier play. The December 11, 1928, premiere of *The Crimson Island* at Tairov's Kamerny Theater marked the beginning of a massive anti-Bulgakov campaign in the press. The harshest criticism came from Vladimir Blum, a literature and theater critic on the staff of Glavrepertkom and one of the proletarian agitators staffing the Khudozhestvennyi sovet, or artistic council, of MAT. Then followed the aforementioned catastrophe of 1929, the cancellation of everything Bulgakov had in production that year.

The Crimson Island is a play within a play about a young writer trying to get his work accepted at a major theater. The censor arrives and the play is presented to him in a panic. That play, also called "The Crimson Island," is about a place of tremendous natural riches located in the middle of nowhere. The ruler is a dimwit who lives fabulously while his people suffer. Eventually he is swallowed up in a volcano and replaced by a smarter but no less corrupt despot. The gullible masses gather around him as the latest hero promising to protect them but who is guaranteed to exploit them.

The play was indeed subversive, and it was condemned. *Molière*, Bulgakov's subsequent attempt to rescue his career, is a subtler and darker provocation. In the opening scene, the protagonist improvises a greeting in verse for the king, in a transparently Mayakovskian idiom. In the finale, he is seen performing in a production of what is supposed to be one of his plays, but the dialogue only vaguely resembles anything the historical Molière wrote.[36] The idea, it would appear, is to demonstrate Molière's skill as an improviser and actor, using texts that have more immediate resonance for the audience of a Soviet theater, and, in doing so, to render irrelevant the impulse to include Molière's actual texts and any questions about what Bulgakov might be trying to do with them. When Molière's plays—*Tartuffe* and *Don Juan*—are mentioned, the focus is their popularity with audiences, not their specific contents. *Molière* avoids what *The Crimson Island* tackled head-on: the workings of the theater. It instead dramatizes events that conventional theatrical productions, and most meta-theatrical plays, decline to take up: censorship versus complete freedom, which Bulgakov suggests is the essential prerequisite for artists to be able to work. A play literally about *a* theater (Molière's), it portrays the theater in a way that downplays the rhetorical potential of onstage action. Instead, the play's claims of dramatic efficacy come from recasting the life of a "remarkable person" as a melodrama of the "theatrical everyday" (in Nemirovich-Danchenko's formulation, *"teatral'nyi byt"*)—with a few glimpses of the tragic thrown in for good measure.

The resulting effect is decidedly ambivalent, which was precisely what Bulgakov strove for in the 1930s, censors notwithstanding. After all, Bulgakov's greatest theatrical—and literary—success, *The Days of the Turbins*, which was once again running at MAT at this time, had triumphed by placing everyday concerns in a historical context. The battle over the *Turbins*' ideological implications, which had seemed suspect to so many Soviet theatrical and literary figures in the 1920s, was ultimately won not in public debates or newspaper discussions but on stage, during the numerous performances of the MAT production attended by Stalin and revived on his orders. *Molière* conceals several things—among them Molière's actual texts. But perhaps the playscript's most important concealment is its reframing of a play about the theater (like *The Crimson Island*) as a play about the everyday (that is, a sequel to *The Days of the Turbins*). The trick of manufacturing another great success worthy of Stalin's approval, the play suggests, involves framing Molière's story as a matter of the theatrical everyday rather than politics.

Teatr i dramaturgiia and other theater publications of the mid-1930s included surveys of goings-on in dozens of theaters across the Soviet Union, sometimes with more information about casting decisions, directorial matters, and rehearsals than facts about actual performances. The theatrical everyday was as much a point of focus as a given play's artistic or ideological implications. *Molière* incorporates this focus, making theatrical *byt* a subversive subspecies of the narrative.

This aspect of the playscript, furthermore, was given special meaning in the crucial final year of *Molière*'s rehearsals at MAT, especially Stanislavsky's work on the play. The stories about the unfortunate but inevitable conflict between Bulgakov and Stanislavsky, so prominent in *Molière*'s production history, imply that Stanislavsky—rightly or wrongly—perceived in Bulgakov's playscript something that it was not. I want to suggest, in contrast, that Stanislavsky's rehearsal experiments pointed to what was most striking and problematic about Bulgakov's project. The focus on the theatrical everyday made it a potential Soviet classic—but also made this classic extremely difficult to perform.

Stanislavsky's technique, parodied later in the *Memoir/Theatrical Novel*, involved reading through the playscript, settling on two or three scenes of interest, and then asking the playwright to make changes to those scenes as needed. At the first rehearsal with Stanislavsky present in the spring of 1935, Bulgakov declared that his work was done and the rest was up to the actors.[37] Still, he changed the text and continued doing so even as he sent formal letters to Gorchakov and Stanislavsky demanding that MAT produce the play as he had conceived it, with no further changes, lest he tear up the contract.³⁸ One of Stanislavsky's requests for a rewrite concerned a scene in the play's second act where Molière discovers his wife/daughter Armande cheating on him with the young actor Moirron. Stanislavsky wanted the passions in this scene intensified, and Bulgakov did as he was asked.³⁹ Stanislavsky had devoted an entire day of rehearsal to the scene on April 15, 1935, seeking to make it resonate with the rest of the play, and Bulgakov recognized that it needed better integration. I want to look briefly at this rehearsal because what Stanislavsky saw in the scene, and what he suggested was not sufficiently emphasized in it, was precisely the combination of the everyday and the theatrical that I consider emblematic of Bulgakov's understanding of the Soviet theater.

The scene takes place at Molière's house; Moirron and Armande are there for a rehearsal, but this point is made in passing. Moirron asks Armande whether she likes keyboard playing (*igra*). He is referring to the harpsichord on the set, but the conversation with Armande takes up the other meanings of the word *igra*: acting, as in a theater, and the sexual act. The connotations of the Russian word *igra* are less overtly sexual than the English equivalent—"performing"—but the connection is nonetheless made: Moirron is a keyboard player, an actor, and a lover. The connection is made more explicit when Moirron and Armande's rehearsal (he is Amour, she is Psyche) segues into a full-blown love scene. Stanislavsky strove to emphasize this amalgamation of various meanings of performance by assigning Moirron the role of the director in the ad hoc rehearsal/seduction. Stanislavsky stopped the rehearsal to go through the intricacies and intimacies with the actors playing Moirron (Boris Livanov) and Armande (Angelina Stepanova):

> A love scene on stage is the most dangerous thing. You have to turn it into a scene that is interesting in itself. *The audience is extremely curious about the behind-the-scenes side of life* [*Publika zakulisnoi storonoi zhizni ochen' interesuetsia*]. There's stroking the hand when you're just stroking it, and then there's the romantic kind of stroking. Maybe Moirron does something funny, and they both burst out laughing. You need something to work with. *He could be showing her how to play some kind of scene*, and in that scene he could show her how to play an embrace. We have to come up with a through line, and only then can we ask Mikhail Afanasievich [Bulgakov] to write more material for this scene.⁴⁰

"Behind-the-scenes," then, Stanislavsky conflates two kinds of ritualized behavior: the rituals/conventions of courtship and the methods of acting. For Bulgakov's play to succeed, this conflation needs to be made explicit. Staged, in accordance with Stanislavsky's instructions, as a "real"-life byproduct of a rehearsal, Moirron's seduction of Armande would quite literally become a backstage event—but one the audience is deliberately, and paradoxically, invited to observe. What matters most to Stanislavsky in rehearsing this scene is that the characters' actions are marked as authentically intimate only when they are presented through the theatrical "behind-the-scenes" perspective. He refines the specifics of Moirron and Armande's exchange, improvising the details of the "rehearsal" with them. The theatrical frame renders this intimate event worthy of the audience's attention. Once the symbolic connection with the "backstage" perspective has been established, it is crucial that the actors stay within the view of the audience, turning the intimate into the public and playing with the voyeuristic appetites of the viewers, which the viewers do not wholly control or wish to acknowledge. This is the aspect of the scene that Stanislavsky wanted Bulgakov to develop further.

In Bulgakov's playscript, the two lovers disappear into a bedroom. When Molière arrives in search of Armande, he rushes to confront Moirron. The confrontation happens offstage, out of sight. Stanislavsky found this sequence of actions unjustified: "Wait, does Molière not walk in on them while they are on stage? It's just amazing how Bulgakov does it: the things you really need he hides backstage [*priachet za stsenoi*]."[41] For Stanislavsky, the beginning of the scene keeps the stage and the *byt* (the "everyday") separate, and then the theatrical and the non-theatrical are aligned and blended into one another.

This vision of theatrical *byt* subsuming the intimate realm returns us to the heart of Stanislavsky's disagreement with Bulgakov. At the first major rehearsal of the play in the spring of 1935 arranged for his benefit, Stanislavsky identified the importance of the scenes of regular life—*byt*—in Bulgakov's conception:

Stanislavsky. At this point I look at Molière and all I see is the life of an ordinary man.

Bulgakov. That's just what I meant to portray: the life of an ordinary man.

Stanislavsky. I couldn't care less about that—about someone marrying his own daughter. What I'm interested in is that he, because of his genius, didn't notice it, didn't even understand it. If this is just about intimate matters—I'm not interested [*Esli eto prosto intim—on menia ne interesuet*]. But if this is about intimate matters, and underneath there is a genius of worldwide significance—that's a different story.[42]

This exchange is usually read as the opening salvo in a protracted battle over Molière the genius whose playwriting transcended his time (Stanislavsky)

Chapter Six

versus Molière the flawed but sympathetic human destroyed by his playwriting (Bulgakov). The ideological conflict (the argument usually goes) led to numerous tensions during rehearsals and reverberated in hostile reviews. And yet, reread in the context of issues raised at rehearsals, this early Stanislavsky-Bulgakov exchange allows us to contemplate the relationship of the stage to the world beyond it.

Stanislavsky's major apprehension about Molière the character and *Molière* the play concerns their "intimate" aspects. He didn't expect Bulgakov to eliminate the motif of incest, as the reviewers of the production claimed he should have done. Stanislavsky instead wanted Bulgakov to address the problem of a person whose "greatness" compromises his personal life.

As a play about fate, *Molière* invokes less the conventions of Romantic drama (acknowledged by Bulgakov himself and echoed in Stanislavsky's evocations of creative genius) or the conventions of Molière's satires (one of which is paraphrased in the play's final scene) than it does the conventions of classical tragedy as reconceived, intimately, in Molière's time. The look of the MAT production—the majestic, opulent, and dazzling costumes praised by reviewers (excluding Kerzhentsev) who otherwise disparaged the performance—amplified its neoclassicism. Spectators watching a conventional tragedy know, or should know, how it will end: the clues are scattered throughout. The first reference to incest in *Molière* would have signaled, to the attentive spectator, that the protagonist's demise is just a matter of time. By retaining the incest motif, then, Stanislavsky endorsed a shift of emphasis from the general shape of the story toward the particulars of its embodiment. He wanted to make it more visceral.

At the beginning of Bulgakov's play, Molière encounters the street urchin Moirron and adopts him. Legally, Moirron is Armande's son as well—a point that he repeatedly brings up as he works to seduce her with his actorly powers:

Moirron. How do you like my performance, Mommy [*mamen'ka*]?

Armande. Monsieur Moirron, I have already asked you not to call me "Mommy" . . .

Moirron. Father's an honorable man, no question about that. But he is jealous like Satan himself. And what a horrible personality!

Armande. I can congratulate my husband. The insolence of his adopted son is truly amazing.

Moirron. Oh sure, I can be obnoxious at times, that's true . . . That's just who I am . . . But what an actor, huh? There's no equal to me in all of Paris . . .

Armande. The nerve! And what about Molière?

Moirron. Well . . . all right . . . There are three of us, then. The maître and I.

Armande. And who's the third?

Moirron. You, Maman [*mama*]. You, my famous actress. You, Psyche . . . Maman, let's go to my room.

Armande. Never in the world! I swear by the Holy Virgin . . .

Moirron. Let's go, Maman . . .

Armande. By the Virgin—no! (*Stands up.*) I won't go. (*She goes and disappears behind the door with Moirron.*)[43]

Here everything is aligned: performance and *byt* (theatrical and romantic), the stage world and backstage world, how things seem and how things truly are.

In Bulgakov's playscript, this second instance of incest, between stepmother and adopted son, leads directly to Molière's downfall. Seething from the confrontation with Molière, Moirron pays a visit to Molière's nemesis, the sinister archbishop, to share the rumor about Molière's relationship with Armande, and so gives the archbishop *kompromat*, the means to blackmail the playwright. As Stanislavsky's interpretation of the Armande-Moirron scene establishes, this incestuous relationship is a product of art. Moirron and Armande are trained in their craft by Molière, who is both a famous playwright and a famous actor. The text they rehearse is (according to the playscript) written by Molière for a production in Molière's theater.[44] Their romantic encounter is presented from the behind-the-scenes perspective associated with theatrical *byt*—the true world, not the world of appearances.

Bulgakov did not make *Molière* as meta-theatrical as *The Crimson Island*, which puts the question of theatrical representation front and center. *Molière* became a play about other ways in which the theater subsumes the world beyond it. It performed the opposite operation, showing how the theater can define the external world.

This is, perhaps, one reason why Molière's discovery of Armande and Moirron's betrayal happens offstage. For Stanislavsky, Bulgakov's emphasis on theatrical *byt* was useful for making the intimate elements of the scene theatrically compelling and for linking them to Molière's peculiar theatrical talent. Stanislavsky wanted the details of the drama that Bulgakov briefly places backstage to be kept in full view of the audience. For Bulgakov, the everyday life of the playwright, especially his complicated relationship with authority, is structured by the ultimately incestuous relationship between the power of behind-the-scenes theatrical *byt* and the finished product of that *byt*—the performance itself. Molière's strength lies in understanding the importance of that relationship and especially of the power of the backstage world. His weakness (a fatal one, in the deterministic rhetoric of the play) is his inability, rather than unwillingness, to fully master it. Paradoxically, this aspect of Bulgakov's play and his worldview came into view most vividly during the Stanislavsky rehearsals, even as the director made suggestions that Bulgakov rejected—including letting the audience witness the moment Molière discovers Armande and Moirron.

Stanislavsky's work on the production ended; Bulgakov didn't make all the changes Stanislavsky desired. The playscript for the production that opened at MAT in 1936 was shorter than the one Stanislavsky used in rehearsal (among other cuts, five speaking roles were eliminated just days before the final dress rehearsals because the performance ran too long: five hours). The scene with Armande and Moirron remained, but the dialogue wasn't expanded, and Molière's discovery of a second incestuous union was not staged. The meta-historical turn in the stories about *Molière*'s lengthy and difficult theatrical trajectory testify to the centrality of Bulgakov's preoccupation with the behind-the-scenes world. Most of these accounts present the meaning of the production and the play as accessible only to those who understand the production's backstage history. Outside the theater, the playwright achieved what he could not prevail upon the theater to perform.

UNEASY AFFINITIES IN ELENA BULGAKOVA'S DIARIES

Bulgakov's wife Elena Sergeyevna began to keep a diary in September 1933 and kept it up until Bulgakov's death in the spring of 1940 with few interruptions, most of them due to travel or sickness. After Bulgakov's personal belongings, including all his manuscripts, were confiscated by the OGPU during a search in 1926, he abandoned diary writing of his own and encouraged her to keep the record of their lives together. "The thought that a writer's diary can be impounded," Elena Sergeyevna explained, became "terrifying and incomprehensible for him."[45] Her diaries would be less about their marriage than his career but would not bear his name.

Unlike Olesha or Afinogenov, Bulgakov didn't think of diaries, his or his spouse's, as any sort of tool for personal development. Elena Sergeyevna tells a tale in the third person about a character named "Misha," "M.A.," or "Mikhail Afanasievich," who is working tirelessly to establish himself as a writer. Her diaries cannot be seen to bear witness to Stalinism. In the 1950s, Elena Sergeyevna rewrote certain passages in the diaries to create a more coherent and consistent account of Bulgakov's efforts to strengthen his standing in Soviet culture. This was the version she intended for posterity.[46]

Elena Sergeyevna recorded Bulgakov's bureaucratic setbacks, disappointments, and humiliations. The first version of the diaries includes several asides in which she decries the "horrifying conditions under which [her] husband has to work" (*D* 354). She charts Bulgakov's attempts to overcome the obstacles blocking his path to success and his hopes of retaining a position of cultural authority. The question I want to pose is whether the tale of

Photograph of Elena and Mikhail Bulgakov. M. Bulgakov Museum Kyiv. Credit: Album / Alamy Stock Photo.

Bulgakov's calamities can be interpreted, paradoxically, as a tale of becoming genuine—as an artist, a person, and a subject of the state.[47]

Throughout the 1930s, Bulgakov dispatched letters to friends and family containing information comparable to that recorded in Elena Sergeyevna's diaries. The impulse to look in the diaries for clues as to what Bulgakov was experiencing at the time is therefore understandable. My interest does not reside, however, in reconstructing what Bulgakov might have expressed in diaries of his own. I am instead interested in the alignment between Elena Sergeyevna's references to the behind-the-scenes workings of the theater world and the biographical information about her husband. Her descriptions of rehearsals, performances, casting decisions, administrative overhauls, battles with the censors, visits from the powers that be—become one with her narrative of Bulgakov's life.

She traces Bulgakov's career as playwright and assistant director. She also chronicles his (and her) social activities: unofficial and usually friendly meetings with other cultural luminaries (theater and film actors, directors, composers, literature scholars, artists, writers, poets), important officials (administrators in the arts, foreign and domestic cultural representatives), and gatherings with friends and family members who have nothing to do with the theater. Lastly, she records the darker sides of Soviet life: arrests of acquaintances, the show trials, and Bulgakov's brushes with the security apparatus, the NKVD. Elena Sergeyevna offers a behind-the-scenes perspective on her and her husband's personal and political realities. Crucial is her account of Bulgakov's efforts to position himself as a major cultural figure in the 1930s even as his career was unraveling.

His writing didn't appear in print in the 1930s. It existed in manuscript and came to the attention of the public in piecemeal fashion: when he hosted informal readings and when he worked at MAT. There his writing had the potential to reach thousands and often did. When the Union of Soviet Writers was formed in 1934, Bulgakov immediately joined, but his interactions with its leadership are incidental to the tale told in Elena Sergeyevna's diaries. He related to those writers who were also involved in the theater, not those who merely published for a living. Marietta Chudakova has suggested that Bulgakov's interest in Molière as a subject for a play came from Mayakovsky, who was likened to Molière by Meyerhold.[48] Like Bulgakov, Mayakovsky tethered himself to the canon, the great books of the past. He also reinvented himself as a playwright and thus became a figure of immense interest to Bulgakov: a rival and a model. Bulgakov's relationship with Afinogenov follows these same contours.

Afinogenov was not a member of Bulgakov's social or intellectual milieu. A committed communist, he served in the late 1920s on the board of RAPP and led the attack against Bulgakov for his ideological failings.

The two of them obviously knew each other, though their paths seldom crossed. In her diaries, Elena Sergeyevna calls Afinogenov one of the most established—successful—"authors of the Art Theater" of all time. Rehearsals for *The Lie* were going well, and the success of *Fear* had given him access to leading cultural officials, including Gorky, who liked Afinogenov enough to invite him to a writers' workshop in September 1933. Bulgakov attended in hopes of consulting with Gorky about his political problems. Gorky was too busy to have a real conversation with him, however, so Bulgakov ended up sitting with Afinogenov. They talked about the new law governing royalty payments, and about Bulgakov's newest play *Flight*. Afinogenov made it clear that he didn't like the play (*D* 36–37).

Afinogenov and his work are regular points of reference for Elena Sergeyevna. The torturous demise of *The Lie* in November 1933 is covered in detail (*D* 44–46), as are the rumors about Afinogenov's next play, *The Portrait* (1934), which MAT considered for production but ultimately rejected (72, 79). Her close attention to the twists and turns in Afinogenov's career is motivated by its implications for Bulgakov's own. One is the foil of the other; their successes and failures happened in counterpoint (85, 354). In one passage, Elena Sergeyevna notes that Afinogenov is struggling; things aren't going well for him. She adds that things are going worse for her husband (354; she later excised this passage). Afinogenov is Bulgakov's shadow in some contexts; in other contexts he becomes Bulgakov's double.

The connection, originally established on theatrical (backstage) turf, resurfaces in accounts of other aspects of Bulgakov's everyday life. As several studies have suggested, one of Bulgakov's most important social relationships in the 1930s was with the US ambassador William Bullitt, an admirer of his work. Bulgakov was fascinated with Bullitt and the lavish events he hosted at the American embassy, where the Bulgakovs were frequent guests.[49] (Bulgakov immortalized a decadent all-night affair at the residence in his novel *Master and Margarita*, nicknaming it "The Spring Ball of the Full Moon.") The length of Elena Sergeyevna's descriptions of Bullitt's soirées varies, but even in the shorter entries she mentions that Afinogenov was also in attendance. She records what he looked like—Afinogenov was famously fastidious in his attire—how he behaved, and what he said (*D* 95, 106–7, 109, 125). Although Bullitt was well known among Moscow's cultural and political elite, obtaining an audience with him was rare—a mark of distinction—and, for Soviet citizens, posed great risks. Afinogenov's second wife, Jenny Marling, was an American citizen, so he received special attention from Bullitt and (accordingly) from the NKVD. On the plus side, Bulgakov and Afinogenov were joined at the hip as members of the cultural elite who also enjoyed the patronage of charismatic foreigners.

When, in 1937, Afinogenov was expelled from the Party and retreated to his dacha in Peredelkino, Elena Sergeyevna recorded the comments of Bulgakov's acquaintances who interpreted the denunciation as a sign that Bulgakov's fortunes were about to improve. Despite the encouragement of others (including, notably, Olesha), Bulgakov refused to settle scores with his RAPP opponents by attending the writers' meetings at which Afinogenov was being attacked together with Kirshon and other former RAPP functionaries (*D* 141). Elena Sergeyevna represents this decision as evidence of Bulgakov's principled character and contrasts it with the behavior of shameful opportunists. Bulgakov emerges as the leading Soviet playwright, in terms of his morality, even though, by 1937, neither he nor Afinogenov were writing for the theater any longer.

Bulgakov worked inside Soviet culture; he had access and authority. Although he represented himself as a persecuted outsider in his letters to the government in the 1930s, he belonged to, and made a difference in, Moscow's theater scene. His work at the Bolshoi Theater is illustrative: his responsibilities included writing his own libretti, as well as ghostwriting and ghost-editing the libretti of some of the most significant productions of the decade, including the refurbished, Sovietized Glinka revival, *Ivan Susanin*.

A few days before Bulgakov left MAT to join the staff of the Bolshoi, Elena Sergeyevna recorded the following aphorism: "In opera, it's not the text that matters, it's the idea of the text" (*D* 122). This formulation belonged to the Bolshoi's principal conductor Samuil Samosud, whose point, in Elena Sergeyevna's interpretation, is that lyrics need not be complicated for an aria to be a success. The spectators' impression, or illusion, of the aria having an important meaning needs to be sustained irrespective of the quality of the lyrics or their repetitiveness. This idea had metaphorical implications for Bulgakov's career.[50]

Bulgakov's decision to leave MAT for the Bolshoi, as opposed to another playhouse, has numerous explanations. Some of them are practical (he had a close friend at the Bolshoi), some aesthetic (Bulgakov loved opera and knew the opera canon well). He was, to be sure, choosing among the most prestigious cultural institutions in the Soviet Union; being involved in a powerful theater, with a distinguished history, appealed to him. No matter how strong Bulgakov's attachment to MAT—something that is always emphasized in Bulgakov studies—or his subsequent unhappiness with it, the concepts explored in *Molière* and the *Memoir/Theatrical Novel* retain their centrality. He was interested in how the backstage position offered access to the elusive mechanisms of theatrical authority and state power, but also in the illusions of agency and autonomy that the theatrical profession nurtures in its artists.

Stalin's visits to the theater are obviously an important point of focus in Elena Sergeyevna's diaries. Even when his attendance has nothing specifically to do with Bulgakov, it affects the people with whom he works in the theatrical establishment. Elena Sergeyevna highlights the directives issued after Stalin takes in a performance and their immediate impact. She uses impersonal constructions to amplify the news coming down from above. (Sometimes Elena Sergeyevna implies that she has been tasked with communicating on behalf of a higher power.) A case in point is her comment about Gorky's *Enemies* (*Vragi*, 1906): "During one of the performances of this play at the Maly Theater recently, a phrase was uttered [*byla proiznesena fraza*] in the Government's box: 'It would be good if this play were mounted at the Art Theater'" (*D* 52). First officialdom's presence, then its verdict. But the causal connection works the other way as well. A few weeks later, she adds: "They ordered [Konstantin Trenev's popular 1920s melodrama] *Liubov' Iarovaia*" performed (54). In this case, Stalin is mentioned as being present at the performance after which the crucial pronouncement is issued, but the command itself is once again framed as an impersonal construction.[51]

When Elena Sergeyevna explicitly identifies Stalin as the source of a comment (sometimes as "the secretary-general" or "I.V."), it usually has something specific to do with Bulgakov's professional activities. Stalin on one occasion asks about the writer's employment at MAT amid some general thoughts about his plays (*D* 55). The place of special honor belongs to *The Turbins*, which Stalin sees several times in the 1930s—including a performance in 1934 in the company of Kirov just before Kirov's assassination (a detail Elena Sergeyevna considers hugely important, 79–81). But the diary also has Stalin asking about the fate of *Minin and Pozharskii*, Bulgakov's libretto for an opera about the Time of Troubles (176), and even lets it be known after *Batum* was banned that he considered it "a very good play" that simply "ought not to be staged" (285). Word of Stalin's interest in Bulgakov's career arrives through the usual "backstage" channels—people whose intimate knowledge of the behind-the-scenes comings and goings is beyond Elena Sergeyevna's doubt, most often her sister (and Nemirovich-Danchenko's secretary) Olga Bokshanskaia, or a close family friend, the Bolshoi (and before that MAT) administrator Yakov Leontiev. Received and reported among the other theatrical news, these items situate Bulgakov's personal tribulations within the context of directives issued from the theaters' "government" boxes. The sense that Bulgakov's immense writerly gifts are underappreciated and unjustly ignored by the Soviet establishment is counterbalanced by entries suggesting that his work is not just an object of the government's attention, but a matter of cultural policy.

Bulgakov's 1930 phone conversation with Stalin boosted Bulgakov's standing for years. The call was received long before Elena Sergeyevna began her diary—indeed, long before she and Bulgakov started living together. But it's mentioned in the diary, and Elena Sergeyevna describes Bulgakov's

Chapter Six

subsequent letters, and drafts of letters, to Stalin—both concerning himself and interceding on behalf of friends, such as the playwright Nikolai Erdman (*D* 184). She also talks about those occasions when friends and acquaintances reached out to Bulgakov for assistance in their dealings with the government. Of the letters to Stalin he helps to write, only one—Akhmatova's, in 1935—produces a result, and Elena Sergeyevna immediately, jubilantly reports it (108). But as with her descriptions of Bulgakov in the government loge, the significance of these gestures resides not merely, and not primarily, in the response they might receive from above. What matters most is the social and cultural position Bulgakov occupies: a backstage, behind-the-scenes position.

To be talked about by the powers that be, and to be able to speak about those powers: engagement with the government determined whether an artist realized their professional aspirations. Bulgakov persisted as a writer despite repeated setbacks and "neurotic fits" (as he put it in the *Memoir/Theatrical Novel*), waiting for additional engagement. But the diary points to another mechanism for renewing and reasserting the connection between the writer and his context—that is, between the artist and the forces of repression. Bulgakov observes Stalin from a uniquely theatrical perspective.

Three days after Akhmatova receives news that her husband and son have been released—a development that Elena Sergeyevna implicitly credits to the letter about which Akhmatova had consulted Bulgakov—Bulgakov sees Stalin. It is the anniversary of the Revolution (November 7, 1935), and Bulgakov is attending the annual parade on Red Square, presumably with other MAT employees. When he returns home, he tells Elena Sergeyevna that he glimpsed Stalin standing atop Lenin's Mausoleum with the other members of the government (*D* 108). This detail follows the description of Akhmatova's surprisingly successful appeal to Stalin, and it confirms that Stalin—from his perch above Red Square—serves as the ultimate, ideally benign, judge and protector of all things within his domain. Here, Bulgakov is just one among the many subjects who observe the most important embodiment of state power participating in a familiar Soviet ritual—the holiday parade.

Consider in this context Elena Sergeyevna's diary entry from some four months later:

March 14, 1936.

At 4:30 P.M. were invited to Bullitt's again. Decided not to go; in no mood to listen to condolences and questions.

In the evening—at the Bolshoi: *Natalka from Poltava* [*Natalka-Poltavka*], Kyiv Opera, here on tour.

We sat in the administration's box, right by the proscenium. The box was just packed with people. Right before the beginning of the second act, in the government box—across from us—there appeared Stalin, Molotov, and Ordzhonikidze.

After it was over, all the performers gathered on stage and started an ovation in Stalin's honor. Then the entire theater took part in it. Stalin greeted the actors by waving his hand, applauded. (*D* 117)

The ritualistic exchange of applause will also happen at a performance of the Glinka opera *Ivan Susanin* (formerly, *A Life for the Tsar*) in April 1939. The public applauds the government officials in attendance before the opera has ended. The clapping, Bulgakov recalls, "grew and grew in intensity and finally turned into a massive ovation, with the Government applauding the stage, the stage applauding the Government, and the audience applauding both ways" (*D* 250).

But the setting and the circumstances make all the difference. As Bulgakov observes and applauds Stalin in March 1936 at the Bolshoi Theater, he is sitting, and then standing, directly across from him, separated only by the stalls. Each of them is in a box, a place reserved for the most important patrons. Bulgakov is watching the performance from Stalin's perspective—the perspective from which the most important behind-the-scenes decisions are made. Physically, Bulgakov may be as far from Stalin, or as close to Stalin, as he is during the Red Square parade. But symbolically he is looking at the production from the same position of authority.

In the opening scene of *Molière*—perhaps the most explicit representation of Bulgakov's understanding of theatrical power mechanisms—the audience watches Molière's improvised performance for the king as if from backstage. The king himself is invisible: all the audience sees is the gilded edge of the royal box (located, like the government box in the Bolshoi, right by the proscenium). This direct line of vision from the backstage area to the king's box is retraced symbolically in the moments when Bulgakov is watching Stalin at the Bolshoi: Stalin's box and Bulgakov's are both part of the "backstage" realm—the shadowy place where the production's future is decided.[52]

Note the date: Bulgakov watches Stalin from the box across the theater on March 14, 1936, just five days after the MAT production of *Molière* was attacked in *Pravda* and canceled; hence Elena Sergeyevna's reference to possible "condolences" from the American embassy at the beginning of her entry. At this point the Bulgakovs suspect that the other plays, *Ivan Vasilievich* and *Alexander Pushkin*, will also be canceled, but they might be wrong and have no knowledge that Stalin personally approved the attack on *Molière*. In Elena Sergeyevna's account, this period of Bulgakov's

Chapter Six

life is a time of despair as well as defiance: she stresses Bulgakov's refusal to repent or apologize for the errors in the play, as colleagues suggested he should (*D* 117). Bulgakov is experiencing firsthand the power of the invisible behind-the-scenes mechanism that he will later reconstruct in his *Memoir/ Theatrical Novel*. In March 1936, this mechanism is in the process of annihilating his plays. Bulgakov applauded Stalin at the Bolshoi that night, ostensibly joining others in celebrating the bright future of the Soviet Union under wise, benevolent leadership. But another ritual was in progress, bringing Bulgakov as cultural actor into contact with Stalin as cultural arbiter. The lights went down, and then the curtain. The power Bulgakov thought he had, and the persona he thought he could adopt, were taken away.

In the final weeks of Bulgakov's illness, three of his former colleagues from the Moscow Art Theater, the famed actors Vassily Kachalov, Alla Tarasova, and Nikolai Khmelev, wrote a letter to Stalin's personal assistant, Aleksandr Poskrebyshev. They described Bulgakov's rapidly deteriorating state and the doctors' pessimistic prognoses. The only thing that his caregivers hoped for, they added, was a "powerful positive shock that could give him new strength to fight his disease, or rather would force him to want to live." Having heard Bulgakov speak so often of his gratitude to Stalin for the attention he'd showed him a decade earlier with his phone call, they wrote to his assistant hoping for an encore performance.

The letter is a remarkable exercise in stylistics and etiquette. Though they make abundantly clear that Stalin, and Stalin alone, has the power to bring the dying author back to life, the authors do not ask for Stalin to pick up the phone and give Bulgakov a call. They merely "inform" and "report," as if they were not pleading for a friend but filing secret surveillance papers. But the letter is also an artifact of the backstage culture into which Bulgakov was initiated and which he tried to master throughout the 1930s. The actors write as part of Bulgakov's support network, and yet they assert their prominence in the Soviet theatrical community: they know his plays better than most. And of course they address the letter not to Stalin but to his chief aide, the person running things behind the scenes at the Kremlin. The seemingly effortless conflation of secrecy, intimacy, and ideological orthodoxy, the quasi-religious feeling, the conspiratorial tone, and the repeated allusions to the theater as the crucial link between all the participants—these things tell us as much about the life of the Soviet citizen as they do the lives of Soviet artists.

The Bolsheviks imagined their expanding realm—the Soviet Union— as a kind of theater. Factories became percussion sessions, sirens and smokestacks became brasses and winds. Representation and enactment changed places. It is still common for scholars of the Stalinist period to see the cultural developments of the 1930s as a kind of extension and mutation of the proletarian movements of the 1920s, with everyone performing for the benefit of everyone else; all the Soviet world becoming a stage. These performances ended, and instead another type of performance happened: the regulation of the behaviors and outlooks of the population through oppressive propaganda. Life was ritualized, a canned performance. The citizen, as actor, had ever less agency, ever less improvisational capacity.

In his *Memoir/Theatrical Novel*, Bulgakov writes about a fictional author's death and a fictional play's demise. It's unpleasant backstage, a place of shameful, self-destructive manipulations. The production is a product of unseemly transactions, performed by turncoats, double-dealers, singers and dancers and orators *en travesti*. The political allegory is obvious: what is seen on the street and printed in the newspapers is the product of unseen operations, hidden processes. No one knows what is happening; no one has access to the truth. Bulgakov tried to expose those processes, first on paper, then on the stage, then again on paper. His playwriting—like the state in which he was fated to live—was radical, maximalist in aspiration and aesthetic, aiming to absorb the entire world.

Conclusion

LIKE LITERATURE AND FILM, Soviet theater gave artists access to the upper ranks of the Soviet government. It also turned their plays into high-risk personal dramas, existential threats. The dangers faced by the dramatis personae in stories for and about the creation of a new world became their own. Such, I have argued, were the disturbing side affects of 1930s theatrical life. On the stage and in the audience, the process of negotiating, judging, evaluating, doubting, and rejoicing accelerated. Soviet theater reached beyond itself, moving from reality into fiction and then presenting audiences with a fictionalization of reality—the reality to come, which was unified in time, space, and event. Success varied.

Olesha, Afinogenov, and Bulgakov explored the tension between the conventional and the unpredictable in their plays. Limitations were transcended by their characters and by themselves as actors employed by the state. In Olesha's case, the theater promised to boost his writing career and helped him to refashion himself. Afinogenov took on the challenge of representing, and bringing into being, another, genuine Soviet existence. Bulgakov found in the theater and its backstage intrigues the skills needed to thwart his detractors on the way to becoming a leading cultural representative. Theater granted these artists access to power, but theater also posed a threat: it could ruin them despite, or because of, their successes as playwrights.

These three writers survived the purges. Though each had obvious reasons to fear for his future, none were arrested. Bulgakov died in March 1940 from a hereditary kidney disease. A Luftwaffe bomb dropped on the Central Committee building in October 1941, killing Afinogenov. Olesha outlived Stalin, dying of a heart attack in May 1960 while finishing up an article on Ernest Hemingway. Each left personal reflections on his experiences in the theater—the good but mostly the bad, their participation in morally questionable, ideologically dangerous, potentially suicidal, and deeply incestuous acts. Each writer, however, persisted, exploring the possibilities of the medium despite the official abolition of anything resembling experiment.

Conclusion

Bulgakov and Olesha produced plays about the theater, and Afinogenov and Bulgakov meditated on acting and actors in their diaries and (unfinished) autobiographical novels. Each of them chronicled the search for self-understanding; explored the ambiguities of the theatrical spectacle; and left behind a surprising and sobering account of life and art under Stalin.

Notes

INTRODUCTION

1. Konstantin Stanislavsky, *An Actor's Work: A Student's Diary*, trans. Jean Benedetti (New York: Routledge, 2008), 11–12. Translation edited for precision and style. Russian original: Konstantin Stanislavskii, "Rabota aktyora nad soboi: Chast' I. Rabota nad soboi v tvorcheskom protsesse perezhivaniia," in *Sobranie sochinenii v vosmi tomakh* (Moscow: Iskusstvo, 1954), 2:19–20. See also Nicholas Ridout, *Stage Fright, Animals, and Other Theatrical Problems* (Cambridge: Cambridge University Press, 2006), 35–69.

2. Julie A. Cassiday, *The Enemy on Trial: Early Soviet Courts on Stage and Screen* (DeKalb: Northern Illinois University Press, 2000), 3–51.

3. The following information and quotations are from K. M. Polivanov, "Gamlet," in *Pasternak i sovremenniki: Biografiia, dialogi, paralleli, prochteniia* (Moscow: GU VShE, 2006), 260–67.

4. Boris Pasternak, *Doctor Zhivago*, trans. Richard Pevear and Larissa Volokhonsky (New York: Pantheon Books, 2010), 612.

5. Julie A. Cassiday, *Russian Style: Performing Gender, Power, and Putinism* (Madison: University of Wisconsin Press, 2023).

6. See Christel Lane, *The Rites of Rulers: Ritual in Industrial Society—The Soviet Case* (Cambridge: Cambridge University Press, 1981); Richard Stites, *Revolutionary Dreams: Utopian Vision and Experimental Life in the Russian Revolution* (Oxford: Oxford University Press, 1989); James von Geldern, *Bolshevik Festivals, 1917–1920* (Berkeley: University of California Press, 1993); and Thomas Seifrid, *Staging the Absolute: Ritual in Russia's Modern Era* (Toronto: University of Toronto Press, 2024).

7. Jeffrey Brooks, *Thank You, Comrade Stalin! Soviet Public Culture from Revolution to Cold War* (Princeton, NJ: Princeton University Press, 2000). Brooks uses the notion of "political theater" and the metaphor of "performance" throughout his study; his most extensive discussion is on pp. 66–69.

8. Malcolm Muggeridge, *Winter in Moscow* (Boston: Little, Brown, 1934), 210.

9. Karen Petrone, *Life Has Become More Joyous, Comrades: Celebrations in the Time of Stalin* (Bloomington: Indiana University Press, 2000), 24.

10. See Cassiday, *Enemy on Trial*, 3–7, 10–19.

11. See Lynn Mally, *Revolutionary Acts: Amateur Theater and the Soviet State, 1917–1938* (Ithaca, NY: Cornell University Press, 2000); Jeffrey Veidlinger, *The Moscow State Yiddish Theater: Jewish Culture on the Soviet Stage* (Bloomington: Indiana University Press, 2000); Eugene Anthony Swift, *Popular Theater and Society in Tsarist Russia* (Berkeley: University of California Press, 2002); Catherine Schuler, *Theatre and Identity in Imperial Russia* (Iowa City: University of Iowa Press, 2009); and Paul Du Quenoy, *Stage Fright: Politics and the Performing Arts in Late Imperial Russia* (University Park: Pennsylvania State University Press, 2009).

12. That performance exists in the moment and "becomes itself through disappearance" is fundamental to Peggy Phelan's writing about the ontology of the theatrical event, what she calls "representation without reproduction" (*Unmarked: The Politics of Performance* [New York: Routledge, 1993], 146).

13. Ridout, *Stage Fright*, 6.

14. Ridout, *Stage Fright*, 4.

15. Heinrich von Kleist, "On the Marionette Theater" (1810), *Southern Cross Review*, https://southerncrossreview.org/9/kleist.htm.

16. Ridout, *Stage Fright*, 40–62.

17. Katerina Clark, *Moscow, the Fourth Rome: Stalinism, Cosmopolitanism, and the Evolution of Soviet Culture, 1931–1941* (Cambridge, MA: Harvard University Press, 2011), 240.

18. Clark, *Moscow, the Fourth Rome*, 241.

19. For a discussion of issues with the first translation of Stanislavsky's book, see Sharon Marie Carnicke, *Stanislavsky in Focus: An Acting Master for the Twenty-First Century*, 2nd ed. (New York: Routledge, 2009).

20. See John Haynes, *New Soviet Man: Gender and Masculinity in Stalinist Soviet Cinema* (Pittsburgh, PA: University of Pittsburgh Press, 2008); and Lilya Kaganovsky, *How the Soviet Man Was Unmade: Cultural Fantasy and Male Subjectivity Under Stalin* (Pittsburgh, PA: University of Pittsburgh Press, 2008).

21. The Russian words for "performance"—*predstavlenie, vystuplenie*, and *ispolnenie*—define the three sections of Julie A. Buckler, Julie A. Cassiday, and Boris Wolfson, eds., *Russian Performances: Word, Object, Action* (Madison: University of Wisconsin Press, 2018).

22. J. L. Austin, "How to Do Things with Words: Lecture II," in *The Performance Studies Reader*, ed. Henry Bial, 2nd ed. (London: Routledge, 2007), 177–83.

23. Quoted in W. B. Worthen, *Shakespeare and the Force of Modern Performance* (Cambridge: Cambridge University Press, 2003), 6–7; see also Andrew Parker and Eve Kosofsky Sedgwick, "Introduction to 'Performativity and Perfor-

mance,'" in *The Performance Studies Reader*, ed. Henry Bial, 2nd ed. (London: Routledge, 2007), 200–207.

24. Worthen, *Shakespeare and the Force of Modern Performance*, 12–13.

25. See Emma Widdis, *Socialist Senses: Film, Feeling, and the Soviet Subject, 1917–1940* (Bloomington: Indiana University Press, 2017), which examines cinema's role in creating a Soviet subject.

26. Leon Trotsky, *Literature and Revolution* (Chicago: Haymarket Books, 2005), 320.

27. These subjects are explored in Katerina Clark, *The Soviet Novel: History as Ritual* (Bloomington: Indiana University Press, 2000); and Hans Guenther and Evgeny Dobrenko, *Sotsrealisticheskii kanon: Sbornik statei* (St. Petersburg: Akademicheskii proekt, 2000).

28. See Christina Kiaer, *Imagine No Possessions: The Socialist Objects of Russian Constructivism* (Cambridge, MA: MIT Press, 2005); and Irina Paperno, *Stories of the Soviet Experience: Memoirs, Diaries, Dreams* (Ithaca, NY: Cornell University Press, 2009).

29. The *"travesti-artist,"* Julie A. Cassiday clarifies, "exhibits ambiguous gender and sexuality in spades and asks that audiences suspend their (dis)belief about prevailing notions of gender and sexuality" for pleasure's sake (*Russian Style: Performing Gender, Power, and Putinism*, 51).

30. Michael Fried, *Absorption and Theatricality: Painting and Beholder in the Age of Diderot* (Berkeley: University of California Press, 1980). Fried's "theatricality" disturbs "absorption," the proper relation of the spectator to the art. Theatrical art exposes itself to its own gaze, and so puts itself, improperly, upon the stage.

31. See Dassia N. Posner, *The Director's Prism: E. T. A. Hoffmann and the Russian Theatrical Avant-Garde* (Evanston, IL: Northwestern University Press, 2016).

32. See W. B. Worthen, *Print and the Poetics of Modern Drama* (Cambridge: Cambridge University Press, 2005).

33. See W. B. Worthen, *Drama: Between Poetry and Performance* (Malden, MA: Wiley-Blackwell, 2010), 28–31.

34. "*na stsene deistvuiut ne tol'ko postupki, no i slova, kotorye, blagodaria stsenicheskoi tekhniki, prevrashchaiutsia postupki: stsena ne govorit slova, a deistvuet imi, b'yot*": "Filosofema o teatre" (1923), in *Sobranie sochinenii v piati tomakh*, by Sigizmund Krzhizhanovskii (St. Petersburg: Symposium, 2001), 4: 78. In English, see "A Philosopheme for the Theater," in Sigizmund Krzhizhanovsky, *That Third Guy: A Comedy from the Stalinist 1930s with Essays on Theater*, trans. Alisa Ballard Lin (Madison: University of Wisconsin Press, 2018), 49. Krzhizhanovskii's theater theory is discussed in Alisa Ballard Lin, *Theatrical Consciousness: The Actor's Mind in Russian Modernism* (Evanston, IL: Northwestern University Press, 2025).

35. Aleksandr Iufit, ed., *Lenin, revoliutsiia, teatr: Dokumenty i vospominaniia* (Leningrad: Iskusstvo, 1970), 159. See also Alisa Ballard Lin, "The 'Miracle' of the Russian Revolution: The Mystery Play in Early Soviet Culture," *Modern Drama* 67, no. 2 (2024): 129–50.

36. Benjamin Bennett, *Theater as Problem: Modern Drama and Its Place in Literature* (Ithaca, NY: Cornell University Press, 1990), 55–92.

37. See Aleksandr Boguslavskii and Vladimir Diev, *Russkaia sovetskaia dramaturgiia: Osnovnye problemy razvitiia, 1917–1935* (Moscow: Izdatel'stvo Akademii nauk SSSR, 1963), 7–60.

38. Lars T. Lih, "Melodrama and the Myth of the Soviet Union," in *Imitations of Life: Two Centuries of Melodrama in Russia*, ed. Louise McReynolds and Joan Neuberger (Durham, NC: Duke University Press, 2002), 178–207; Cassiday, *The Enemy on Trial*, 83–94.

39. The standard English-language account of the transition from the 1920s to the 1930s in Soviet theater is Harold B. Segel, *Twentieth-Century Russian Drama: From Gorky to the Present*, 2d ed. (Baltimore, MD: Johns Hopkins University Press, 1993; orig. ed., New York: Columbia University Press, 1979). See also Vladimir Zhidkov, *Teatr i vlast': 1917–1927, do "osoznannoi neobkhodimosti"* (Moscow: Aleteia, 2003).

40. See Anna Muza, "The Tragedy of a Russian Woman: 'Anna Karenina' at the Moscow Art Theater, 1937," *Russian Literature* 65, no. 4 (May 2009): 467–506.

41. The theater was renamed the USSR Maksim Gorky Moscow Academic Art Theater (MKhAT SSSR imeni Maksima Gor'kogo).

42. Ilya Zilbershtein and Evgeny Tager, eds., *Gor'kii i sovetskie pisateli: Neizdannaia perepiska*, Literaturnoe nasledstvo, vol. 70 (Moscow: Izdatel'stvo AN SSSR, 1963), 30.

43. Zilbershtein and Tager, eds., *Gor'kii i sovetskie pisateli*, 387.

44. See A. Belinkov, *Sdacha i gibel' sovetskogo intelligenta: Iurii Olesha* (Moscow: RIK Kul'tura, 1997).

45. Mikhail Gundarin, "Iurii Olesha: Chelovek s chetyr'mia tainami," livejournal, March 12, 2024, https://rewizor-ru.livejournal.com/11534.html.

46. See Jochen Hellbeck, *Revolution on My Mind: Writing a Diary under Stalin* (Cambridge, MA: Harvard University Press, 2006), 285–346.

47. Elena Bulgakova, *Dnevnik* (Moscow: Knizhnaia palata, 1990), 169.

48. Iurii Olesha, "Zapiski Zanda," Materialy, Olesha Papers, Moscow, Institut mirovoi literatury (IMLI) f. 161, op. 1, ed. khr. 8, l. 8; Bulgakova, *Dnevnik*, 141, 210.

49. Most of the theaters discussed in this book are in Moscow. After the announcement of the "General Plan for the Reconstruction of Moscow" in 1931, Moscow became the main site of, and model for, Stalinist culture.

50. Il'ia Veniavkin, "*Rasshirovka* Afinogenov: 'Strakh,'" Arzamas, https://arzamas.academy/materials/1224.

51. Veniavkin, "*Rasshirovka* Afinogenov."

CHAPTER ONE

1. Veronique Garros, Natalia Korenevskaya, and Thomas Lahusen, eds., *Intimacy and Terror: Soviet Diaries of the 1930s* (New York: New Press, 1995), 169.

2. Garros et al., *Intimacy and Terror*, 172–73, 167–68.

3. Nataliia Sats, "Tsentral'nyi detskii teatr," *Pravda*, February 28, 1936, p. 4.

4. For a chronicle of the events leading to the closing of MAT 2 and the founding of the TsDT, see Z. P. Udal'tsova, ed., *MKhAT Vtoroi: Opyt vosstanovleniia biografii* (Moscow: Moskovskii Khudozhestvennyi teatr, 2010), 520–76.

5. "Sumbur vmesto muzyki: Ob opera 'Ledi Makbet Mtsenskogo Uyezda,'" *Pravda*, January 28, 1936, p. 3; "Baletnaia falsh,'" *Pravda*, February 6, 1936, p. 3.

6. [Associated Press], "Natalya Sats, 90, Dies; Children's Opera Head," *New York Times*, December 22, 1993, Section B, p. 8.

7. On the educational function of the children's theaters, see Gene Sosin, "Children's Theater and Drama in the Soviet Union (1917–1953)" (PhD diss., Columbia University, 1958), 12–33. On children's involvement in theatrical design and production, see Leonid Makar'ev's short book *S utra do vechera v teatre: Dlia detei srednego i starshego vozrasta* (Moscow: Molodaia gvardiia, 1930); and also the accounts included in Dina Shvarts, *Dnevniki i zametki* (St. Petersburg: Inapress, 2001).

8. Sosin, "Children's Theater," 356, 219–25; L. Shpet, *Sovetskii teatr dlia detei: Stranitsy istorii, 1918–1945* (Moscow: Iskusstvo, 1971), 299–338.

9. Omri Ronen, "Detskaia literatura i sotsialisticheskii realizm," in *Sotsrealisticheskii kanon*, ed. Hans Guenther and Evgeny Dobrenko (St. Petersburg: Akademicheskii proekt, 2000), 969–79; M. O. Chudakova, "Skvoz' zvyozdy k terniiam," in *Literatura sovetskogo proshlogo* (Moscow: Iazyki russkoi kul'tury, 2001), 339–66.

10. See Benjamin Bennett, *Theater as Problem: Modern Drama and Its Place in Literature* (Ithaca, NY: Cornell University Press, 1990).

11. Lev Cherniavskii and Sergei Rozanov, eds., *The Moscow Theatre for Children* (Moscow: Cooperative Publishing Society of Foreign Workers in the USSR, 1934), 4.

12. Cherniavskii and Rozanov, eds., *Moscow Theatre for Children*, 30–32; translation adjusted, replacing "Negro" with "African."

13. Sats called the production a musical pantomime with animation. Nataliia Sats, *Zhizn'—iavlenie polosatoe* (Moscow: Novosti, 1991), 150–51.

14. Nataliia Sats, *Novelly moei zhizni* (Moscow: Iskusstvo, 1979), 289–91; Sats, *Zhizn'—iavlenie polosatoe*, 239–40.

15. Sats, *Zhizn'—iavlenie polosatoe*, 239–40.

16. Sats, *Zhizn'—iavlenie polosatoe*, 239–40. The Central Children's Theater is discussed in Manon van de Water, *Moscow Theatres for Young People: A Cultural History of Ideological Coercion and Artistic Innovation, 1917–2000* (New York: Palgrave Macmillan, 2006), 113–36.

17. There had been some alternatives to *The Blue Bird* in Moscow. The private, imperial-era Korsh Theater and the Nezlobin Theater (whose troupe was housed in the building that would eventually be occupied by the Central Children's Theater) put on productions for children, especially around the holidays (Shpet, *Sovetskii teatr dlia detei*, 8–10).

18. In her memoirs, Sats framed the trip to see *Blue Bird* as a conversion experience that determined her career in theater. She cultivated the connection to the play, and to MAT, throughout her life, supervising and directing an opera and a ballet based on it, and selecting the figure of the blue bird as the logo of the Moscow Musical Theater for Children (which she founded in 1962, after her years in prison and exile). Sats, *Zhizn'—iavlenie polosatoe*, 40–43, 500–502, 532–43.

19. Shpet, *Sovetskii teatr dlia detei*, 21–28.

20. For an early, influential articulation of this narrative, see Aleksandra Brushtein, "Sovetskii teatr dlia detei," in *Sovetskii teatr*, ed. M. S. Grigor'ev (Moscow: VTO, 1947), 551–84.

21. Brushtein, "Sovetskii teatr dlia detei," 56–57, 67–69.

22. Galina Semyonovna Mironova, "P'esa-skazka E. L. Shvartsa 'Golyi korol': Satiricheskaia komediia ili antifashistskii pamflet?" *Vestnik Kostromskogo gosudarstvennogo universiteta* 28, no. 2 (2022): 155–59.

23. In 1928, Pavel Aleksandrovich Markov (1897–1980) was one of MAT's repertoire managers. Nikolai Mikhailovich Gorchakov (1898–1958) had arrived at the theater some three years earlier from the Vakhtangov Studio and had directed two other productions before being assigned to *Three Fat Men*. Both became actively involved in commissioning plays on Soviet themes for MAT.

24. A stage adaptation of *Envy* titled *A Conspiracy of Feelings* (*Zagovor chuvstv*) opened at the Vakhtangov Theater in the spring of 1929 and received a glowing review from the People's Commissar of Enlightenment, Lunacharsky. See A. V. Lunacharskii, "Zagovor chuvstv," in *Sobranie sochinenii, Tom 3: Stat'i, doklady, rechi, retsenzii (1904–1933)*, ed. G. I. Vladykin and U. A. Gural'nik (Moscow: Khudozhestvennaia literatura, 1964), 418–21.

25. The connection between *Three Fat Men* and *Blue Bird* was picked up by the critics, including V. Blium, "Na smenu 'Sinei ptitse,'" *Vecherniaia Moskva*, June 10, 1930, p. 3. As to the intended audience of *Three Fat Men*, Blium felt that it had none: "The production, in the end, is suitable neither for our children nor our adults."

26. A. V. Lunacharskii, "'Tolstiaki' i 'chudaki': Po povodu p'esy Oleshi v

MKhT," in *Sobranie sochinenii. Tom 2: Sovetskaia literatura: Stat'i, doklady, rechi (1904–1933)*, ed. V. R. Shcherbina (Moscow: Khudozhestvennaia literatura, 1964), 462–68.

27. Lunacharskii, "'Tolstiaki' i 'chudaki,'" 465–66.

28. "Eccentric"/"Chudak" was a condescending term for a member of the intelligentsia, as Aleksandr Afinogenov's 1929 eponymous play demonstrates. That play was still running when Lunacharsky's review of *Three Fat Men* appeared.

29. Lunacharsky's Russian is severe: "*proizvedenie . . . proizvodit vpechatlenie otsutstviia nasiliia nad soboi*" (Lunacharskii, "'Tolstiaki' i 'chudaki,'" 465). The word *nasilie* is defined as "violence," "coercion," and/or "abuse."

30. Lunacharskii, "'Tolstiaki' i 'chudaki,'" 464–65.

31. See Iurii Olesha, "Tri tolstiaka," in *Izbrannoe* (Moscow: Khudozhestvennaia literatura, 1974), 95–188, 183–84. The play follows the novel closely; there were just a handful of changes.

32. Lunacharsky describes the grotesquerie as an homage to E. T. A. Hoffmann ("'Tolstiaki' i 'chudaki,'" 466). In the failed revolt depicted in the first act, a haughty aristocrat loses her prosthetic body parts one by one. At the end of the play, she reappears intact.

33. The production relied on a revolving platform cued by the performers.

34. Iurii Olesha, "Igra v plakhu," in *Mnemozina: Dokumenty i fakty iz istorii otechestvennogo teatra XX veka*, ed. V. V. Ivanov, vol. 3 (Moscow: Artist. Rezhissyor. Teatr, 2004), 68–86.

35. The most detailed description of the production concept is in Nikolai Gorchakov's press release for *Three Fat Men*, Muzei Moskovskogo Khudozhestvennogo Akademicheskogo teatra f. 1, op. V. Zh., ed. khr. B/N, l. 1.

36. "At that time Stanislavskii was in France. In Paris he saw [Firmin] Gémier [a popular actor at the Théâtre Antoine]. During one conversation with him, he was talking about how theater has been deteriorating in the West, how it only thrives in the Soviet Union—and then mostly at MAT. So then he showed [Gémier] a magazine with a picture of some production that annoyed him to no end. 'Look!' he said. 'Look what they've come to, what a disgrace!' Gémier glanced at it and said: 'But wait, this is *Three Fat Men* at MAT.' Stanislavskii ordered the show canceled having never seen it himself" (Mikhail Ianshin, "[Vospominaniia ob Oleshe]," in *Vospominaniia o Iurii Oleshe*, ed. Olga Olesha-Suok [Moscow: Sovetskii pisatel', 1975], 122–23).

There were several reasons for the cancellation, including Stanislavsky's antagonism toward Nemirovich-Danchenko (who had signed off on *Three Fat Men*) and changes in cultural politics during the rehearsal period. The reviews of the production wouldn't have mattered; even those critics who considered Olesha's play "too idealistic" considered it better than *Blue Bird*, and the reviews were generally positive. Perhaps Stanislavsky felt that the moment for the production had passed; what seemed timely back in 1928 was old hat in 1930. Stanislavsky's refusal to give Erdman and Gorchakov (not to mention Olesha) the benefit of the doubt by watching an actual performance of *Three Fat Men* suggests concerns about the loss of creative consistency at MAT. Lunacharsky, for his part, saw no contradiction in having *Three Fat Men* appear at MAT at the same time as the theater's uncontroversially "realistic" productions, including Kirshon's *Bread*. See A. V. Lunacharskii, "O novykh p'esakh i osnovnykh liniiakh proletarskogo iskusstva," in *Sobranie sochinenii. Tom 2*, 469–76, esp. 473.

37. P. Baranchikov, "Moskovskii teatr dlia detei," *Izvestiia*, December 14, 1929, p. 3.

38. Sosin, "Children's Theater," 94–95; Shpet, *Sovetskii teatr dlia detei*, 137.

39. D. Luk'ianov, "Spektakl' o sovetskom shkol'nike," *Pravda*, February 11, 1936, p. 6.

40. Valentina Liubimova, "Seryozha Strel'tsov," in *P'esy dlia detei* (Moscow: Iskusstvo, 1975), 3–83.

41. Shpet, *Sovetskii teatr dlia detei*, 134.

42. Sosin, "Children's Theater," 160–62; Shpet, *Sovetskii teatr dlia detei*, 260.

43. G. W. F. Hegel, *Lectures on the Philosophy of History*, trans. John Sibree (New York: Dover, 1956), 167–68.

44. Karl Marx, *Capital: A Critique of Political Economy*, trans. Ben Fowkes, 3 vols. (London and New York: Penguin Books and New Left Review, 1981), 1: 270, 677.

45. Sats, *Zhizn'—iavlenie polosatoe*, 273–86.

46. Though children's theater was not one of Stanislavsky's main interests, he had an important indirect influence on its development through his mentorship in the late 1930s of Boris Zon, the artistic director (after 1935) of Leningrad's Theater for the Young Spectator. Zon directed most of the original productions of Evgeny Shvarts's plays in the 1920s and 1930s.

47. Sats, *Zhizn'—iavlenie polosatoe*, 279.

48. Sats never reconciled this stance with the fact that she began to write and direct plays for children when she was just a teenager.

49. Shpet, *Sovetskii teatr dlia detei*, 9.

50. "Travesty actress" is how the Russian term is rendered in Miriam Morton, ed., *Through the Magic Curtain, Theater for Children, Adolescents, and Youth in the USSR* (New Orleans, LA: Anchorage, 1979), a translation of Ol'ga Iarmolinskaia, ed., *Teatr detstva, otrochestva i iunosti* (Moscow: VTO, 1972). English-language theater does not, as a rule, use this term: an actress who performs a male role is known as a "breeches" actress; see Elizabeth Reitz Mullenix, *Wearing the Breeches: Gender on the Antebellum Stage* (New York: St. Martin's Press, 2000).

51. Children's theaters were the professional starting points for a significant

number of prominent actors, directors, and playwrights. The men among the actors employed by children's theaters moved on to "adult" theaters more frequently than the women, especially the travesty actresses.

52. Morton, ed., *Through the Magic Curtain*, 105; Iarmolinskaia, ed., *Teatr detstva*, 144.

53. N. I. Sats, *Deti prikhodiat v teatr: Stranitsy vospominanii* (Moscow: Iskusstvo, 1961), 214–21.

54. Emilii Mindlin, *Valentina Aleksandrovna Sperantova* (Moscow: Iskusstvo, 1951), 17, 33.

55. Mindlin, *Valentina Aleksandrovna Sperantova*, 17, 33.

56. V. Ashmarin, "Zdes' nastoiashchee" (1928), quoted in Sats, *Deti prikhodiat v teatr*, 217.

57. Mark Lipovetskii, "Utopiia svobodnoi marionetki," *Novoe literaturnoe obozrenie* 60 (2003): 263.

CHAPTER TWO

1. "*Ia sygrala Vas, Iurochka. Radek skazal, chto sebia—neverno. Khochu sebia. Eshcho raz khochu somknut'sia s Vami v tvorchestve. Zinaida.*" Violetta Gudkova, *Iurii Olesha i Vsevolod Meierkhol'd v rabote nad spektaklem "Spisok blagodeianii": Opyt teatral'noi arkheologii* (Moscow: Novoe literaturnoe obozrenie, 2002), 588, 594.

2. See Sheila Fitzpatrick, *Tear Off the Masks! Identity and Imposture in Twentieth-Century Russia* (Princeton, NJ: Princeton University Press, 2005).

3. Iurii Olesha, *Kniga proshchaniia*, ed. Violetta Gudkova (Moscow: Vagrius, 1999), 35–36. References to this book in the main text are given as *KP* followed by the page numbers from this 1999 edition and (where there are differences) those from the edition published a year before.

4. Iurii Olesha, *Ni dnia bez strochki* (Moscow: Khudozhestvennaia literatura, 1965); English translation: Yury Olesha, *No Day without a Line: From Notebooks*, trans. Judson Rosengrant (Evanston, IL: Northwestern University Press, 1998; orig. ed., Ann Arbor, MI: Ardis, 1979).

5. Gudkova contrasts the goals of her editorial project with those of *No Day without a Line*. The diary entries that appeared in that collection were heavily edited by the renowned literary theorist (and Olesha's brother-in-law) Viktor Shklovsky, Olesha's widow Olga Suok, and the literary critic Mikhail Gromov. In addition to excising those passages that detracted from the more conventionally "optimistic" (as Gudkova puts it) and ideologically unproblematic image of Olesha, the man and the writer, the editors sorted and reordered Olesha's fragments using necessarily artificial, often inconsistent, categories (Gudkova, "O Iurii Karloviche Oleshe i ego knige, vyshedshei bez vedoma avtora," *KP* 5–24, esp. 6, 21, 23). Judson Rosengrant offers a similar account of that publication in the pref-

ace to his translation of *No Day*, xv–xvii. Moreover, the material for *No Day* was drawn almost exclusively from Olesha's diaries of 1953 and 1960; the material from two earlier periods—1929–37 and 1939–46—was largely ignored. Using the manuscripts preserved at the Russian State Archive of Literature and Art (RGALI), Gudkova made public many (though still not all) of the diary entries from the 1930s and 1940s and restored the passages deleted in 1965. She also adopted what she claimed was a more flexible and authentic structure meant to allow "the complexity of Olesha's personality" to shine through (*KP* 24). Gudkova didn't attempt to reconstruct the chronology of the diaries (a task that, as she points out, is inherently complicated by Olesha's erratic date-keeping). Whatever their aesthetic value, her editorial decisions created several problems for the readers of *Kniga proshchaniia* (*A Book of Farewell*). Some records from 1931, for instance, precede those for 1930, whereas excerpts from 1929 appear, unmarked, in the middle of what looks like a coherent set of entries from the 1930 diary. Still, Gudkova appears to have adhered to the fundamental divisions between the three eras in Olesha's diary-keeping: 1929–1937, 1939–1946, and 1953–1960. My strategy in reading Olesha's diaries from the 1930s—the focus of this section—has been to indicate specific dates when they are clearly marked by Olesha or can be incontrovertibly established from the context.

6. On the banal aspects of the purges, see Sheila Fitzpatrick, *Everyday Stalinism: Ordinary Life in Extraordinary Times: Soviet Russia in the 1930s* (New York: Oxford University Press, 2000), 19–21; and Igal Halfin, *Stalinist Confessions: Messianism and Terror at the Leningrad Communist University* (Pittsburgh, PA: University of Pittsburgh Press, 2009).

7. For example: "*poiavliaetsia seriia rasskazov*"; "*neobkhodimo literature otrazhat'*"; "*kak chistilsia geroi*"; "*tekh, kto podvergalsia chistke.*"

8. *KP* 98/86. Judging by its location in *A Book of Farewell*, this entry was most likely made in 1930–31.

9. "I'm a very organic writer. I sit down to write—nothing. Absolutely nothing! Then something somewhere deep inside my brain starts slowly moving—and the knowledge of what I need and want to write arises from my physiology in utterly mysterious ways, which can never be perceived" (*KP* 36/21).

10. On temporality in diaries, and Olesha's in particular, see Irina Paperno, "What Can Be Done with Diaries?" *Russian Review* 63, no. 4 (October 2004): 561–73.

11. Jochen Hellbeck (whose pioneering study of diaries of the 1930s informs my own analysis) has argued that "the problem that Olesha grappled with . . . had less literary and more personal resonance; aesthetics formed a part of this problem, yet they were but an expression of an overriding problem of existential proportions," namely "capturing 'objective reality'" ("The Diary between Literature and History: A Historian's Critical Response," *Russian Review* 63, no. 4 [October 2004]: 624–25).

12. An earlier entry, from April 13, already included a version of the crucial formulation about the need to escape the world of conventional "literature," that is, belles lettres. Compare: "*April 13*. Instead of beginning a novel, I started a diary. It's much more interesting than belles lettres, more captivating. This sort of book produces incomparable interest. May Fate keep me away from fiction" (*KP* 33/17).—"*May 5*. Instead of beginning a novel, I started a diary. Readers are captivated by memoir literature. Speaking for myself, I find it much more pleasant to be writing memoirs than belles lettres. (I despise the latter)" (35/20). Note that in the May 5 entry, the distinctions between diary-keeping and memoir-writing are obliterated *en passant*.

13. "We, who are living in the era of the founding of the new human society, must leave copious testimony" (*KP* 35/20).

14. Elda Garetto and Irina Ozernaia, "Iz perepiski Iu. K. Oleshi s V. E. Meierkhol'dom i Z. N. Raikh," *Minuvshee* 10 (1992): 142–57, esp. 145–49.

15. The Olesha archive at RGALI contains two versions of the same letter, both dated April 30 (Garetto and Ozernaia, "Iz perepiski Iu. K. Oleshi," 147). Garetto and Ozernaia conclude that Olesha mailed another, at least third version of the letter.

16. Olesha voices this anxiety again in a later entry: "in the diaries, too, they try their belletristic tricks [*belletristicheskie shtuchki*] . . . And so—the diary, too, is a work of fiction [*proizvedenie belletristicheskoe*]" (*KP* 47/32). Here the term "belletristic" emphasizes contrivance as endemic to diary-writing. At the same time, the passage can be read as contrasting Olesha with writers who succumb to belletristic tricks. Olesha himself, after all, does not need to rely upon such tricks because he is writing a different kind of narrative. Still, the desire to purge belletrism is voiced again and again in the 1930s diaries (compare: "Oh how difficult it is to escape from belles lettres [*bezhat' ot belletristiki*]!" (93/79); "How boring. This is all fiction—and bad fiction at that [*Belletristika. I plokhaia*]" (103/90).

17. "The news of Mayakovsky's death has spread; the death that was the result of a misunderstanding . . . (how trite is this thing I'm writing . . .)"; and "[Mayakovsky] would get fixated on some line, and would then keep repeating it for days (Dear God, what is this wooden language I've got!)" (*KP* 38/23, 46/31).

18. This is not to say that Olesha preserves everything. Gudkova's introduction to the first edition of *A Book of Farewell* (*KP* 23–24) lists words and phrases that were deleted, restored, and deleted again. This habit explains Olesha's problems getting his diaries going. On October 28, 1940, for example, he writes: "This is a diary. There will be no style here. More than that—even if I feel that something is ungrammatical, I won't pay any attention to it. I want to express thoughts in whatever way need be, and not to have to waste any time on correcting an entry, even if I don't like the form it takes" (157/147).

19. On writing about death in diaries, see Irina Paperno, "Tolstoy's Diaries: The Inaccessible Self," in *Self and Story in Russian History*, ed. Laura Engelstein and Stephanie Sandler (Ithaca, NY: Cornell University Press, 2000), 242–65, esp. 244.

20. Aleksei Anastas'ev ("Stenogramma soznaniia," *Druzhba narodov*, no. 7 [July 1999]: 217–20) notes several instances of Olesha censuring himself and engaging in self-surveillance: "I drank not because I liked to drink; I drank because I didn't know what to do in between. That's nonsense, too, actually." "What a marvelous actor! A magician! I'm probably exaggerating."

21. In addition to routinely writing articles and giving interviews about their "artistic plans" and creative methods ("*Kak ia pishu*"), Soviet writers generated lengthier autobiographical or "personal" texts for public consumption: see Jochen Hellbeck, "Working, Struggling, Becoming: Stalin-Era Autobiographical Texts," *Russian Review* 60, no. 3 (July 2001): 340–59, esp. 355. Olesha acknowledges his interest in what he calls "memoir literature" in the April 13 and May 5, 1930, diary entries. The generic range of the diaries published in the 1930s can be gauged by comparing two texts: Marietta Shaginian, *Dnevniki, 1917–1931* (Leningrad: Izdatel'stvo pisatelei, 1932), and Viktor Shklovskii, *Dnevnik* (Moscow: Sovetskii pisatel', 1939). Shaginian's robust publication is a meticulous record of everything she's read, the trips she's taken, and the illnesses she's battled through. In the preface, she highlights the authenticity and immediacy of the material she is presenting to the public (pp. 8–10). Shklovsky's book, in contrast, is essentially a collection of polished essays on literature and the arts; it doesn't pretend to be a diary. In the preface, Shklovsky declares: "My diary—the record of my thoughts [*zapisi myslei*]—is devoted to history. I don't keep any other kind of diary" (p. 4).

22. On pilots as heroes, see Fitzpatrick, *Everyday Stalinism*, 72–73.

23. "Must find the New Person! Where is he? That very *muzhik* in European dress who was getting a shave yesterday next to me" (*KP* 39/23). Physicality and ideology are frequently aligned in Olesha's fiction. On masculinity in *Envy*, see Eliot Borenstein, *Men without Women: Masculinity and Revolution in Russian Fiction, 1917–1929* (Durham, NC: Duke University Press, 2000), 125–90. Olesha returns more than once to the image of the ideal man coming to the rescue when an electric cable falls on the street. See his "Strogii iunosha" ("The Strict Young Man," 1935), in *Izbrannoe*, ed. T. Sumarokovo (Moscow: Khudozhestvennaia literatura, 1974), 299–340, esp. 330–31.

24. On the complicated tradition of intelligentsia criticism and self-identification in the 1920s, see Igal Halfin, *From Darkness to Light: Class, Consciousness, and Salvation in Revolutionary Russia* (Pittsburgh, PA: University of Pittsburgh Press, 2000). See also Tatiana Smirnova, *"Byvshie liudi" Sovetskoi Rossii: Strategii i puti integratsii, 1917–1936 gody* (Moscow: Mir istorii, 2003).

25. Olesha's entry reads "January 20, 1930," but, as Gudkova points out

Notes to Pages 57–59

(*KP* 443/446), the context and the contents suggest a later date: 1931. Gudkova opens *Kniga proshchaniia* with this entry.

26. In his obituary of Stanislavsky, Olesha recalls his first impression of MAT: a touring production of *The Blue Bird* ("O velikom artiste," *Iskusstvo i zhizn'*, no. 9 [1938]: 338–46, esp. 338–39).

27. This entry is undated, but it begins with a description of Olesha praising the performance of the actress Bendina during a rehearsal. Vera Dmitrievna Bendina (1898–1974) played Suok in *Three Fat Men*.

28. MAT has been described as a collection of "people who neither belonged to neat *soslovie* categories nor defined themselves in other recognizable ways—neither gentry nor bureaucrat nor worker nor peasant." They were unified in their general distaste for "philistinism," "*meshchanstvo*," as an ethical rather than a social category. Edith W. Clowes, "Social Discourse in the Moscow Art Theater," in *Between Tsar and People: Educated Society and the Quest for Public Identity in Late Imperial Russia*, ed. Edith W. Clowes, Samuel D. Kassow, and James L. West (Princeton, NJ: Princeton University Press, 1991), 286.

29. The term Olesha uses, "*peredovoi*," connotes literary prominence, aesthetic experimentation, and (moderately) progressive political views.

30. *Three Fat Men* had a four-person directorial team. Nikolai Gorchakov (who initiated the project) and Elizaveta Telesheva held the titles of director and ran most of the rehearsals; Nemirovich-Danchenko and Ivan Moskvin were appointed the production's "artistic supervisors" and charged with providing guidance to, and approving the specific directorial choices of, the junior members of the team. According to Nemirovich-Danchenko's secretary Olga Bokshanskaia, the director had little interest in the production (Olga Radishcheva, *Stanislavskii i Nemirovich-Danchenko: Istoriia teatral'nykh otnoshenii, 1917–1938* [Moscow: Artist. Rezhisser. Teatr, 1999], 259), but nonetheless led several rehearsals in the spring of 1930 and supervised the final dress rehearsals. In a May 31 letter to Bokshanskaia, he complained that the theater was "dealing with an incredibly difficult set of circumstances. *Three Fat Men* was allowed to open before it was ready [*pushcheny syrymi*] . . . As a result I consider this season to have been full of unforgivable errors" (Liubov' Freidkina, *Dni i gody Vl. I. Nemirovicha-Danchenko: Letopis' zhizni i tvorchestva* [Moscow: Vserossiiskoe teatral'noe obshchestvo, 1962], 435).

31. "Where is the capital of the new world? Construction of new cities is being planned. So will the brightest minds perhaps converge upon an ore-mining hub?! It used to be that if a provincial town, Kazan or some other place, generated intellectual opposition to the capital, it thereby only helped solidify the authority of the capital. The capital reigned, and one wanted to overthrow it, to conquer it. Now, when there's only one truth, one opinion about what needs to be done, no single town can be in intellectual ascendancy. All towns are equal!" (*KP* 44/29).

32. At stake here is more than acknowledging the imperfection of one's social origins (though that alone, of course, is politically hazardous). The language of class struggle conflates ideological and aesthetic categories—the "bourgeois" is both a representative of the exploiting class ("proprietor [*sobstvennik*]") and a metaphor for mediocrity, a philistine (*obyvatel'*). Olesha's verdict, then, portends artistic failure as much as political unreliability.

33. As we saw, Lunacharsky uses the same categories as Olesha does—"new human being" and "bourgeois"—but his response to the question of Olesha's sociocultural identity also includes the category of "speaking on behalf of the 'eccentrics.'"

34. This mode is evident in other instances, like the passage where Olesha dismisses his affection for actors and writing parts for them with a curt "How sentimental" (*KP* 101/89).

35. Writing a new play while the previous one was in rehearsal was not unusual for Olesha: a year earlier, in the spring of 1929, he had been revising the playscript of *Three Fat Men* (he read it to the cast on March 2) just as *A Conspiracy of Feelings* was about to open at the Vakhtangov Theater. See Iurii Olesha, *P'esy. Stat'i o teatre i dramaturgii* (Moscow: Iskusstvo, 1968), 374–76, 381.

36. "Parallel to it, there exists an *obshchestvennost'* [community / public opinion] which is ignored, but which comprises the judgments and beliefs of a great number of people who continue to participate in the life of the nation by working for state agencies, at construction sites, you name it, even though they have no say in governing and regulating general need [*upravlenie i regulirovanie obshchei neobkhodimosti*] . . . This second *obshchestvennost'*, this second public opinion, which exists in the soviet state, is the primary material for my play" (*KP* 40/25). See Joseph Bradley, "Voluntary Associations, Civic Culture, and Obshchestvennost' in Moscow," in *Between Tsar and People*, ed. Clowes et al., 131–48.

37. Not naming the community is equivalent to renouncing one's status as an *intelligent*. To wit, "I'm tired of being an *intelligent*" (*KP* 37/22, 39/24, 55/41).

38. The term is "*sovetsko-chelovecheskaia komediia*," mixing "*sovetskii chelovek*" ("Soviet human being") with "*chelovecheskaia komediia*" ("human comedy").

39. It has been suggested that the diary entry where Olesha details his plans for the future play amounts to a précis of *A List of Good Deeds*. See Violetta Gudkova, "Golos fleity: O rannem variante p'esy, napisannoi Iuriem Oleshei dlia GosTIMa," in *Meierkhol'd i drugie: Dokumenty i materialy*, ed. O. M. Fel'dman (Moscow: OGI, 2000), 665–672, esp. 666; and Violetta Gudkova, *Iurii Olesha i Vsevolod Meierkhol'd v rabote nad spektaklem "Spisok blagodeianii"* (Moscow: Novoe literaturnoe obozrenie, 2002), 178–79. Subsequent references to the latter publication are abbreviated as *OM*. Features of character types Two

and Three recur, almost verbatim, in the drafts of *A List of Good Deeds*. Character types One, Three, Four, and Five resurface in the drafts of *The Death of Zand*, the play that had been commissioned by MAT before Stanislavsky canceled *Three Fat Men*.

40. Character One's slogan "You can't build a state if you are going to destroy the society at the same time" (*KP* 40/25) reprises the ambivalent dichotomy of the previous paragraphs. But this character has been fired from his job as part of a purge. According to Olesha's own stipulation a few lines above, this makes him less than an ideal spokesman for the *"obshchestvennost'"* whose representatives work diligently within the system. Character Five confronts his physical and moral degeneration and bemoans the poverty of his mind and spirit (41/26). Character Two, a woman, dreams of Europe—but only because it will make her "famous and rich"; Character Four decides to join the Communist Party because it will help his career prospects and hurt a rival (40/25). The characters' common predicament is never explicitly named. But in the description of Character Three, who hates himself for his "Hamletism" and "duality," being a member of the intelligentsia is singled out as the problem.

41. The sociological meaning of the term *kulak*—a rich peasant—is overshadowed by the word's larger metaphorical significance in the Soviet discourse of class struggle. In the 1930s, anyone accused of resisting or merely resenting the abolition of private property and forced collectivization could be described as a *kulak*; and all *kulaks*, no matter where they lived or what they did, were enemies of the Soviet way of life. See Fitzpatrick, *Everyday Stalinism*, 122–23.

42. This formulation is intricate wordplay: the abstract notion of the self (*sobstvennoe ia*, or *one's own I*) is linked to the taboo term for private property (*sobstvennicheskaia suchchnost'*) and, by extension, the will to possess, to make one's own, which defines the bourgeois worldview.

43. In Olesha's novel and play, Tutti the Heir Apparent is told by the Fat Men that his real heart has been replaced with a heart of steel, and so is incapable of feeling anything other than cruelty. The play's finale has Doctor Gaspar announcing that Tutti's heart is in fact real and he can be kind as well as cruel.

44. The bit of staging to which Meyerhold reacts is an homage to "biomechanics," Meyerhold's school of stylized theatrical movement.

45. *Uvidel dobrotu moego serdtsa // Meierkhol'd vseponimaiushchii, genii, ditia, ia sam.*

46. The accusation in question concerns Meyerhold's cold-heartedness. He was "a cool, aloof craftsman, an egotist. That's what they say about him. They don't like him, they want to laugh at him all the time, to surpass him and then have him considered *passé*. And this is Meyerhold we're talking about, the man who had provided them all with their daily bread. And they wolf down whatever he gives them and then condescend to him . . . Nonentities! Oh, they are doing

very well for themselves! Pathetic! Their tedious, petty affairs: always about their own selves, their own selves, and their own selves only . . . this fixation on being possessive . . ." (*KP* 104/91).

47. An entry about the *Three Fat Men* rehearsal (May 7, 1930) includes a satirical description of Ivan Moskvin, one of MAT's elders and the production's "artistic supervisor." He has a "big head, wide forehead—a nutcracker" (*KP* 42/27). Olesha then corrects himself: "My first impression was erroneous. I thought: an actor! That is—like all actors. Maybe this one a little higher: an 'itinerant' ['*peredvizhnik*']. Then I realized I was wrong" (42/27). By correcting his "first impression," Olesha explains the scale he's used to rank Moskvin: "an itinerant" (a reference to proponents of a realistic, socially engaged tradition in nineteenth-century Russian visual art) scores just above "an actor" but below a person with a genuine sense of humor, a person of dignity and palpable masculinity.

48. Olesha's diaries related the enormous impression left on him by Meyerhold's 1926 production of *The Inspector General* (*KP* 105/92). Later, in an article written for Meyerhold's sixtieth birthday, Olesha describes his lifelong fascination with Meyerhold (Iurii Olesha, "Liubov' k Meierkhol'du," in *Vstrechi s Meierkhol'dom*, ed. Mariia Valentei et al. [Moscow: Vserossiiskoe teatral'noe obshchestvo, 1967], 361–64, esp. 361).

49. The downturn in Meyerhold's fortunes and the tragedy of his arrest and execution in 1940 are well known. Still, a few details merit recapitulating to illustrate the radicality of the shift in Soviet culture between the first and second halves of the 1930s. In 1937, Platon Kerzhentsev published an article in *Pravda* about Meyerhold's activities and plans for a new theater. Kerzhentsev began with the devastating statistic that just one of the 700 theaters operating in the Soviet Union had failed to put on a production marking the twentieth anniversary of the Great October Socialist Revolution. That theater belonged to Meyerhold, who had failed in his effort to rid himself of the "mysticism, symbolism, and God-seeking stupefaction" of the theater of the pre-1917 period. The censors had instructed him to fall in line, to get with the ideological program by staging plays about the Soviet experience. Meyerhold had responded with an adaptation of Nikolai Ostrovskii's 1936 novel *How the Steel Was Tempered*, which had been published in serial form in a magazine (before being rewritten to accord with the artistic doctrine of Socialist Realism). It's a tale of overcoming: growing up in rags in the twilight of the tsarist era, getting thrown of school and finding purpose with the Bolsheviks. The hero, Pavka Korchagin, gets the girl (though, in the first version of the novel, he also loses her) and fights in the Civil War. He loses his vision and the use of one of his hands and both of his legs but nonetheless works in construction, tempering railroads as he himself has been tempered. It's about hard times, but the man and the epoch create each other and there's more to life than the pursuit of comfort. Meyerhold made it all seem "depress-

ing," in Kerzhentsev's opinion, and so it was pulled from the repertoire after its second official viewing. Meyerhold missed the big picture: the triumph of history over nature, and he turned the dream of socialism into a nightmare of suffering and disability. "Does Soviet art, do Soviet audiences, need such a theater?" Kerzhentsev asked. The answer was obvious, and it was the beginning of the end of Meyerhold's career. P. Kerzhentsev, "Chuzhoi teatr," *Pravda*, December 17, 1937, p. 4.

50. Tairov was written out of theater histories for decades after antisemitic campaigns resulted in closing the Kamerny Theater in 1950. Research by Dassia Posner and Svetlana Sboeva over the past couple of decades has revealed what a powerful, popular, and innovative director Tairov was, equal to if not surpassing Meyerhold.

51. Olesha emphasized this aspect of their relationship in a 1934 tribute: "Sometime later, Meyerhold directed a play of mine. I am proud of the fact that my thoughts provoked a response from this brilliant man of the stage . . . Once in rehearsal he suddenly said to me: "Cinderella!" That is, he saw in my concept something that escaped me—*he saw something I wanted to include in my concept and could not*" (Olesha, "Liubov' k Meierkhol'du," esp. 362; emphasis added).

52. The two complete translations of the play into English give the title as *A List of Blessings* (Michael Green and Jerome Katsell, in *The Complete Plays* [Ann Arbor, MI: Ardis, 1983], 69–126) and *A List of Good Deeds* (Andrew R. MacAndrew, in *Envy and Other Works* [Garden City, NY: Doubleday, 1967], 221–88). Both translations are based on the 1931 Russian edition. The Green-Katsell translation is hereafter referenced with the abbreviation *CP*, and the MacAndrew translation is referenced using the abbreviation *MA*.

53. Helen Muchnic, "Stories of Intrigue and Love," *New York Review of Books*, March 28, 1968, https://www.nybooks.com/articles/1968/03/28/stories-of-intrigue-and-love/.

54. I follow Violetta Gudkova's reconstruction of the genesis of the playscript (*OM* 166). There are two full drafts, the first submitted to the censor in October 1930, and the second (overhauling the first) included in the production promptbook. The latter text differs in important respects from the published versions (in *Krasnaia nov'*, 1931, no. 8, and the separate book edition issued simultaneously in Moscow, by Federatsiia, and in Berlin by Buch und Bühne); several scenes and passages from the October 1930 draft were reinserted into what is essentially the June 1931 playscript. This is the version reprinted in *KP* 91–169. When quoting from the playscript, I mark the discrepancies between the theatrical and the printed versions and address some of the crucial changes. Gudkova's book includes hundreds of pages of hitherto unpublished materials, most from the GosTIM collection at RGALI.

55. For an analysis of the changes demanded by Glavrepertkom, and an

account of the transformation of the play's ideological and dramatic structure, see *OM* 133–68, esp. 163.

56. *OM* 150–53. Olesha's previous theatrical efforts were also heavily censored. For a sampling of objections to *A Conspiracy of Feelings*, see A. Ia. Trabskii, ed., *Russkii sovetskii teatr 1926–1932: Chast' pervaia, Sovetskii teatr: Dokumenty i materialy* (Leningrad: Iskusstvo, 1982), 233–34. The "censor's copy" of *A Conspiracy of Feelings'* playscript is held by the Vakhtangov Theater Museum (op. 1, sviaz. 15, arkh. 471). The playscripts of *Three Fat Men* belong to the MAT Museum (the censorship copy of the first version is f. 1, op. BRCh, ed. khr. 460; the promptbook of the second version is f. 1, op. LCh, ed. khr. 509). In part because *A List of Good Deeds* was written specifically for the stage rather than being an adaptation of an existing work, the anxiety about the play's ideological and aesthetic suitability was much greater—as was the author's willingness to make changes to it.

57. Gudkova considers such editorial changes typical for a play written by a "thoughtful writer" of the period (*OM* 166). She admits, however, that the new dialogue created problems for the theater (168). The October 1930 playscript vetted by Glavrepertkom was hardly subversive: Lelia was not excessively idealized by the author; the Bolshevik she meets in Paris (in the first draft he is the Soviet ambassador) was in some ways even more likable than in the final version; and the treacherous émigré was sufficiently negative (163–64).

58. Gudkova (who edited *Kniga proschaniia*) pays special attention to the parallels between Olesha's diaries and the early drafts of *A List of Good Deeds* (*OM* 169–75, 233–37).

59. Those concerned with the latter question at times rehearsed, almost verbatim and rather unselfconsciously, the complaints leveled at Lelia in the prologue to Olesha's play. For Gudkova's detailed summary of the critical reception of the play, see *OM* chapter 10. She includes the transcripts of several discussions ("public" and "closed") of the playscript and the production in chapters 5 and 8; reviews are reprinted in chapter 8. For other reviews of the production, see Tatiana Lanina, ed., *Meierkhol'd v russkoi teatral'noi kritike: 1920–1938* (Moscow: Artist. Rezhisser. Teatr, 2000), 348–60.

60. Gudkova catalogs the responses of the critics to "the unity of the writer's and the director's visions" in *OM* 556.

61. In a brief study of the Hamlet motif in *A List of Good Deeds*, Sally Margaret O'Dell lists the places where Olesha cites Shakespeare's play but does not consider the implications of the allusions ("Yuri Olesha's Play 'Spisok Blagodeyaniya' [*sic!*] ('A List of Blessings,' 1931): Hamlet and the Artist in Soviet Society," *Proceedings of the Pacific Northwest Conference on Foreign Languages* 29, no. 1 [Spring 1978]: 136–39).

62. The Russian *Hamlet* tradition is the focus of Eleanor Rowe, *A Window on Hamlet* (New York: New York University Press, 1976).

63. "Hamlet's revolt questions the Good, but it knows the meaning of Evil, and engages in a ferocious fight with it": I. S. Turgenev, "Gamlet i Don-Kikhot," rvb.ru, https://rvb.ru/turgenev/01text/vol_05/01text/0181.htm. Turgenev acknowledges that Hamlet is capable of scheming and even cruelty, but he sees these qualities as remnants of a medieval worldview.

64. *"Gamlet, veroiatno, vel dnevnik": Turgenev, "Gamlet i Don-Kikhot."* Turgenev's reading of *Hamlet* is influenced by the early nineteenth-century German interpretations of the play, as well as his own studies of Schopenhauer.

65. The diary also symbolically links her self-image as an *intelligent* to her professional interests as an actress. "*Lelia.* Here's the notebook I've told you about . . . // *Semenova.* An actress's diary [*dnevnik aktrisy*]? // *Lelia.* No, this is no actress's diary. It's the secret of the Russian intelligentsia" (Olesha, *P'esy,* 98). Here "*dnevnik aktrisy*" refers to a notebook for character studies; the subtitle of Stanislavsky's book is "An Actor's Diary"—"*Dnevnik aktyora.*" The motif of Lelia confusing her acting notes/playscript with her diary appears in the earliest drafts (*OM* 52–53).

66. This parallel was noticed by the audience. See Aleksandr Orlinskii's discussion of the play at the FOSP Writer's Club, *OM* 491–92.

67. This version of Goncharova's monologue appeared in the final theatrical redaction; the passage in brackets was cut by Glavrepertkom and then restored by Olesha in the play's published edition (*P* [Olesha, *P'esy*] 110 / *CP* 82–83 / *MA* 237). For the original version of the monologue, see *OM* 202. An earlier version of the scene was published before the play opened (Iu. Olesha, "Tema intelligenta," *Stroika*, March 31, 1930, p. 2). As with *Three Fat Men*, the English version of the play is based on the two available published translations, by Green and Katsell and by MacAndrew.

68. "*Lelia . . .* A set of familiar associations has been destroyed . . . Many concepts just drift around, bouncing off the eye and the ear, failing to penetrate one's consciousness" (*P* 100 / *CP* 76 / *MA* 228).

69. Gudkova suggests that Chaplin's films weren't shown in the Soviet Union because the government couldn't afford the rights for them (*OM* 235). On Chaplin in the Soviet theater, including the Meyerhold connection, see Spencer Golub, *The Recurrence of Fate: Theatre and Memory in Twentieth-Century Russia* (Iowa City: University of Iowa Press, 1994), 100–122.

70. *Pokazyvat' "Gamleta" novomu chelovechestvu* (*OM* 193, 199; the October 1930 version).

71. "*Lelia (reading the note) . . .* 'The play we have been shown, *Hamlet,* was obviously written for the intelligentsia. A working man can't understand a thing in it, it's foreign and belongs to ancient history. Why bother doing it?'—*Hamlet* is the finest work created by the art of the past. That's my opinion. In all probability, Russian audiences will never see *Hamlet* again, so I decided to do it one more time" (*P* 93 / *CP* 71 / *MA* 223).

72. See Yana Meerzon, "On Expressionistic Mysterium: Michael Chekhov's Tragic Character on Page and on Stage," *Stanislavsky Studies* 4, no. 2 (2016): 137–55.

73. Chekhov's defection is a subject of Stalin's 1929 letters to the RAPP leadership and to the playwright Bill'-Belotserkovskii. "There can be no doubt that Chekhov went abroad not out of love for the Soviet public [*obshchestvennost'*; this is the same term that Olesha uses to denote his idea of the new intelligentsia] and, in general, behaved like a swine—although that, in turn, does not mean that we have to kick all the Chekhovs out of here [*vsekh Chekhovykh gnat' v sheiu*]" (Andrei Artizov and Oleg Naumov, eds., *Vlast' i khudozhestvennaia intelligentsiia: Dokumenty TsK RKP(b)-VKP(b), VChK-OGPU-NKVD o kul'turnoi politike, 1917–1953 gg.* [Moscow: Demokratiia, 1999], 109–12). On Mikhail Chekhov's interpretation of *Hamlet*, see Vladislav Ivanov, "Michael Chekhov and Russian Existentialism," in *Wandering Stars: Russian Emigre Theatre, 1905–1940*, ed. Laurence Senelick (Iowa City: University of Iowa Press, 1992), 140–57, esp. 149–54.

74. Evgeniia V. Brodskaia, "P'esa Iu. K. Oleshi 'Spisok blagodeianii' v zerkale sovetskoy kritiki: O statuse sovetskoi intelligentsii v nachale 1930-x gg.," *Vestnik RGGU: Seriia 'Istoriia, Filologiia, Kul'turologiia, Vostokovedenie,'* no. 11 (2018): 20.

75. Nikolai Akimov's 1932 production at the Vakhtangov Theater was a short-lived scandal. Though the idea of staging *Hamlet* was mooted by several Moscow directors in the 1930s and 1940s, including Meyerhold and Nemirovich-Danchenko, it wasn't staged again in Moscow until 1954. (It had been produced in a few provincial theaters before then.)

76. Aleksandr Gladkov, *Meierkhol'd, Tom. 2: Piat' let s Meierkhol'dom, Vstrechi s Pasternakom* (Moscow: Soiuz teatral'nykh deiatelei, 1990), 156–64. Meyerhold even planned to celebrate the opening of his new theater space with *Hamlet*, and commissioned Boris Pasternak to translate it.

77. After *The Inspector General* and *Woe from Wit*, Meyerhold staged a series of Soviet plays; *A List of Good Deeds* was preceded by Ilya Selvinskii's *Second Army Commander* (*Komandarm 2*, 1929), Vladimir Mayakovsky's *The Bathhouse* (*Bania*, 1930), and Vsevolod Vishnevskii's *The Ultimate Battle* (*Poslednii reshitel'nyi*, 1931).

78. *P* 94 / *CP* 71 / *MA* 223.

79. The Lelia-Margerette exchange was based upon an anecdote concerning Mikhail Chekhov's attempts to establish himself as an actor in Berlin. Chekhov, too, thought he was being asked to play Hamlet; but his manager wanted him to do a cabaret act. Olesha heard the story from Meyerhold, who visited Chekhov in Berlin in 1930. Some fifteen years later, Chekhov described the incident in "Zhizn' i vstrechi" (1944–45), reproduced in M. A. Chekhov, *Literaturnoe nasledie*, ed. N. B. Volkova et al., 2 vols. (Moscow: Iskusstvo, 1995), 1: 182–83.

The language of Chekhov's written account echoes the dialogue of the scene from *A List of Good Deeds*, and it seems plausible that Chekhov's recollections were in turn influenced by Olesha's play (which was published in Berlin in 1931 and available abroad).

80. This is how Margerette's monologue appears in the production promptbook. In the published redaction of the play, the final lines are: "Get it? The crowd goes wild, laughter, standing ovation" (*P* 134 / *CP* 100 / *MA* 259).

81. *OM* 421, 425–26. One of Meyerhold's additions, in rehearsal, was Lelia's line "I thought this was a theater, but this is a torture chamber" (*OM* 337–38).

82. Meyerhold himself emphasized the meta-theatrical elements during rehearsals.

83. While the Russian spelling of Ulalume's name—*Ulialium*—is identical to the spelling (in the Russian translation) of the title of Edgar Allan Poe's well-known ballad, there is little evidence of an allusion to Poe. The singer's name is more likely derived from the Russian spelling of "ooh la la!"—*"ulialia"*—with its connotations of stereotyped (decadent) French culture. At the same time, his name is a kind of parodic refraction of Lelia's (emphasized by the presence of the *–lia-* syllable and the doubling of the 'l' in both names: ***Lyolia*** / ***Ulialium***).

84. In the earlier versions of the playscript (and later in the published edition), Olesha has Lelia mistakenly assume that "the great artist" to whom Margerette is referring is her hero, Charlie Chaplin. This line was cut late in the rehearsal process, but in the following scene, during Lelia's wanderings through Paris, she meets a homeless man dressed up like Chaplin.

85. The length and the content of the Margerette monologue about Ulalume varied in rehearsal and in performance; the version I reference here comes from the final printed redaction (*P* 137 / *CP* 102 / *MA* 262 and *OM* 211). The production promptbook shows the cuts in the monologue; in a characteristic move, Meyerhold shifted the emphasis from talking about Ulalume's technique (in the monologue) to showing him in action (in Ulalume's seduction of Lelia) (*OM* 337–39).

86. This could be seen as a theatrical paraphrase of the motif in Olesha's diaries: "Drumroll, please! Creativity is a profoundly physiological activity!" (*KP* 36/21).

87. In the original, Ulalium's name ends in a consonant (м), which is masculine. The performers who played him at the Meyerhold Theater were male.

88. Nicholas Ridout analyzes the destabilizing and empowering effects of face-to-face encounters in the theater (based in part on his analysis of Kleist's "Marionette Theater" essay) in *Stage Fright*, 15–30.

89. The two most important moments, in this respect, occur in the prologue in Moscow (*P* 93 / *CP* 71 / *MA* 223) and during Lelia's conversation with a Soviet representative in Paris: "*Lelia.* These days a woman must think like a man. Men's accounts are being settled" (*P* 145 / *CP* 107 / *MA* 268). For an illuminat-

ing discussion of gender in Olesha's plays, see Borenstein, *Men without Women*, 125–90.

90. Ulalume, the paradigmatic "representative of the decadent and vulgar bourgeois art," was, according to one response, "lyrical" and "appealing" in manner; according to another, he had "grandeur, elegance and beauty, power and superiority" (*OM* 531).

91. When Ulalume entered, Margerette quite literally offered Lelia to him: "I've prepared her for you!" (*OM* 338).

92. In the words of critic Iurii Yuzovskii, Ulalume is "the only human being who is Lelia's kin [*rodnoi*]. Essentially, Ulalume *is* Lelia" (review of June 15, 1931; quoted in *OM* 531).

93. Before the rehearsals began, Meyerhold described the play to Olesha as "your new major tragedy" (*OM* 141). At the cast meeting, with Olesha present, he described the revisions moving the play from a "heroic poem" to "a tragedy" (159). During the rehearsals, Meyerhold introduced what he called "gestures of ancient tragedy" into several scenes, including Lelia's visit to the Globe Music Hall (411, 422).

94. Creating the design and supervising set construction was the responsibility of Sergei Vakhtangov, who was listed as the "architect" of the production in the program (*OM* 507; *KP* 32–33/17).

95. The "lever" metaphor belongs to Nikolai Tarabukin: "Right when the building of the State Meyerhold Theater was due for a major renovation, Meyerhold could stand it no longer and *turned the stage with a lever* [*povernul rychagom stsenu*]. Not only did he 'squeeze' ['*smial'*] the floor, but he also broke apart [*razlomal*] the frame [of the conventional proscenium]" (Nikolai Tarabukin, "Zritel'noe oformlenie v GosTIMe; K desiateletnemu iubileiu teatra," in *Meierkhol'd i khudozhniki*, ed. Alla Mikhailova [Moscow: Galart, 1995], 315–21, esp. 320; emphasis added). On the critics' reaction to Meyerhold's set, see *OM* 517–19.

96. "This community [*obshchestvennost'*] is regulated by no one . . . it is supported by a powerful mechanism which everyone knows about—a mechanism whose gears shift on their own, even though no one is standing by the lever [*rychag*] waiting to push it; in fact, it's not even clear where that lever is or what it looks like" (*KP* 40/25).

97. Tony Howard, *Women as Hamlet: Performance and Interpretation in Theatre, Film and Fiction* (Cambridge: Cambridge University Press, 2007), 160–82.

98. Compare Olesha's declaration, "I want to write a book about Meyerhold directing my play" (*KP* 25/9), with his earlier attempt to account for his relationship with Meyerhold as part of his new, non-belletristic project: "I'm beginning a book *about my own life* [*o moei sobstvennoi zhizni*]. Look: I just came home—tonight, December 10, 1930—and I'm starting to write a book about my own

life. Starting by writing down that I came back tonight . . . Alright then: I came back in the evening. I was at Meyerhold's" (*KP* 103/90; emphasis added). In this conception, Meyerhold is one of a long list of topics: "So then quite a few things are piling up: on Z. Raikh, on smoking, on how far I've come" (105/93).

99. Even the entry in which Olesha announces the beginning of his work on a documentary account (on January 20, 1931) is bound by the limitations of the diary's narrative strategies and fails to serve as an account either of Meyerhold or his production. Olesha begins to explain that the play whose production he will be documenting examines the notions of "the Soviet" and "the European." But that generalization leads Olesha to a passage of self-surveillance. While he doesn't feel the need to justify his attempt at examining the meaning of "the Soviet," writing about "the European" is suspect: "I've never been to Europe. To go there, to travel to Germany, France, Italy is a dream of mine. Sometimes I even see the Abroad in my sleep. What kind of a dream is this? A reactionary one, perhaps? Let me try to sort it all out" (*KP* 9). To ease his suspicions Olesha goes all the way back to his childhood, to the first images of the West he remembers. His impressionistic sketch of an imagined Europe explicitly evokes the central themes and metaphors of *A List of Good Deeds* (and so might be considered appropriate subject matter for a book about the play). But the play itself is never brought up; nor is Olesha able to convince himself that the European myth is not a "reactionary" topic, and the narrative trails off. In the next entry, Olesha begins the documentary account from scratch.

100. This account is given in an entry dated March 15, 1931, about two months after Olesha said that he would be writing a book about Meyerhold directing the production. The version Olesha read to the cast on March 14 was revised before the production opened (*OM* 166).

101. "The table was lit by an instrument from the wings, and in the light Meyerhold's face had a greenish tint . . . Silence. The lighting instrument is blinding me. I turn my head in that direction and I can see a lamp which seems to me to have melted; my eyes, which are unused to this lighting, perceive not one but several lamps, all of them wired together" (*KP* 29/13, 30–31/15). In addition to echoing the Stanislavsky passage quoted in my introduction, the motif of blindness by light evokes a central theme of Olesha's fiction: vision as a metaphor for the artistic process. See Nils Ake Nilsson, "Through the Wrong End of Binoculars: An Introduction to Jurij Olesa," in *Major Soviet Writers*, ed. Edward J. Brown (London: Oxford University Press, 1973), 254–79.

102. Olesha insists upon Meyerhold's metaphorical "centrality": "There are people who stand in the middle [*posredine*] of a family, in the middle [*posredi*] of a household—at an intersection of other family members' sympathies and disappointments, the struggles of their predilections and character traits—these people stand in the middle of the household, and without them the household ceases to function. If our artistic community, our Art, is a household, Meyerhold

stands in that middle [*posredi*] of that household" (*KP* 30/14). Even though Olesha sits in the middle of the stage during the reading, in his account Meyerhold occupies that position.

103. There are several references to *Hamlet* in Olesha's plays. The drafts of *A List of Good Deeds* include references to the act 5 gravediggers' scene and Hamlet's discovery of Yorick's skull (*OM* 229).

104. It is unclear when or how the decision to close the production was made (*OM* 581). The play was still part of the Meyerhold Theater's repertoire through the 1932–33 season and could have been performed into 1934.

105. For the most overtly polemical reading of Olesha's career, see A. Belinkov, *Sdacha i gibel' sovetskogo intelligenta: Iurii Olesha* (Moscow: RIK Kul'tura, 1997). As the book's title, "The Capitulation and Demise of a Soviet *Intelligent*," attests, Belinkov's Olesha is a collaborator. *A List of Good Deeds* (discussed in the chapter entitled "The Swallowed Flute" ["Proglochennaia fleita," 297–411]) represents, for Belinkov, the lowest point of Olesha's journey from a sensitive and sincere writer to a hack ideologue. Violetta Gudkova's studies of Olesha's *Kniga proshchaniia* and *A List of Good Deeds* ("Mechta o golose," *Novoe literaturnoe obozrenie*, no. 38 [1999]: 143–65, esp. 143–44, and 162–63; and "O Iurii Karloviche Oleshe i ego knige, vyshedshei bez vedoma avtora," in Iurii Olesha, *Kniga proshchaniia* [Moscow: Vagrius, 1999], 5–24, esp. 12) dispute Belinkov's claims. "With respect to Olesha's and Meyerhold's joint production of *A List of Good Deeds*," she writes, "I see not their 'capitulation and demise' (A. Belinkov), but a persistent, not entirely futile struggle in unfair circumstances, the struggle of the private individual against the emergent totalitarian regime" (*OM* 12).

106. Hellbeck, "The Diary between Literature and History." According to Hellbeck, the quote is from a draft of this paper; it does not appear in the version published in the *Russian Review* in 2004 (personal communication with Simon Morrison, August 26, 2024).

CHAPTER THREE

1. I. K. Luppol, M. M. Rosental', and S. M. Tretiakov, eds., *Pervyi vsesoiuznyi s'ezd sovetskikh pisatelei, 1934: Stenograficheskii otchyot* (Moscow: Sovetskii pisatel', 1990), 395. Subsequent references to this report are listed as *SSP* with the corresponding page number(s).

2. Violetta Gudkova, *Rozhdenie sovetskikh siuzhetov: Tipologiia otechestvennoi dramy 1920-kh-nachala 1930-kh godov* (Moscow: Novoe literaturnoe obozrenie, 2008).

3. "*Est' khoroshie p'esy, no oni bol'shie, nam poka s nimi ne spravit'sia*" (*SSP* 395).

4. Gorky's 1933 article "On Plays" ("O p'esakh," in M. Gor'kii, *Sobranie sochinenii v tridtsati tomakh* [Moscow: Khudozhestvennaia literatura, 1949–56],

26: 425–29) explains his political position and includes passages of self-criticism along with words of advice for young writers. He remained an enthusiastic theatergoer in the years ahead and offered advice on draft plays. Save for defending his RAPP protégés against attack, he stayed out of the debates about the future of Soviet theater.

5. "O zadachakh RAPP na teatral'nom fronte: Postanovlenie Sekretariata RAPP," *Sovetskii teatr* 2, no. 10–11 (1931): 4–16.

6. See A. N. Anastas'ev, ed., *Istoriia sovetskogo dramaticheskogo teatre v shesti tomakh* (Moscow: Nauka, 1966–71), 3: 34–35.

7. The production is discussed in Nick Worrall, *Modernism to Realism on the Soviet Stage: Tairov, Vakhtangov, Okhlopkov* (Cambridge: Cambridge University Press, 1989), 161–66.

8. V. Kirpotkin, *Nasledie Pushkina i kommunizm* (Moscow: Khudozhestvennaia literatura, 1936), 5.

9. *SSP* 409. The word Kirshon uses here—*chudak*—is code for an intellectual, a member of the intelligentsia.

10. Valerii Kirpotin, *Rovesnik zheleznogo veka: Memuranaia kniga* (Moscow: Zakharov, 2006), 177–206.

11. "Rech' Stalina na sobranii pisatelei-kommunistov na kvartire Gor'kogo 20 oktiabria 1932 g.," in *Bol'shaia tsenzura: Pisateli i zhurnalisty v Strane Sovetov 1917–1956*, ed. Leonid Maksimenkov (Moscow: Materik, 2005), 261–66.

12. Kornelii Zelinskii, "Odna vstrecha u Gor'kogo (Zapis' iz dnevnika)," *Voprosy literatury*, no. 5 (1991): 144–70.

13. Zelinskii, "Vstrecha u Gor'kogo," 160–61.

14. Kirpotin, *Rovesnik zheleznogo veka*, 188–89.

15. Kirpotin, *Rovesnik zheleznogo veka*, 185–86.

16. m-jake, "Dzhugashvili tozhe kritik—2," livejournal, September 11, 2016, https://m-jake.livejournal.com/523807.html.

17. "Rech' Stalina 20 oktiabria 1932 g.," 261–66.

18. "Rech' Stalina 20 oktiabria 1932 g.," 263.

19. "Rech' Stalina 20 oktiabria 1932 g.," 264.

20. "Rech' Stalina 20 oktiabria 1932 g.," 264.

21. "Kirshon-Stalinu o svoei novoi p'ese: Otvet Stalina," in *Bol'shaia tsenzura: Pisateli i zhurnalisty v Strane Sovetov 1917–1956*, ed. Leonid Maksimenkov (Moscow: Materik, 2005), 302–3.

22. Vishnevskii picked up on this detail in a diary entry dated April 3, 1934: "Art here is now moving toward more or less omnivorous use, anything is fair game: classics, vaudevilles in underpants (Kirshon, 2nd prize), music-hall, variety shows, radio, 'Europe' . . .—The organism of the USSR is getting healthier—it wants to eat, eat, and eat" (RGALI f. 1038, op. 1, ed. khr. 2071, courtesy of Il'ia Veniavkin, trans. Dassia Posner).

23. These were the two plays running in Moscow's theaters in advance of

the First All-Union Congress of Soviet Writers. Leonid Maksimenkov, "Ocherki nomenklaturnoi istorii sovetskoi literatury (1932–46): Stalin, Bukharin, Zhdanov, Shcherbakov i drugie. I," *Voprosy literatury*, no. 4 (2003): 212–58.

24. Elena Bulgakova, *Dnevnik* (Moscow: Knizhnaia palata, 1990), 117.

25. Quoted in Ridout, *Stage Fright*, 49.

CHAPTER FOUR

1. Aleksandr Afinogenov, "Avtobiografiia," *Edinyi front: Gazeta Khar'kovskogo teatra russkoi dramy*, November 1, 1933, p. 3. Two earlier versions of the text, not intended for publication and excluding this detail, are compiled as "Avtobiografii Afinogenova Aleksandra Nikolaevicha. 3 iiulia 1926–1931," RGALI, f. 2172, op. 1, ed. khr. 11, ll. 2–3.

2. Aleksandr Afinogenov, "Otkrytoe pis'mo moim budushchim rezhissyoram," *Edinyi front*, November 1, 1933, pp. 3–4. The same letter was published in a special brochure: Andrei Bartoshevich, *Dramaturgiia Aleksandra Afinogenova* (Kharkov: Teatr russkoi dramy, 1933), 100–112.

3. Il'ia Veniavkin, "'Nebogatoe oformlenie': 'Lozh' Aleksandra Afinogenova i stalinskaia kul'turnaia politika 1930-kh godov," *Novoe literaturnoe obozrenie* 108, no. 2 (2011): 140.

4. "Rech' Stalina 20 oktiabria 1932 g.," in *Bol'shaia tsenzura: Pisateli i zhurnalisty v Strane Sovetov 1917–1956*, ed. Leonid Maksimenkov (Moscow: Materik, 2005), 264.

5. W. B. Worthen, *Modern Drama and the Rhetoric of Theater* (Berkeley: University of California Press, 1992), 1.

6. Lars T. Lih, "Melodrama and the Myth of the Soviet Union," in *Imitations of Life: Two Centuries of Melodrama in Russia*, ed. Louise McReynolds and Joan Neuberger (Durham, NC: Duke University Press, 2002), 178–207; Julie A. Cassiday, *The Enemy on Trial: Early Soviet Courts on Stage and Screen* (DeKalb: Northern Illinois University Press, 2000), 83–94.

7. After chatting with his neighbor Vsevolod Ivanov in the writers' enclave of Peredelkino about everything "that was happening" in Moscow in 1937—the show trials, the arrests of "wreckers," saboteurs in the state "apparatus"—Afinogenov extolled Stalin's resolve: "Only he could have decided on such a pitiless, massive eradication of everything that's grown over, become offensive, putrid. This is the best proof that our government belongs to the masses and relies on the masses to fuel the apparatus with new energy . . . But if our government relied exclusively on the apparatus, it would never have embarked on such a general purge, a genuine smoking out of enemies from every nook and crevice. We still don't know much, or rather we know very little, almost nothing—we can only speculate from the outside about the scope of the cleansing operation. But how I want to know more, to know the roots and causes of everything—

because then the wisdom and genius of Stalin will emerge even brighter, more complete! . . . If only we were allowed to read one of the many interrogation reports of one of those who did terrible harm in secret as members of the apparatus!" RGALI f. 2172, op. 3, ed. khr. 5 (August 29, 1937, diary entry, courtesy of Il'ia Veniavkin).

8. Aleksandr Karaganov, *Zhizn' dramaturga: Tvorcheskii put' Aleksandra Afinogenova* (Moscow: Sovetskii pisatel', 1964).

9. On the rhetoric of stage realism more generally, see Worthen, *Modern Drama and the Rhetoric of Theater*, 12–29, 54–62. On Stanislavsky's technique as applied to "realistic" productions, see Sharon Marie Carnicke, *Stanislavsky in Focus: An Acting Master for the Twenty-First Century* (New York: Routledge, 2009).

10. Osip Mandel'shtam, "Khudozhestvennyi teatr i slovo," in *Sobranie sochinenii*, vol. 2 (Moscow: Art-Biznes-Tsentr, 1993), 333–35.

11. Just five days before reading the first draft of *Fear* to MAT actors, Afinogenov attacked Stanislavsky at a RAPP conference on theater ("V reshitel'noe nastuplenie na teatral'nom fronte," *Vecherniaia Moskva*, January 27, 1931, p. 3). *Fear* was MAT's second peace offering to RAPP. Earlier in 1931, the theater had staged Kirshon's *Bread*.

12. Valerii Kirpotin, "U istokov," *Novyi mir*, no. 8 (August 1984): 205–16, esp. 209. Gorky often got emotional in the theater.

13. A. Charnyi, "Pochemu 'Strakh'?" *Izvestiia*, January 7, 1932, p. 3.

14. The standard Russian edition of *Strakh* is in Aleksandr Afinogenov, *Izbrannoe v dvukh tomakh: P'esy, stat'i, vystupleniia*, ed. K. N. Kirilenko and V. P. Korshunova (Moscow: Iskusstvo, 1977), 1: 185–244. It matches the second edition of the play published by GIKhL in Leningrad in 1932. In this chapter I quote from the English translation (Eugene Lyons, *Six Soviet Plays* [Boston: Houghton Mifflin, 1934], 393–469) with some refinements. After each quotation, and using the abbreviation S, I list the page number from the English translation in parentheses before the page number from the standard Russian edition.

15. In the first edition of the play—A. Afinogenov, *Strakh* (Leningrad: GIKhL, 1931), 69—Klara went even further, stating that the current level of fear felt by "class enemies" needed to be multiplied tenfold. This edition was used for the production in Leningrad. The production in Moscow relied on the second edition completed at the end of 1931.

16. The promptbook for the MAT production includes a brief exchange, at the end of the interrogation scene, in which the OGPU investigator tells Borodin that he is free to go—"out on the street, back home, wherever you want" (Muzei Moskovskogo Khudozhestvennogo Akademicheskogo teatra f. BRCh, ed. khr. 287, l. 131). This ending was not included in the published editions of the play.

17. Lih, "Melodrama and the Myth of the Soviet Union," 188–89.

18. See Igal Halfin, *From Darkness to Light: Class, Consciousness, and Sal-*

vation in Revolutionary Russia (Pittsburgh, PA: University of Pittsburgh Press, 2000).

19. Letter of October 4–5, 1931, in I. N. Solov'yova, ed., *Pis'ma O. S. Bokshanskoi Vl. I. Nemirovichu-Danchenko v dvukh tomakh (1922–1942)* (Moscow: Moskovskii Khudozhestvennyi teatr, 2005), 2: 12.

20. Cassiday, *Enemy on Trial*, 175–81.

21. One of the first reviews of the play conflated Borodin's lines with statements attributed to Pavlov to make a point about the play's topicality: Isaak Kruti, "Strakh," *Sovetskii teatr* 2, no. 7 (July 1931): 20–25, esp. 20.

22. Radishcheva, *Stanislavskii i Nemirovich-Danchenko*, 280–83.

23. Afinogenov changed the playscript based on suggestions from both Gosdrama and MAT, since they were rehearsing *Fear* at the same time. Elena Poliakova, *Teatr i dramaturg: Iz opyta raboty Moskovskogo Khudozhestvennogo teatra nad p'esami sovetskikh dramaturgov, 1917–1941 gg.* (Moscow: Vserossiiskoe teatral'noe obshchestvo, 1959), 180–223.

24. *O "Strakhe": Obrabotannaia stenogramma vyezdnogo zasedaniia prezidiuma leningradskogo oblastnogo otdela soiuza rabotnikov iskusstv v Gosudarstvennom teatre dramy 15 i 27 iiunia 1931 goda* (Leningrad: Lenoblrabis, 1931), 14–15. Additional references to this edition are given in parentheses, with the abbreviation *OS*.

25. Worthen, *Modern Drama and the Rhetoric of Theater*, 15–19.

26. Petrov relied on the precepts of theatrical realism. He took his cast on a field trip to Ivan Pavlov's laboratory at the Academy of Sciences to observe the behavior of actual scientists; the actress playing the part of Makarova snuck into one of Pavlov's seminars to observe him teaching (*OS* 70).

27. N. V. Petrov, *50 i 500* (Moscow: VTO, 1960), 316–20; Vasilii Rafalovich, *Vesna teatral'naia: Vospominaniia* (Leningrad: Iskusstvo, 1971), 157–60.

28. Afinogenov, *Izbrannoe v dvukh tomakh*, 1: 500.

29. Petrov, *50 i 500*, 316.

30. Petrov, *50 i 500*, 313. On the touring version of the Gosdrama production of *Fear*, see Aleksandr Borisov, *Iz tvorcheskogo opyta* (Moscow: Iskusstvo, 1954), 167–70.

31. S. Amaglobeli et al., "'Strakh' v Leningrade i 'Strakh' v Moskve," *Literaturnaia gazeta*, December 23, 1931, p. 4; M. Charnyi, "Miting spektaklei," *Izvestiia*, April 3, 1932, p. 4.

32. Osaf Litovskii, "Pis'mo zaveduiushchemu khudozhestvennoi chast'iu MKhAT i V. G. Sakhnovskomu 27 dekabria 1931 g.," Muzei Moskovskogo Khudozhestvennogo Akademicheskogo teatra f. 1, sezon 1931/32, 1.1 ob. For the details of the administrative maneuvering, see Radishcheva, *Stanislavskii i Nemirovich-Danchenko*, 282–83.

33. Inna Solov'yova, "Strakh," in *Moskovskii Khudozhestvennyi teatr: Sto*

let, vol. 1, ed. Anatolii Smelianskii (Moscow: Moskovskii Khudozhestvennyi teatr, 1998), 128–30.

34. On Stanislavsky's participation in the rehearsals of *Fear*, see Irina Vinogradskaia, *Zhizn' i tvorchestvo K. S. Stanislavskogo: Letopis'*, 2nd ed., 4 vols. (Moscow: Moskovskii Khudozhestvennyi teatr, 2003), 4: 162–83.

35. These reports are contained in the letters sent to Nemirovich-Danchenko by his assistant Olga Bokshanskaia. Solov'yova, ed., *Pis'ma O. S. Bokshanskoi Vl. I. Nemirovichu-Danchenko*, 1: 791–94, 2: 11–15, 45–65.

36. On Leonidov's career, see Mikhail Rogachevskii, *Tragedia tragika: Leonid Leonidov, Dokumental'noe povestvovanie* (Moscow: Iskusstvo, 1998).

37. On the 1904 production of *The Cherry Orchard*, see Laurence Senelick, *The Chekhov Theatre: A Century of the Plays in Performance* (Cambridge: Cambridge University Press, 1997), 67–79.

38. Nikolai Gorchakov, *Rezhissyorskie uroki K. S. Stanislavskogo: Besedy i zapisi repetitsii* (Moscow: Iskusstvo, 1950), 534.

39. Gorchakov, *Rezhissyorskie uroki K. S. Stanislavskogo*, 536.

40. This suggestion is more remarkable given the exclusion (in the MAT production) of lines in which Borodin expresses admiration for the Soviet system. Karaganov, *Zhizn' dramaturga*, 156.

41. Gorchakov, *Rezhissyorskie uroki K. S. Stanislavskogo*, 535.

42. Bokshanskaia to Nemirovich-Danchenko, letter of December 6, 1931, in Solov'yova, ed., *Pis'ma O. S. Bokshanskoi Vl. I. Nemirovichu-Danchenko*, 2: 53–55. See also Marianna Stroeva, *Rezhissyorskie iskaniia Stanislavskogo, 1917–1938* (Moscow: Nauka, 1977), 319; and Vinogradskaia, *Zhizn' i tvorchestvo K. S. Stanislavskogo: Letopis'*, 177. The next day, Stanislavsky tried putting a cast member in the audience and having him interrupt Leonidov's monologue. He wasn't satisfied with the result. Solov'yova, "Strakh," 129. One of the regional productions of *Fear*, in Magnitogorsk, relied on "provocateurs" in the audience. "Stenogramma diskussii po pis'mu tov. Amaglobeli po p'ese 'Strakh' 16 fevralia 1932 g. pri Sekretariate [Vseroskomdrama]," Afinogenov papers, IMLI f. 371, op. 1, ed. khr. 2, l. 11.

43. Vinogradskaia, *Zhizn' i tvorchestvo K. S. Stanislavskogo: Letopis'*, 179.

44. Aleksandr Afinogenov, "Tvorcheskii universitet," *Teatr i dramaturgiia* 2, no. 3 (March 1934): 23–27.

45. Ia. Grinval'd, "'Strakh': P'esa A. Afinogenova v MKhAT I," *Vecherniaia Moskva*, December 24, 1931, p. 4; Iu. Iuzovskii, "'Strakh' Afinogenova v MkhAT," *Literaturnaia gazeta*, December 28, 1931, p. 3; Litovskii, "Pis'mo zaveduiushchemu khudozhestvennoi chast'iu MKhAT i V. G. Sakhnovskomu 27 dekabria 1931 g.," l. 1 ob.

46. Amaglobeli et al., "'Strakh' v Leningrade i 'Strakh' v Moskve," 4; Osaf Litovskii, "'Strakh' v MKhATe," *Sovetskoe iskusstvo*, December 30, 1931, p. 4.

47. Amaglobeli et al., "'Strakh' v Leningrade i 'Strakh' v Moskve," 4; Solov'yova, "Strakh," 130.

48. Iu. Olesha, "O 'Strakhe' A. Afinogenova," in *P'esy: Stat'i o teatre i dramaturgii* (Moscow: Iskusstvo, 1968), 265–66. This article was originally published on January 16, 1932.

49. RGALI, f. 2172, op. 1, ed. khr. 13, l. 3.

50. Afinogenov to Stanislavsky, February 2, 1932, in Afinogenov, *Izbrannoe v dvukh tomakh*, 2: 35.

51. "Ia khochu ne verit' v sotsializm!": A. N. Afinogenov, "P'esa 'Lozh' i perepiska s I. V. Stalinym," RGALI f. 2172, op. 3, ed. khr. 10, l. 7. This document is also held at the Rossiiskii gosudarstvennyi arkhiv sotsial'no-politicheskoi istorii, f. 558, op. 1, d. 5088, with the same pagination. References to this document are henceforth given as *Lozh' I* with the folio number.

52. "Ia ne khochu verit' v sotsializm," *Lozh' I*, l. 22.

53. "Ia khochu ne tol'ko verit' v sotsializm, ia khochu eshcho znat', pochemu my ego stroim i za chto boremsia," *Lozh' I*, l. 20.

54. *Lozh' I*, ll. 75–76.

55. *Lozh' I*, l. 22.

56. In a letter to another young writer, in early 1932, Gorky suggests that Afinogenov, "the author of *Fear*," would be the best person to consult on matters of playwriting. Ilya Zilbershtein and Evgeny Tager, eds., *Gor'kii i sovetskie pisateli: Neizdannaia perepiska*, Literaturnoe nasledstvo, vol. 70 (Moscow: Izdatel'stvo AN SSSR, 1963), 28. Afinogenov and Gorky spent time together in the summer of 1932 in Italy.

57. Afinogenov to Gorky, April 6 (?), 1933, in *Gor'kii i sovetskie pisateli*, ed. Zilbershtein and Tager, 30.

58. Natal'ia Larionova, "Genseku-redaktoru ne ponravilas' 'Lozh': Neizvestnye stranitsy iz perepiski dramaturga A.N. Afinogenova s I.V. Stalinym," *Pravda*, April 17–24, 1998, pp. 6–7; see also Karaganov, *Zhizn' dramaturga*, 289.

59. *Lozh' I*, l. 25. This character confesses, upon reading Nina's diary, that she "recognizes herself" in Nina's description of her doubts (l. 47), a detail that is used to (1) undermine the validity of Nina's concerns; (2) further discredit the spinster's judgment; and (3) turn the diary into a kind of compendium of subtexts.

60. Afinogenov to Stalin, April 2, 1933, in *Lozh' I*, l. 1.

61. Afinogenov to Stalin, April 2, 1933, in *Lozh' I*, ll. 118–19; emphasis in the original.

62. See Mikhail Vaiskopf, *Pisatel' Stalin* (Moscow: Novoe literaturnoe obozrenie, 2001).

63. Zilbershtein and Tager, eds., *Gor'kii i sovetskie pisateli*, 32.

64. *Lozh' I*, l. 27; Stalin's handwritten changes are emphasized.

65. A comparison with Stalin's response illustrates Gorky's ambiguity. The

latter writes: "Perhaps I will never be able to portray a Bolshevik the way he deserves to be portrayed. But I have every reason to say that you don't have a very clear picture of this type of person. Why? I am really not sure [*zatrudniaius' skazat'*]" (Zilbershtein and Tager, eds., *Gor'kii i sovetskie pisateli*, 34).

66. "*Kriminal'nyi giperbolizm*": Vaiskopf, *Pisatel' Stalin*, 94.

67. *Lozh' I*, l. 90. The note in the margin reads "*Sovetuiu peredal* [*sic*; must be *peredelat'*] *vse ostal'noe i oboitis' bez vystrela Niny i ego posledstvii, kak sovershenno sluchainago* [*sic*], *nadumannago* [*sic*], *ne sviazannago* [*sic*] *s ideei p'esy elementa.*" The orthographic inconsistencies make the "advice" more immediate and emphatic.

68. The second version of the playscript has been published as Aleksandr Afinogenov, "Lozh' (Sem'ia Ivanovykh): P'esa v chetyrekh aktakh," *Sovremennaia dramaturgiia*, no. 1 (1982): 191–220.

69. To interpret the decision to preserve the shot as an act of defiance would be ahistorical. Speculation of a different kind—that Afinogenov was too naive to understand the consequences of disobeying Stalin's instructions—is likewise hard to sustain, especially considering the playwright's work as a cultural official and the support his decision received from fellow playwrights, directors, and actors.

70. Petrov, *50 i 500*, 359.

71. In October 1932, the Politburo issued a resolution ending theatrical monopolies and directing theaters to mount "parallel productions" of popular plays (Artizov and Naumov, eds., *Vlast' i khudozhestvennaia intelligentsiia*, 185). The First and Second Moscow Art Theaters settled on parallel productions of *The Lie*.

72. Petrov had been appointed the artistic director of the theater, the best one in Kharkiv. He took several Gosdrama actors with him and asked Akimov to design several productions. Petrov, *50 i 500*, 356–59.

73. *Lozh' I*, l. 28.

74. Afinogenov, "Lozh' (Sem'ia Ivanovykh)," 199.

75. Afinogenov, "Otkrytoe pis'mo," 4.

76. Afinogenov, "Otkrytoe pis'mo," 4.

77. Petrov, *50 i 500*, 361–62; Karaganov, *Zhizn' dramaturga*, 334–35.

78. *Lozh' I*, l. 121.

79. Afinogenov's next play, *The Portrait* (*Portret*, 1934), about a former White Sea Canal convict who is unable to make the transition to regular life owing to abuse from her relatives, was staged in Leningrad and Kharkiv and several provincial theaters, but its playscript was criticized by Gorky and Petrov (in private letters to Afinogenov) and ultimately rejected by MAT. His play *Distant Point* (*Dalyokoe*, 1935; also translated as *Far Taiga*), about a Red Army commander dying of cancer in a train station in the Far East, was a major success and received the personal endorsement of the Soviet politician Kliment Voroshilov,

Notes to Pages 119–120

in whose apartment Afinogenov organized the first reading of the playscript. The positive and negative characters both make controversial statements, as they do in *Fear* and *The Lie*.

80. Afinogenov kept diaries from the mid-1920s until his death. The earliest of them chronicle general developments in his career (often without dates). The diaries of 1937–38, a period of crisis, are introspective and exceptionally detailed. The diaries of the last years of his life are detached and intermittent. There are four different Soviet editions of the 1937–38 diaries (1957, 1960, 1977, and 1990), each heavily censored. There is no mention of Afinogenov's expulsion from the Communist Party and Union of Soviet Writers; nothing about treacherous colleagues; and nothing about the Stalinist purges. The edition of the 1937–38 diaries published in 1993 (in the January, February, and March/April issues of the journal *Sovremennaia dramaturgiia*) excludes Afinogenov's expressions of devotion to Stalin and his belief that Stalin's pursuit of traitors and other "enemies of the people" was justified. Jochen Hellbeck included several annotated, translated passages from the 1937–38 diaries in *Revolution on My Mind: Writing a Diary under Stalin* (Cambridge, MA: Harvard University Press, 2006), 285–346. To date, the full unexpurgated text of the diaries has not been published. I refer in this chapter to the excerpts published in Afinogenov, *Izbrannoe v dvukh tomakh*, and to the RGALI typescript.

81. The following poem is a variation of A. K. Tolstoy's "Ioann Damaskin" ("John of Damascus"), from 1859. Afinogenov writes in the headnote that what he used to consider outdated had become relevant to him, including Tolstoy's "inquisitive penetration into the depths of time and life."

> *Ostav', uidi, zhadnoi slavoi,*
> *Ne bleskom vysprennikh rechei—*
> *Ia porazhen—inoi otravoi,*
> *I etot iad mne goriachei,*
> *Ia prokhozhu v tumanakh ulits,*
> *Ia vizhu obliki vysot,*
> *I nikuda ne zavernuli*
> *Dorogi naidennykh krasot,*
> *I nikomu ne govorili,*
> *Chto proidena bol'shaia strast',*
> *Strastei vysokikh volny plyli—*
> *Nad serdtsem prostiraia vlast',*
> *Ia vizhu milyi oblik dalei,*
> *Tropinku vizhu ia puti—*
> *I nikomu moikh pechalei—*
> *So mnoiu vmeste—ne proiti,*
> *I nikogda ne svergnut' snega,*

> S vershiny mira moego—
> Pust' budet v'iuga, svetit Vega—
> Ne zakryvaia nichego—
> Eshcho upast', eshcho razbit'sia,
> Eshcho podniat'sia—i togda—
> Ot snega mokrye resnitsy—
> Glaza zakroiut—navsegda . . .

> Leave me, go away; Not by greedy glory or
> by the allure of lofty rhetoric—
> I am defeated by another poison,
> And this toxin scorches me still more.
> I wander in the haze of streets,
> I see the faces of the heights,
> The paths of new-found beauties
> Never went astray,
> And never told anyone
> That a great passion had passed,
> The waves of lofty passions moved,
> Extending their power over the heart,
> I see a dear face of the distances,
> I see the footpath of a way
> And no one can avoid my sadness
> Together with me,
> Nor can the snow ever be removed
> From the heights of my world—
> Let there be a blizzard, let Vega shine brightly
> Not obscuring anything;
> To fall, to break to pieces,
> To rise up once again—and then
> My eyelids, wet from snow
> Will close my eyes—forever . . .

RGALI f. 2172, op. 3, ed. khr. 5 (January 1 and February 8, 1937, diary entries, courtesy of Il'ia Veniavkin).

82. Afinogenov's September 4, 1937, diary entry (in RGALI f. 2172, op. 3, ed. khr. 5) contains the longest and richest of the imagined interrogations. It reads like an actual transcript, and as Thomas Seifrid notes (personal communication with Simon Morrison, July 31, 2024), it anticipates the interrogation protocols as summarized or reconstructed by Aleksandr Solzhenitsyn, Varlam Shalamov, Lidiia Ginzburg, and others. In its ultimate absurdity, Afinogenov's protocol can be likened to fictional tales by Gogol or Kafka. Afinogenov's admiration

of the OGPU and its agents also suggests—seriously—the postmodern burlesques of Vladimir Sorokin.

83. Afinogenov, *Izbrannoe v dvukh tomakh*, 2: 485.

84. RGALI f. 2172, op. 3, ed. khr. 5, l. 267.

85. RGALI f. 2172, op. 3, ed. khr. 5, l. 267; I reference *Oedipus the King*, ll. 36–68 and 377–78, in *Sophocles I*, ed. and trans. Mark Griffith, Glenn W. Most, David Grene, and Richmond Lattimore (Chicago: University of Chicago Press, 1991), 26–27.

86. RGALI f. 2172, op. 3, ed. khr. 5, l. 269; I reference Seneca, *Oedipus*, ll. 681–84 and 687, in *Four Tragedies and Octavia*, trans. E. F. Watling (New York: Viking, 1966), 235–36.

87. Afinogenov, *Izbrannoe v dvukh tomakh*, 1: 511–16.

CHAPTER FIVE

1. Iurii Olesha, "Zametki dramaturga," *Teatr i dramaturgiia*, no. 5 (1933): 1–4; reprinted in Iurii Olesha, *P'esy. Stat'i o teatre i dramaturgii* (Moscow: Iskusstvo, 1968), 291–302. The article is based on a June 12, 1933, conversation between Olesha and an unidentified interlocutor ("'Beseda S. i O.' o dramaturgii," RGALI, f. 358, op. 2, ed. khr. 490) that expands on Olesha's observations and includes specific mention of *Hamlet* to illustrate his point about the destruction of characters in the "theater of the old days" (l. 2).

2. The most detailed accounts of the play's prehistory are given in Vladimir Rogovin, "Iz tvorcheskoi istorii p'esy 'Smert' Zanda,'" *Teatr*, no. 1 (1993): 144–47; and Irina Ozernaia, "Vchityvaias' v rukopisi," *Sovremennaia dramaturgiia*, no. 3 (1985): 217–19. On the versions of the play, see Iurii Olesha, "'Smert' Zanda': P'esa v tryokh deistviiakh, shesti stsenakh (opyt rekonstruktsii)," *Teatr*, no. 1 (1993): 149–91; and Iurii Olesha and Mikhail Levitin, "'Smert' Zanda.' Kompozitsiia po chernovikam p'esy," *Sovremennaia dramaturgiia*, no. 3 (1985): 190–217.

3. "Pis'mo K. S. Stanislavskogo I. V. Stalinu 29 oktiabria 1931 g. (No. 67); Pis'mo I. V. Stalina K. S. Stanislavskomu 9 noiabria 1931 g. (No. 69)," in Artizov and Naumov, eds., *Vlast' i khudozhestvennaia intelligentsiia*, 157–58.

4. Mikhail Bulgakov, *Zapiski pokoinika: Teatral'nyi roman*, ed. Aleksandr Kobrinskii (St. Petersburg: Akademicheskii proekt, 2002); henceforth ZP. English translation: Mikhail Bulgakov, *Black Snow: A Theatrical Novel*, trans. Michael Glenny (London: Harvill, 1996). In the main text, where relevant, I provide the page numbers of both the Russian and English versions in parentheses.

5. The commentaries in ZP (182–203) give the most detailed account to date of the prototypes of the novel's characters.

6. On the reactions to Bulgakov's parodies, including the traditional reading of the novel as a narrative version of a theatrical *kapustnik*, see Susan Kirsten

Larsen, "The Poetics of Performance in the Works of Mixail Bulgakov" (PhD diss., Yale University, 1993), 213–15.

7. According to Elena Bulgakova, the writer's wife, the plans for the novel's finale involved Maksudov committing suicide in reaction to his disappointment with the production and attacks from the critics (Vladimir Lakshin, "Elena Sergeyevna rasskazyvaet . . . ," in *Vospominaniia o Mikhaile Bulgakove*, ed. Elena Bulgakova and Semen Liandres [Moscow: Sovetskii pisatel', 1988], 412–20, esp. 417).

8. According to his wife, Bulgakov believed that the cut was demanded by the censors, and it was not until 1935 that he realized that the idea belonged to Stanislavsky himself. For the most detailed account of the circumstances surrounding the cut, see Mikhail Bulgakov, *P'esy 1920-kh godov* (Leningrad: Iskusstvo, 1989), 530–31.

9. My analysis derives from Mikhail Iampolskii, "'Ia ne uvizhu znamenitoi Fedry': Zametki o reprezentatsii smerti v barochnoi tragedii," *Novoe literaturnoe obozrenie*, no. 4 (2000): 5–42.

10. Elena Vasilyeva, "Two Decades of Soviet Biographical Film: From Revolutionary Romanticism to Epic Monumentalism" (PhD diss., University of Southern California, 2009), 3, 15.

11. Bert O. States, "The Phenomenological Attitude," in *Critical Theory and Performance*, ed. Janelle G. Reinelt and Joseph R. Roach (Ann Arbor: University of Michigan Press, 2007), 28.

12. Muza, "The Tragedy of a Russian Woman," 494–95.

13. Jodi Kantor, "Death Becomes Performance: The Reciprocal Usefulness of Death and Performance," *Theatre Annual* 54 (2001): 25–42, esp. 25–26.

14. Philippe Ariès, *Western Attitudes toward Death: From the Middle Ages to the Present* (Baltimore, MD: Johns Hopkins University Press, 1974), 13–14, 55–56.

15. Iurii Olesha, "Smert' Zanda," *Teatr*, no. 1 (1993): 170–71.

16. Iurii Olesha, "Koe-chto iz sekretnykh zapisei poputchika Zanda," *Tridtsat' dnei*, no. 1 (1932): 11–17.

17. Olesha, "Zametki dramaturga," 4.

18. Personal communication with the author, July 10, 2004.

19. Iurii Olesha, "Igra v plakhu: Tragikomediia: Dlia repertuara maloi formy," *Tridtsat' dnei*, no. 5 (1934): 35–48.

CHAPTER SIX

1. Mikhail Bulgakov, *P'esy 1930-kh godov* (St. Petersburg: Iskusstvo, 1994), 105.

2. Elena Bulgakova, *Dnevnik* (Moscow: Knizhnaia palata, 1990), 164.

3. See Irina Erykalova's analyses in Bulgakov, *P'esy 30-kh godov*, 587–92;

and Mikhail Bulgakov, *Sobranie sochinenii v piati tomakh* (Moscow: Khudozhestvennaia literatura, 1989), 3: 657–66.

4. Anatolii Smelianskii, "Dramy i teatr Mikhaila Bulgakova," in Bulgakov, *Sobranie sochinenii v piati tomakh*, 3: 573–609, esp. 602.

5. See J. A. E. Curtis, *Mikhail Bulgakov* (London: Reaktion Books, 2017).

6. Bulgakova, *Dnevnik*, 300.

7. For information about Bulgakov's life I consulted Marietta Chudakova, *Zhizneopisanie Mikhaila Bulgakova*, 2nd ed. (Moscow: Kniga, 1988); Anatolii Smelianskii, *Mikhail Bulgakov v Khudozhestvennom teatre*, 2nd ed. (Moscow: Iskusstvo, 1989); Lesley Milne, *Mikhail Bulgakov: A Critical Biography* (Cambridge: Cambridge University Press, 1990); and Marie-Christine Autant-Mathieu, *Le Theatre de Boulgakov* (Lausanne: L'Age d'Homme, 2000).

8. *Flight* is set in the Crimea at the end of the Civil War. It focuses, sympathetically, on the "Whites" and the people whose lives have been upturned by the Revolution and the "spontaneous, irresistible" might of the Bolsheviks. Stalin didn't like the play, arguing, in a 1928 letter circulated throughout the cultural establishment, that Bulgakov should have devoted more attention to the self-delusions of the Whites rather than justifying their anti-Soviet conduct. Gorky, however, came to Bulgakov's defense, which left the production of *Flight* in limbo pending an expert review of the playscript. This fell to Platon Kerzhentsev, a high-ranking government official who was also a playwright. (In 1935, he would become head of the all-powerful Committee on Arts Affairs.) Kerzhentsev did what he knew Stalin wanted him to do. He wrote a scathing report condemning Bulgakov's support of the "bastards, whores, embezzlers," and "scum" on the wrong side of the Revolution. *Flight* "justifies those who consciously or unconsciously served as foot soldiers of class enemies. For three or four hours of the performance, the minds of the viewer will be dulled, desensitized, and destroyed by the play's alien elements." The play, Kerzhentsev added, is "an unfounded, unprincipled concession to the most conservative and reactionary groups and will make it all the harder for Soviet theater to appeal to the working-class viewer." On January 30, 1929, the Central Committee affirmed the "inadvisability" of staging *Flight*. Rossiiskii gosudarstvennyi arkhiv noveishei istorii (RGANI) f. 89, op. 51, d. 17, ll. 1–13 (Kerzhentsev's report); RGANI f. 89, op. 51, d. 18, l.1 (Kliment Voroshilov's recommendation for the play's cancellation).

9. There are competing accounts of the telephone conversation with Stalin. See Chudakova, *Zhizneopisanie Mikhaila Bulgakova*, 437–40.

10. See Julie Curtis, *Bulgakov's Last Decade: The Writer as Hero* (Cambridge: Cambridge University Press, 1987).

11. See Boris Gasparov, "Novyi Zavet v proizvedeniiakh M. A. Bulgakova," in *Literaturnye leitmotivy: ocherki russkoi literatury XX veka* (Moscow: Vostochnaia literatura, 1993), 83-123; and the same author's "Mikhaïl Boulgakov," in *His-*

toire de la litterature russe, vol. 3, part 3 ("Le XXe Siecle, Gels et Degels"), ed. Efim Etkind (Paris: Fayard, 1990), 211–29; and Kamil Ikramov, "'Postoite, polozhite shliapu . . .': K voprosu o transformatsii pervoistochnikov," *Novoe literaturnoe obozrenie*, no. 4 (1993): 177–96.

12. Violetta Gudkova, "From Salon to Samizdat," in *Bulgakov: The Novelist-Playwright*, ed. Lesley Milne (Luxembourg: Harwood, 1995), 15–28.

13. On Bulgakov's interactions with Gorky and Nemirovich, see Bulgakova, *Dnevnik*, 36, 214–15, 251.

14. Bulgakova, *Dnevnik*, 222.

15. Chudakova, *Zhizneopisanie Mikhaila Bulgakova*, 474–75.

16. Bulgakova, *Dnevnik*, 226.

17. M. O. Chudakova, "Osvedomiteli v dome Bulgakova v seredine 1930-kh godov," in *Sed'mye Tynianovskie chteniia: Materialy dlia obsuzhdeniia*, ed. M. O. Chudakova, E. A. Toddes, and Yu. G. Tsivian (Kaluga: Poligrafist, 1996), 385–463.

18. See Larsen, "Poetics of Performance," 220–22.

19. The name "Ivan Vasilievich" recalls Tsar Ivan IV, aka Ivan the Terrible, who featured in a Bulgakov comedy of the 1930s. The director's initials—I. V.—match Stalin's.

20. See Larsen, "Poetics of Performance," 222.

21. On Bulgakov's complicated relationship with the censors, especially during the staging of *The Days of the Turbins*, see Steven Richmond, "Ideologically Firm: Soviet Theater Censorship, 1921–1928" (PhD diss., University of Chicago, 1996).

22. The original title referred to the secret society involved in Molière's downfall and death. For an analysis of the ideological ambiguity of Bulgakov's use of the word *"kabala,"* or "servitude," and a reading of the original title as an allusion to a *"sotsial'nyi zakaz"* (a demand formulated by a social class), see Larsen, "Poetics of Performance," 188–89; and Angela Brintlinger, *Writing a Usable Past: Russian Literary Culture, 1917–1937* (Evanston, IL: Northwestern University Press, 2000), 120–39.

23. On Stanislavsky's involvement in the rehearsals for Molière, see Vinogradskaia, *Zhizn' i tvorchestvo K. S. Stanislavskogo: Letopis'*, 306, 317–31.

24. [Platon Kerzhentsev], "Vneshnii blesk i fal'shivoe soderzhanie," *Pravda*, March 9, 1936, p. 3. For context, see Leonid Maksimenkov, *Sumbur vmesto muzyki: Stalinskaia kul'turnaia revoliutsiia, 1936–1938* (Moscow: Iuridicheskaia kniga, 1997), 182–96.

25. Osaf Litovskii wrote the first negative review of the MAT production for the February 11, 1936, issue of *Sovetskoe iskusstvo*. He had attacked Bulgakov before. Afinogenov, Olesha, and Vsevolod Ivanov criticized the play in the February 22, 1936, issue of the MAT newsletter *Gor'kovets*. See Smelianskii, *Mikhail Bulgakov v Khudozhestvennom teatre*, 309–10. For Kerzhentsev's report to the

Politburo and Stalin's response to it, see Artizov and Naumov, eds., *Vlast' i khudozhestvennaia intelligentsiia*, 298–300.

26. Bulgakov, *P'esy 30-kh godov*, 62.

27. On February 6, after the first dress rehearsal, Bulgakov's wife wrote: "This was not the production we had dreamed about" (Bulgakova, *Dnevnik*, 111).

28. The history of the production of *Molière*, like that of Afinogenov's *Fear*, finds Stanislavsky more attuned to political realities than generally assumed. In 1934, he told the director Ilya Sudakov that, in selecting plays for production, the Kremlin was his "compass" (Smelianskii, *Mikhail Bulgakov v Khudozhestvennom teatre*, 271).

29. On the editorial cuts, see Bulgakov, *P'esy 30-kh godov*, 559.

30. Bulgakova notes the inclusion of *Molière* in a lavish volume dedicated to MAT's fortieth anniversary in 1938, but also several instances when the play was purposely excluded from the theater's press releases (*Dnevnik*, 143, 212).

31. Nikolai Gorchakov, *Rezhissyorskie uroki K. S. Stanislavskogo: Besedy i zapisi repetitsii* (Moscow: Iskusstvo, 1950).

32. Gorchakov, *Rezhissyorskie uroki K. S. Stanislavskogo*, 388.

33. Gorchakov, *Rezhissyorskie uroki K. S. Stanislavskogo*, 356–57.

34. In subsequent editions of his book, Gorchakov eliminated the summary of the rehearsal of *Molière*, replacing it with a description of Stanislavsky's collaborations with other Soviet playwrights and information about Afinogenov's *Fear*.

35. Smelianskii, *Mikhail Bulgakov v Khudozhestvennom teatre*, 257.

36. On Bulgakov's use of Molière's writings and on Molière as the protagonist of Bulgakov's play, see Larsen, "Poetics of Performance," 176–77. On Mayakovsky's influence on Bulgakov's conception of the Molière play, see Chudakova, *Zhizneopisanie Mikhaila Bulgakova*, 403–5, 413–16, 450–51. Chudakova does not discuss this more obvious reference to Mayakovsky in the playscript.

37. Irina Vinogradskaia, *Stanislavskii repetiruet: Zapisi i stenogrammy repetitsii* (Moscow: Soiuz teatral'nykh deiatelei RSFSR, 1987), 350–51. Bulgakov's argument is repeated in several accounts, including his own letters and his wife's diary. It is central to the story of the demise of *Molière*.

38. Bulgakov, *P'esy 30-kh godov*, 557.

39. This detail is from Boris Livanov, who played Moirron and served as one of the production's assistant directors (Vinogradskaia, *Stanislavskii repetiruet*, 394). In the end, Bulgakov didn't change the Armande-Moirron scene. The next rehearsal, on April 17, provoked Bulgakov's furious letters to Stanislavsky and Gorchakov.

40. Vinogradskaia, *Stanislavskii repetiruet*, 394; emphasis added.

41. Vinogradskaia, *Stanislavskii repetiruet*, 397.

42. Vinogradskaia, *Stanislavskii repetiruet*, 353.

43. Bulgakov, *P'esy 1930-kh godov*, 41–42.

44. They seem to have been rehearsing a scene from *Psyche*, a play-cum-

ballet coauthored by Molière, Corneille, and Lully (Bulgakov, *P'esy 30-kh godov*, 578).

45. Bulgakova, *Dnevnik*, 34. Subsequent references to this edition, with the abbreviation *D*, are given in parentheses.

46. On problems in the published edition of Bulgakova's diary, see Chudakova, "Osvedomiteli v dome Bulgakova v seredine 1930-kh godov," 391–93.

47. This coinage, however awkward, is more accurate than "Stalinist playwright" would have been. As this chapter argues, Bulgakov held different positions in the theater.

48. Chudakova, *Zhizneopisanie Mikhaila Bulgakova*, 403–5, 413–16.

49. Leonid Parshin, *Chertovshchina v amerikanskom posol'stve v Moskve, ili Trinadtsat' zagadok Mikhaila Bulgakova* (Moscow: Knizhnaia palata, 1991); Aleksandr Etkind, *Tolkovanie puteshestvii: Rossiia i Amerika v travelogakh i intertekstakh* (Moscow: Novoe literaturnoe obozrenie, 2001), 215–43.

50. Compare Samosud's reaction, in August 1939, to the news of *Batum*'s demise, recorded in Bulgakova's diary: "'What is the plot? Why has it been banned?' And of course: 'We should do an opera. How about Shostakovich?'—Misha: 'Samuil Abramovich, I am warning you, the play has been banned by the Central Committee.'—'But what about music? There is music, after all. A play is something entirely different. Is there a good female part?'" (Bulgakova, *Dnevnik*, 283).

51. In a speech given at a Kremlin awards ceremony, Nemirovich-Danchenko credited Stalin with these recommendations. "One cannot fail to recall that among the recent productions for which we received this honor, the two most significant were suggested [*podskazany*] to us by comrade Stalin. These were *Enemies* and *Liubov' Iarovaia*" ("Zasedanie Prezidiuma TsIK Soiuza SSR," *Pravda*, May 8, 1937, p. 1).

52. Compare the entry in Bulgakova's diary from a decade earlier (March 4, 1936): "Then—toward the end of the show—we made it to *Molière*. Full house. In the government box, in the shadows [*v polut'me*] we saw Litovskii who was writing something" (*Dnevnik*, 116). Litovskii—an old nemesis of Bulgakov's—is writing a negative review of the production (published immediately after *Molière* was canceled). The government box, though not physically located behind the stage, becomes part of the "backstage" world that determines what happens, when, and how.

Index

Page numbers in *italic* refer to images.

acting: realistic, 104; Stanislavsky on, 94, 154–55; training for, 71
actor: and authors, 17–23; and bourgeois culture, 11; fear and, 102; as force, 18; and kinds of performers, 79; power of, 5; in rehearsal, 154; side affects and, 12; and Stalinism, 16; Stanislavsky on, 5–6, 11–12. *See also* stage fright; travesty actor/actress
Actor's Work Upon the Self, An (Stanislavsky), 4–6, 11–12, 42
Adam and Eve (Bulgakov), 138
Aeschylus, 120–21
Afinogenov, Aleksandr: adolescence of, 92; audience in work, 23; and Bulgakov, 22, 160–61; and children's theater, 34, 42, 44; death of, 22, 168; denunciation of, 22, 114, 161–62; expelled from Party, 24; at First Congress, 23, 83, 84, 122; and Gorky, 113–14, 200n56, 201n79; and MAT, 95; and melodrama, 93; prominence of, 21, 94; in RAPP, 81, 100; on Sophocles, 120–22; and Stalin, 23, 114–17, 118, 119, 196n7; and Stanislavsky, 106, 197; and the unpredictable, 168. *See also* Afinogenov diaries; *Black Ravine*; *Eccentric*; *Fear*; *Lie*; *Mashen'ka*; *Moscow, Kremlin*; "Open Letter to My Future Directors"
Afinogenov diaries, 93, 119–22, 202–4nn80–82
Akhmatova, Anna, 164
Akimov, Nikolai, 101, 104, 117, 201n72
Alexander Nevsky (Eisenstein), 124, 132; filming of, *126*

Alexander Pushkin (Bulgakov), 165
Anna Karenina (Tolstoy), 20
Anna Karenina (Volkov), 20, 134–35
Ariès, Philippe, 134–35
Aristocrats, The (Pogodin), 83
Artaud, Antonin, 134
audience: bodies of, 72; for children's theater, 28–29; elite, 19; of *Fear*, 110–11; fears of, 95–96; and fourth wall, 102; guiding to conclusion, 38; as part of spectacle, 96, 110–11; power of, 79; relation to art, 173n30; for show trials, 3–4, 110; Stalin as, 90–91; tears of, 103; theater's challenge to, 118–19; transformation of, vii
Austin, J. L., 12

Batum (Bulgakov): banning of, 134; MAT and, 140, 142; Stalin and, 25
Belinkov, Arkady, 21–22
Berezovskii, Feoktist, 85
Bezhin Meadow (Eisenstein), 135
biographies, staged, 132–34
Black Ravine, The (Afinogenov), 34, 42, 44
Blue Bird, The (Maeterlinck): mysticism in, 33; productions of, 34, 176n17; and *Three Fat Men*, 40, 57, 176n25, 177n36; Stanislavsky and, 43
Blum, Vladimir, 152
Bokshanskaia, Olga, 128
Bolshevik Revolution, 42, 57, 59, 68, 81–82, 99, 164
Bolsheviks: and intelligentsia, 69; theatricalizing reality, 6–7, 166–67; Tolstoy and, 83

211

Index

Bolshoi Dramatic Theater (Leningrad), 81, 146
Bolshoi Theater (Moscow): Bulgakov at, 24, 141, 162; and TsDT, 27
Bread (Kirshon), 20, 93
"breeches" actress, 16, 45, 74–75, 178n50. *See also* travesty actor/actress
Briantsev, Aleksandr, 34, 42
Bright Stream, The (Shostakovich), 27
Brushtein, Aleksandra, 35
Building Number Five (Shtok), 35, 44
Bukharin, Nikolai, 82
Bulgakov, Mikhail: and Afinogenov, 22, 160–61; alternative readings of, 140–41; backstage in, 19, 23, 24, 127, 140–41, 142, 146–58, 163–67; and Bullitt, 141, 161–62; career and productions, 24, 138–41, 152; critical reputation, 137; on death, 126–28, 129–32; death of, 140, 168; and diary writing, 158; and Dostoevsky, 144, 145; and Olesha, 22, 144, 145; plays about Pushkin, 132–34, 139, 142; prominence of, 21, 162; as radical, 167; and RAPP, 139; refusal to apologize, 166; and Stalin, 25, 138, 139, 150, 163–67, 206nn8–9; and Stanislavsky, 131, 147, 155–56, 158; subversiveness in, 138; and theatrical everyday, 137–69; and the unpredictable, 168; work for hire, 140; 159. *See also Adam and Eve; Alexander Pushkin; Batum;* Bulgakova diaries; *Crimson Island; Days of the Turbins; Dead Man's Memoir; Dead Souls; Don Quixote; Flight; Ivan Vasilievich; Last Days of Pushkin; Master and Margarita; Memoir/A Theatrical Novel; Minin and Pozharskii; Molière; Pickwick Papers; War and Peace; Yegor Bulychov and Company; Zoyka's Apartment*
Bulgakova, Elena: diaries of, 22, 141, 143–46, 158–67; and *Molière* publication, 150; on Stalin, 90; 159. *See also* Bulgakova diaries
Bulgakova diaries: Afinogenov in, 160–61; denunciation in, 165–66; language of, 143; *The Lie* in, 161; *Memoir/A Theatrical Novel* in, 143–46; *Molière* in, 158–67, 209n52; NKVD in, 160; rewriting of, 159; Stalin in, 162–65
Bulgakov studies, 162

Bullitt, William, 141, 161–62
Burke, Kenneth, 18

Cassiday, Julie, 5
censorship: and culture of duplicity, 7; vs. freedom, 152; in Leningrad vs. Moscow, 100, 103; and Olesha, 188n56; permitting criticism, 138; and Stanislavsky, 131
Central Children's Theater (TsDT), 26–27, 29, 31–32, 43, 44
Chaplin, Charlie, 68, 189n69, 191n84
Chekhov, Anton, 57, 59, 84, 94, 106–7, 125
Chekhov, Mikhail: defection of, 68–69, 190n73; and Olesha, 190n79
Cherry Orchard, The (Chekhov), 107, 108
children's theater: audience for, 28–29; coercion in, 42; Constructivist designs in, 35, 40; ideology in, 31, 32–33, 37, 44; Olesha in, 23, 35–42; performed by children, 43; racism in, 30; range of works in, 28, 33–35; Sats in, 26–27, 42–45; Stanislavsky on, 42, 178n46
Chudakova, Marietta, 160
Chuprunenko (worker at First Congress), 80
cinema, as religion, 19
Clark, Katerina, 11
Committee on Arts Affairs, 27, 148
communist development, 82–83
Communist Party: Afinogenov and, 24, 25, 92, 100, 119, 202; as family, 27; at First Congress, 84; and purges, 51; and writers, 80
Conspiracy of Feelings, A (Olesha), 25, 61, 124
Constructivist stage designs, 35, 40, 74
contemporary Russian performing arts, vii
creative unions, 27, 48, 141
Crimson Island, The (Bulgakov), 137, 139, 151
cross-dressing, 16, 44–45

Days of the Turbins, The (Bulgakov): murder scene cut, 131; RAPP critique of, 20, 139; revival of, 141
Dead Man's Memoir, A (Bulgakov), 4, 24, 126. *See also Memoir/A Theatrical Novel* (Bulgakov)
Dead Souls (Bulgakov), 139
Death of Zand, The (Olesha), 124, 135–36
deaths, staged, 123–36

Index

denunciation: of Afinogenov, 22, 114, 161–62; of *Molière*, 148, 149, 165–66; of Second Moscow Art Theater, 27; of Shostakovich and Sats, 27–28
diaries: of Afinogenov, 119–22, 202–4nn80–82; Bulgakov on, 158; of Bulgakova, 22, 141, 143–46, 158–67; of Olesha, 49–78, 179n5, 181n12, 181n16, 181n18; publication of, 182n21; of Shtange, 26–27, 29
director, the: performing the will of, 5; personality of, 19
Doctor Zhivago (Pasternak), 3–5
Don Quixote (Bulgakov), 140
Dostoevsky, Fyodor, 54, 144, 145
drama, Romantic, 156
drama, Soviet: and death, 135–36; at First Congress, 84–85; journal issue on, 123; melodrama in, 93; theory of living human being in, 81–82

Eccentric, The (Afinogenov), 20, 25, 114, 117
Eisenstein, Sergei, 124, 132, 135; *126*
Enemy on Trial, The (Cassiday), 5
Envy (Olesha): power in, 55; stage adaptation, 36, 176n24; success of, 49, 50
Erdman, Boris, 40
Erdman, Nikolai, 125
Expressionism: RAPP rejection of, 81; in stage effects, 70–71, 83

Fadeev, Aleksandr, 86, 89
Fairy Tale (Svetlov), 35
"'Fat Men' and 'Eccentrics'" (Lunacharsky), 37–38
fear: of audience, 95–96; in *Fear*, 95, 104, 116; of fear, 108; in Soviet society, 104
Fear (Afinogenov): audience for, 110–11; designs of, 101–2, 104, 105–6; dramatic structure, 108; elite audience for, 19; extra-textual meanings in, 100; Klara-Borodin scene, 101, 102–3, 106, 109; Leningrad production, 100–105, 109; maquette of, *106*; at MAT, 24, 94, 100, 105–11, 197n15; as melodrama, 98, 103; OGPU scene, 104, 105, 108, 111, 197n16; and Party, 100; plot and characters, 96–100; rehearsals of, 102–3, 106; responses to, 109, 110–11, 198n21; rewrites of, 101, 102, 198n23, 199n40,

199n42; Stalinism in, 97–99; Stalin on, 89, 92–93; Stanislavsky and, 105–11; success of, 23, 94; touring, 105, 110–11
Fighters (Romashov), 90
First All-Union Congress of Soviet Writers: Afinogenov at, 122; and best play competition, 123; biographic plays and, 132; debates on theater, 23; earlier meetings and, 90; Olesha at, 78; RAPP and, 81–82; remarks at, 79–80; Zhdanov speech, 15
First Five Year Plan, 48, 55, 99
First State Theater for Children, 34
Flight (Bulgakov), 139, 206n8
formalism, war on, 27
Fritz Bauer (Sats), 35

genuine Soviet person/citizen: Afinogenov as, 93; as cultural imperative, 14, 17; and death, 135–36; and intelligentsia, 74; in *List of Good Deeds*, 64; Olesha as, 59, 78; performer as, 81, 132; and self-doubt, 144; and side affects, 16; and subtexts, 113
Glavrepertkom, 65, 105, 146, 152, 187n55, 189n67
Golden Key, The (Tolstoy), 43, 44, 45
Gorchakov, Nikolai, 36, 40, 147, 150–51
Gorky, Maxim (Alexei Maximovich Peshkov): and biographies, 132; and Afinogenov, 113–14, 200n56, 201n79; and MAT, 20–21; on melodrama, 20; and Stalin, 80, 88; in writers' meetings, 85, 88; with Zhdanov, 15
Gosdrama (Leningrad State Academic Drama Theater), 100–105
Griunzaid, Valentina, 36
Gudkova, Violetta, 80, 179n5, 187n54, 188nn57–60, 189n69, 194n105
Gudok newspaper, 22, 137
Gumilevskii, Lev, 34

Hamlet (Shakespeare): in *Doctor Zhivago*, 3–5; in *List of Good Deeds*, 46, 64, 66–70, 194n103
"Hamlet and Don Quixote" (Turgenev), 66–67
Hamlet character: and intelligentsia, 66–67, 73, 74; in Olesha diary, 76–77; and Soviet life, 70; and travesty actress, 72, 74–75

213

Index

Hargreaves, James, 42
Hellbeck, Jochen, 78, 180n11
Hitler, Adolf, 82

intelligent, 55–56, 60–61, 66–67, 73, 74, 78, 184n37, 189n65
intelligentsia: and *Fear*, 107; and genuine Soviet person, 13, 74, 110; and Hamlet character, 66–67; in *Memoir/A Theatrical Novel*, 144; Olesha and, 58, 60–62
Ivanov Family, The (Afinogenov). See *Lie, The* (Afinogenov)
Ivan Vasilievich (Bulgakov), 165
Izvestiia newspaper, 27, 40, 46

Juggernaut's Chariot (Shcheglov), 42

Kachalov, Vassily, 166
Kamerny Theater, 152
Kapital, Das (Marx), 42
Kerzhentsev, Platon, 148, 186n49
Kharkiv Theater of Russian Drama, 92
Khmelev, Nikolai, 166
Kirov, Sergei, 100
Kirpotin, Valery: at First Congress, 84; in writers' meetings, 85, 86, 89
Kirshon, Vladimir: best play prize, 90; at First Congress, 82, 83, 84, 89, 195n9; on individual, 20; on playwriting, 85; in RAPP, 81
Kleist, Heinrich von, 10
Knipper-Chekhov, Olga, 106, 108
Korchagina-Aleksandrovskaia, Ekaterina, 100–101, 102–3
Koreneva, Klavdia, 43–45
"Kirilka" (Gorky), 88
Kron, Aleksandr, 34, 44

Lady Macbeth of the Mtsensk District, The (Shostakovich), 27
Lady of the Camellias, The (Dumas), Meyerhold production, 124
Last Days of Pushkin, The (Bulgakov), 133–34, 142
Lenin, Vladimir: on cinema, 19; death of, 86–87, 88, 89; dramas about, 82; Stalin on, 218
Leonidov, Leonid, 106–7
Lie, The (Afinogenov): confessions in, 113–14; ideology in, 113; at MAT, 111–19; plot and characters, 111–13; shooting scene, 116–17, 125–26, 131, 201n69; Stalin edits, 23, 114–17, 118, 119, 125; withdrawal of, 92–93, 119
Lipovetsky, Mark, 45
List of Good Deeds, A (Meyerhold and Olesha), 48; aftereffects of, 75–78; ambiguous death in, 124; criticism of, 65–66, 77–78, 188n57; director's personality, 19; genuineness in, 23; *Hamlet* in, 64, 68–69; *Izvestiia* review, 46, 47; kiss in, 72–73; Lelia character, 63–64, 66–70, 71–73, 77, 78, 188n57, 191–92nn89–92; Margerette character, 70–73, 191nn80–87; meta-theatrical in, 66, 69; Meyerhold role in, 62, 63, 65, 73–75; in Olesha diary, 60, 65; Raikh in, 46; rehearsals of, 73, 192nn93–94
literature: and objective reality, 50–51; Olesha on, 135, 181n12; Stalin on, 88
Literature and Revolution (Trotsky), 14
Litovskii, Osaf, 81, 207n25
Little African Boy and the Monkey, The (Rozanov and Sats), 30–32, 34, 43, 44; cover of children's book, 32
Little Humpbacked Horse, The (Saint-Léon), 34
Little Humpbacked Horse or The Tsar Maiden, The (Briantsev), 34
Little Red Riding Hood (Shvarts), 35
Liubimova, Valentina, 35
Livanov, Boris, 154
Lives of Remarkable People series, 132
Lunacharsky, Anatoly: biographical plays by, 132; on melodrama, 20; on *Three Fat Men*, 37–38, 40, 58, 60, 177nn28–29, 177n32, 178n36, 184n33

Maeterlinck, Maurice, 33
Magnificent Alloy, The (Kirshon), 90
Makar'ev, Leonid, 34, 43
Markov, Pavel, 36
Marling, Jenny, 161
Marshak, Samuil, 82
Marx, Karl, 42, 101
Marxism: fiction and, 50–51; of RAPP era, 37, 81
Mashen'ka (Afinogenov), 22
Master and Margarita, The (Bulgakov), 22, 140, 142, 161

Index

Mayakovsky, Vladimir: and Meyerhold, 63, 160; suicide of, 52
melodrama: *Fear* as, 98, 103, 108; Gorky on, 20; at MAT, 94–95; and show trials, 93
Memoir/A Theatrical Novel (Bulgakov): backstage in, 127, 142, 166, 167; Bulgakova diaries on, 143–46; in Bulgakov studies, 162; on cultural authority, 128–29; death in, 126–28, 129–32; plot and characters, 129–31; Socialist Realism in, 145
meta-theatrical, the: in *Crimson Island*, 157; in *Lie*, 119; in *List of Good Deeds*, 66, 69; in *Molière*, 152, 156; in *Three Fat Men*, 38
Meyerhold, Vsevolod: arrest of, 25, 186n49; Constructivist staging by, 74; on *Hamlet*, 69; Expressionist effects by, 70–71; illusion in, 17; and *Lady of the Camellias*, 124; and *List of Good Deeds*, 62, 63, 65, 73–75; and Mayakovsky, 63, 160; and Olesha, 62–78, 185n44, 185n46, 186n48, 187n51, 192–93nn98–102; as performance artist, 77; power of, 63; and Raikh, 46; as revolutionary, 75; with Yuri Olesha, 47
Meyerhold Theater, 46, 66, 75, 124
Minin and Pozharskii (Bulgakov), 140, 141
Molière (Bulgakov): backstage in, 19, 152–58, 209n52; in Bulgakov studies, 162; censors on, 146, 205n8; costume design for, *147*; cuts in, 158; denunciation of, 148, 149, 165; everyday in, 142, 146; incest theme, 150, 156; Moirron and Armande scene, 154–58, 208n39; publication, 148, 150; rehearsals of, 139–40, 153–58, 208n34; reviews of, 22, 148, 207n25; revolutionary in, 149–50
Moscow Art Theater (MAT): and *Batum*, 140, 142; and *Blue Bird*, 33,176n18; Bulgakov and, 24, 129; *Death of Zand* at, 124; *Fear* at, 24, 94, 100, 105–11, 117, 197n16, 199n40; and Gorky, 20–21, 81; *Lie* at, 93; *List of Good Deeds* at, 123; *Molière* at, 24, 146–47, 149, 156, 208n30; in Olesha diaries, 56–62; and Pasternak, 5; as preeminent, 25; and RAPP, 81; realism and, 94; *Three Fat Men* at, 36, 39, 45, 176n23, 183n28, 183n30

Moscow, Kremlin (Afinogenov), 120
Moscow Realistic Theater, 83
Moscow Theater for Children (MTD), 30, 31, 32, 33, 40
Moscow Theater for Children, The (album), 29–30
Muchnic, Helen, 64
Muggeridge, Malcolm, 7–8, 9, 13, 123

Naked King, The (Shvarts), 35
Nemirovich-Danchenko, Vladimir: and *Anna Karenina*, 134–35; and Bulgakov, 128; and *Fear*, 106; and Gorky, 21; and MAT, 94; and *Molière*, 139, 152, 209n51; with Stanislavsky, 95; and *Three Fat Men*, 183n30
Nesbet, Anne, 135
New Economic Policy (NEP), 34
New Soviet Child, 33
New Soviet Man/New Person, 13, 14, 57
NKVD secret police: and Afinogenov, 120, 122, 161; and Bulgakov, 138, 142, 160; and Olesha, 51; and RAPP, 119
Notes from Underground (Dostoevsky), 144

Oedipus the King (Seneca), 121
OGPU, 104, 105, 108, 138, 158, 197n16
Okhlopkov, Nikolai, 83
Olesha, Yuri: and Afinogenov, 22; ambiguity and, 78; and Bulgakov, 22, 144, 145; career of, 49; death of, 168; on *Fear*, 110; fiction by, 49; at First Congress, 83; and MAT, 49; and Mayakovsky, 52; and Meyerhold, 47, 49; posthumous reputation, 21; self-criticism of, 53–54, 60; and Raikh, 78; and Shakespeare, 46–47; and Socialist Realism, 37; as Soviet citizen, 49; stage in, 23; on staged death, 123–24; and the unpredictable, 168. See also *Conspiracy of Feelings*; *Death of Zand*; *Envy*; *List of Good Deeds*; Olesha diaries; *Playing Execution*; *Three Fat Men*
Olesha diaries: on belles lettres, 49, 51, 53, 181n12, 181n16; and the fictional, 51; Hamlet in, 66; key words in, 68; Meyerhold in, 62–78; publication of, 50, 179n5, 181n18; rehabilitation through, 52–56; theatrical productions in, 56–62

215

Index

"Open Letter to My Future Directors" (Afinogenov), 92, 117–19
Optimistic Tragedy, An (Vishnevskii), 20, 93

Parker, Andrew, 12
Pasternak, Boris, 3–5
People's Commissariat of Communication and Transportation, 26–27
People's Commissariat for Enlightenment Moscow, 34
performance: and death, 134–35; and event, 18; and Putinism, 5; and Stalinism, 7–8; as term, 11–12, 172n21; text vs. act in, 66; vs. theater, 10–11, 172n12; and torture, 70–71; as transformative, 77; and violence, 73
Peshkov, Alexei Maximovich. *See* Gorky, Maxim
Peter and the Wolf (Prokofiev), 27
Petrograd Theater for Young Spectators, 34
Petrov, Nikolai, 100–101, 104, 117, 198n26, 201n72
Pevtsov, Illarion, 102–3
Pickwick Papers, The (Bulgakov), 139
Playing Execution (Olesha), 39–40, 135–36
Poem About an Axe, A (Pogodin), 20
Pogodin, Nikolai: epic style of, 20, 21; at First Congress, 83, 84
Poskrebyshev, Aleksandr, 166
power: of actor, 5; of audience, 79; backstage, 164–67; of Bulgakov on, 144; of embodiment, 59; of Meyerhold, 63; playwrights on, 137; of spectacle, 96; of state and stage, 22
Pravda newspaper, 27, 40–41, 148
Prokofiev, Sergei, 24, 27
proletarian organizations, community of, 61
Puchner, Martin, 10
puppet theater, 10
purges, Stalinist: Afinogenov and, 24, 121–22, 202n80; and *Fear*, 110, 121; and First Congress, 79; Olesha and, 51; survivors of, 168
Pushkin, Alexander, 132–34, 139

Radek, Karl, 46, 47, 82
Raikh, Zinaida: as Lelia, 74, 78; and Meyerhold, 46
Ramzin, Leonid, 4

RAPP (Russian Association of Proletarian Writers): attack on MAT, 20, 95; dissolving of, 15, 35; and First Congress, 81; Marxism of, 37; as repressive, 81; and show trials, 119–20; Stalin on, 88; as union prototype, 48; and Writers' Union, 86
Red Famine, 141
reeducation: militaristic, 34; and violence, 41–42
rehabilitation, through diary writing, 52–56
Ridout, Nicholas, 10, 11, 13
Rifle 492116 (Kron), 34, 44
Romashov, Boris, 90
Rozanov, Sergei, 30
Rozanov, Vasilii, 53
Rudin (Turgenev), 67
Russian Style (Cassiday), 5
Rykov, Aleksei, 4

Saint-Léon, Arthur, 34
Samosud, Samuil, 141
Sats, Ilya, 33
Sats, Nataliia: aesthetic of, 30–31; arrest of, 28, 42; and children's theater, 26–27, 175n13, 176n18; 178n48; *31*
Shcheglov, Dmitri, 42
Second Moscow Art Theater, 20, 25, 27, 93–94
Sedgwick, Eve Kosofsky, 12
self: and death, 53; and the fictional, 51; made legible, 62; and performance, 11; as radically mutable, 54–55; in Stalinist era, 16; writing vs. staging of, 57, 60
self, Soviet: and aesthetics, 15; creating, 135; in Lelia character, 72–73; and performer, 79; and Soviet theater, 22. *See also* genuine Soviet person/citizen
self-coercion, 44
self-criticism, 53–56
self-surveillance, 60, 182n20
self-understanding, 122, 169
Seneca, 120–21
Seryozha Strel'tsov (Liubimova), 35, 40–41
Shakespeare, William: and Olesha, 46–47, 68; in Russian culture, 66–67
Shostakovich, Dmitri, denunciation of, 27, 83
show trials: audience for, 3–4; of bour-

Index

geois specialists, 48; and *Fear*, 110; and genuine Soviet person, 13–14; and melodrama, 93; and RAPP, 119–20
Shtange, Galina, 26–27, 29
Shtok, Isidor, 35, 44
Shtraukh, Maksim, 70
Shvarts, Evgenii, 35, 44
side *a*ffects: and actors, 12; in children's theater, 23; and convention, 17; and genuine Soviet person, 16; as high risk, 168; and Stalin, 89; of theater, 11
Snitch, The (Vepritskaia), 40
Snow Queen, The (Shvarts), 35, 44
Socialist Realism: as evolving, 80; in fiction, 145, 186n49; at First Congress, 83; and genuine Soviet person, 13–14; Gorky in, 85; and Olesha, 37; and plays for children, 34–35; writers' meetings on, 85–91
Sokolovskaia, Nina, 108–9
Sophocles, 120–22
Soviet Art journal, 27
spectacle: ambiguities of, 169; audience in power of, 96, 110–11; of death, 131–32; of execution, 39; spectator reaction to, 19; and Stalinism, 8, 96
Sperantova, Valentina, 43–44
stage fright: and Great Terror, 11, 16; Ridout on, 10, 11, 13; and Stalin, 91; Stanislavsky on, 3, 4, 5–6, 10, 13, 79, 91
Stage Fright (Puchner), 10
Stage Fright, Animals, and other Theatrical Problems (Ridout), 10, 11, 13
Stalin, Joseph: and Afinogenov, 23, 114–17, 118, 119, 196n7; and Akhmatova, 164; appeal to write plays, 123; art under, 169; and backstage channels, 163, 164; and *Batum*, 140; and Bukharin's beard, 87, 88, 89; and Bulgakov, 25, 138, 139, 150, 163–67, 206nn8–9; and children, 26, 27; and *Days of the Turbins*, 141, 153; death of, 7; and edits of *The Lie*, 114–17, 118, 119, 125–26; and Gorky, 80; and *Molière*, 148, 149; as mythical, 87; and Pasternak, 5; performing for, 79–90; on shooting scenes, 131; on *The Suicide*, 125; as superhuman, 8; at theater, 14, 90, 95, 162–65; with writers, 23, 86–91, 92–23
Stalinism: and Bulgakova diary, 159; and childhood, 28, 29; and dissidence, 134;

in *Fear*, 24, 97–98; and film, 19; and history, 3, 133; in Moscow, 174; and Olesha, 20–21; and parades, 8; scholarly debate on, 7–8; and show trials, 3–4; theatricality in, 6–7; as worldview, 16
Stalin Prize, 151
Stanislavsky, Konstantin: on acting, 5, 11–12; and Afinogenov, 111, 197n11; and *Blue Bird*, 33; and Bulgakov, 131, 147, 155–56, 158; on children's theater, 42, 178n46; and *Fear*, 24, 100, 105–11, 199n42; and *The Lie*, 111–19; and *Molière*, 139, 147–48, 149, 153–58, 208n28; with Nemirovich-Danchenko, 95; and Olesha, 66; and Pushkin, 133; on realism, 17, 108; and Ridout, 10, 11, 13; and Sats, 42; on stage fright/ "curtain of light," 3, 4, 5–6, 10, 13, 79, 91; and *Three Fat Men*, 40, 177n36
State Central Theater for Young Spectators, 42
State Meyerhold Theater, 20
Stepanova, Angelina, 154
stock type, 17
Sudakov, Ilya, 106
Suicide, The (Erdman), 125
Sulerzhitskii, Leopold, 33
Svetlov, Mikhail, 35

Tairov, Aleksander: as authoritative, 63; and illusion, 17; as leader, 25, 71, 187n50
Tarasova, Alla, 166
theater: as challenge to audience, 118–19; as circus, 70–71; and cultural authority, 77; experience of, 12–13, 29; vs. literature, 19; vs. performance, 10–11; power of embodiment in, 59, 61–62; as rhetorical art, 17; side *a*ffects of, 11; and Soviet history, 6–8, 166–67; writers reflecting on, 16–17. *See also* theater, Soviet
theater, Soviet: effects of, 9; elite audience for, 19; as engine of discomfort, 13; and First Congress, 23; and fourth wall, 102; as high risk, 168; representing power, 79; and Soviet self, 22; staged deaths in, 123–36; transformation of the audience, vii; writers' perspectives on, 22
"theater for young spectators" term, 43
theater history, limitations on, 8–9

Index

This Is the Way It Was (Brushtein and Zon), 35
Three Fat Men (Olesha): and *The Blue Bird*, 40, 57, 176n25; coercion in, 35–42; directorial team, 183n30, 186n47; embodiment in, 62; first edition of, 36; Lipovetsky on, 45; Lunacharsky on, 37–38, 40, 58, 60, 177nn28–29, 177n32, 178n36, 184n33; meta-theatrical in, 38; in Olesha diaries, 57–58, 77; plot and characters, 38–39, 185n40, 185n43; visuals in, 40, 185n44
Timoshka's Mine (Makar'ev), 34, 43
To a Secret Friend (Bulgakov), 139
Tolstoy, Aleksei, 45, 83, 132
Tolstoy, Leo, 20, 93, 134, 139
TRAM (Workers' Youth Theater), 139
travesty actor/actress: in children's theater, 23, 43, 179n51; defined, 16, 178n50; and disruption, 17; and Hamlet role, 72; as ideal, 44–45; training of, 43
Treasure, The (Shvarts), 44
Trotsky, Leon, 14
Turgenev, Ivan, 66–67, 189n64

Ultimate Battle, The (Vishnevskii), 124
Uncle Vanya (Chekhov), 125
Union of Soviet Writers: Afinogenov expelled, 119, 202; best play competition, 123; Bulgakov and, 141–42, 160; Central Committee and, 19; Gorky and, 84; Kirpotin and, 84; Playwrights' Section, 22; and RAPP, 81, 86

Vakhtangov Theater, 25, 80, 176n24, 190n75
Vecherniaia Moskva newspaper, 110
Vepritskaia, Liudmila, 40
violence: and performance, 73; and reeducation, 41–42; in theater, 40; transformative, 60
Vishnevskii, Vsevolod, 125; deaths in, 124; epic style of, 20, 21; at First Congress, 84; and melodrama, 93
Volkov, Nikolai, 20, 81
Vyshinsky, Andrei, 4

War and Peace (Bulgakov), 139
"Winter Evening" (Pushkin), 132
Winter in Moscow (Muggeridge), 7–8
words vs. acts, 18, 113–14
worldview, Soviet, 118
Worthen, W. B., 12–13
writer, the: and cultural policy, 18; as ideological overseer, 15–16; reflecting on theater, 16–17
writers' meetings on Socialist Realism, 85–91, 92–93

Yagoda, Genrikh, 119
Yegor Bulychov and Company (Gorky), 80–81

Zelinskii, Kornelii, 85, 86, 89
Zhdanov, Andrei, 15; with Gorky, 15
Zon, Boris, 35, 178n46
Zoyka's Apartment (Bulgakov), 137, 139